Leadership Greatness

Best Practices to Become a Great Leader

Tri Junarso

iUniverse, Inc.
New York   Bloomington

Leadership Greatness
Best Practices To Become A Great Leader

iUniverse books may be ordered through booksellers or by contacting:

iUniverse
1663 Liberty Drive
Bloomington, IN 47403
www.iuniverse.com
1-800-Authors (1-800-288-4677)

Because of the dynamic nature of the Internet, any Web addresses or links contained in this book may have changed since publication and may no longer be valid. The views expressed in this work are solely those of the author and do not necessarily reflect the views of the publisher, and the publisher hereby disclaims any responsibility for them.

ISBN: 978-1-4401-1298-0 (sc)
ISBN: 978-1-4401-1300-0 (dj)
ISBN: 978-1-4401-1299-7 (ebook)

Printed in the United States of America

iUniverse rev. date: 3/5/2009

FOREWORD

Can you become a great leader? If you have the leadership greatness, the answer is "Yes, Why Not." Great leadership doesn't start with what you know. To be a great leader is not what you say about your leadership style and achievements, but what the people say. Great leaders act with sense of greatness.

A leader is a sense-maker; know that the way they view, review; reframe and build on past experiences - how they make sense of things - influences how successful they will be in setting positive, realistic expectations and successful outcomes.

Sense of greatness that creates great leaders is GREAT (Growth, Responsibility, Entrepreneurship, Authenticity, and Trust). We are all born with the potential for greatness. The GREAT describes:

a. Sense of Growth: Leaders focus on the needs and growth of those being led, not the needs of those who are leading.

b. Sense of Responsibility: Leadership that is rooted in one's free will, which underpins both responsibility and accountability.

c. Sense of Entrepreneurship: Leaders possess traits which motivate others and lead them in new directions.

d. Sense of Authenticity: Leaders display genuineness - knowing he/she is born an original, and show his/her best-self.

e. Sense of Trust: Leadership that implies followers to respect and trust their leader, as well as the leader believes in people.

This book is aimed to help you spread the practice of leadership greatness throughout your organization, which provides you with strategies on how to become a great leader.

The book focuses on perspective of greatness, especially leadership greatness. It's not merely discussing about competency, i.e. skill knowledge and attitude, in which a highly effective leader should possess. But more than this is how a person to demonstrate his/her greatness to becoming a great leader.

By reading this book you will experience a journey to greatness, in which great leaders have practiced successfully and been called as a true great leader.

No one can stop you becoming a great leader. Show your own GREAT. Act with sense of greatness. And be ready for your next destiny – be a GREAT leader!

Author

ACKNOWLEDGEMENT

This book is inspired by the leadership practiced in my previous company. The President is a strongest top level person I find during my service there, i.e. he has personal capability, displays high productivity and with high profit, maintains good interpersonal relationship, etc. No one or situation can rock him, because he owns complete reason to stand, e.g. high level of competency and back up from the stockholders. The question is why employees are not satisfied and organizing two times of demonstrations and one time of strike?

I try to compile all the root causes to know his failures and successes. There is no doubt he is excellent in five aspects of GREAT (Growth, Responsibility, Entrepreneurship, Authenticity, and Trust). In my personal observation, he is lacking in insincerity to the employees, particularly sense of giving, and not making sure that he surrounds himself with great people. I believe, if he would like to improve these lacks, he would be potential to becoming a GREAT leader.

The Author understands there will be errors, misspellings, or omissions. For the time being it is the best the Author could do. If you find any error, please do not hesitate to let us know so that we can improve this book performance in future.

The Author would also like to thank the many people who have supported, and helped with this book, especially my family, my wife, and my colleagues.

CONTENTS

INTRODUCTION

Leaders create conditions under which all the followers can perform independently and effectively toward a common objective. Success in leadership comes when the leadership style meets with the characteristics of the follower. Leadership is

a. Behaviors: The process of directing the behavior of others toward the accomplishment of common objectives.

b. Actions: Direct, supervise, encourage, inspire, and co-ordinate

c. Inspiration: Leaders articulate their vision and ideals to others, convincing them of the value of their ideas.

d. Self-images and moral codes: Leaders engage emotional contents, norms and values.

e. Ethics: Know what he/she ought to do when no one is watching. The leader will showcase their ethics and values.

f. Not an authority, technical skill, nor one's I.Q: People trust and respect leader, not for the skills he/she possesses.

Leadership, like beauty, might be difficult to define, but most people will recognize it when they see it.

Greatness displays a fascinating perspective on one's character. Greatness is dependent on a person's perspective; a state of mind.

Some people are born great which would be defined by heredity, possess natural talents and/or virtues of an exceptional kind; *some achieve greatness* - self-made, achiever, a lot of work to get done, *and some have greatness thrust upon them* – be in the right place at the right time.

Leaders don't have to be perfect, but to be great.

Greatness comes from persistent quality - even in the most mundane actions. Leadership greatness describes the extraordinary qualities of one's leadership, in which the person brings out greatness throughout the organization.

Sense is one's capacity for displaying a perception, that implies the faculty of thinking, reasoning, and acquiring and applying knowledge. It demonstrates the condition of being aware; capacity to make judgment and sensible decisions. Sense of greatness makes people want to do more than what they are currently doing.

The world needs leaders who lead with moral, ethical and values. Attitude seems to be the defining factor that separates leadership-mediocrity and leadership-greatness. Great organizations are created by great leaders. Some great leaders become so by being great followers. They are perceived as great leaders because they have great followers.

Great leaders recognize an important measure of leadership success is the growth.

Organizations need great leaders in order to create the performance, future, and fulfillment that everyone desires. No one will be called a great leader unless he/she demonstrate leadership greatness – act with sense of greatness.

Leadership can be learned, practiced, and developed; by training, by choice and by strength of character, people become leaders. A leader develops personal leadership skills and encourages and trains new leaders who will follow.

A leader who is aspiring to reach great heights can succeed through effective leadership training and executive coaching programs. One way to follow your path for greatness is to focus on your growth through work. Development is to produce confident, knowledgeable and courageous leaders and others.

Greatness emphasizes perceived superiority of a person or thing. Great leaders demonstrate actions that indicate sensitivity to and regard for the feelings and needs of others and an awareness of the impact of one's own behavior on them; being supportive of and fair with others.

Great organizations need great leaders - who act with sense of greatness.

Leaders are motivated by the wish to empower others. Empowerment exists when members have the authority to make decisions and take appropriate actions without first seeking approval from others. Empowerment allows a member to act quickly, improve satisfaction and boost morale.

Having a purpose is the difference between making a living and making a life. Leaders have a clear sense of purpose. From your sense of purpose, you can set goals and align them with that purpose - goals that serve as a blueprint to others. Great leaders work effectively with others to create a clear and compelling purpose.

Leadership is very much about performance. Leadership is a key to member engagement, innovation and success. To create a successful organization, a leader should be investing in building his/her leadership ability. Great leaders must be regarded as achievers. The great leaders always make sure that they surround themselves with great people.

Leadership starts with having a vision; the key to getting started as a leader. A vision that is likely to come true has to take account of the culture of the organization. Great leaders have vision and the ability to take people toward that vision. A leader's vision needs to be shared by those who will be involved in the realization of the vision.

Leaders who operate with a sense of vision demonstrate to others an understanding of how to get things done effectively within the organization and how to get the most out of the capabilities of the organization.

A sense of hope gives organization and members the impetus to keep moving ahead. They give people a sense of hope. Great leaders tend to be optimists and purveyors of hope. Great leaders are dealers in hope.

Leaders must have passion. Leaders' passion inspired them to take on new and very dangerous challenges. Passion - The drive and desire to do something extraordinary and powerfully well. Leadership is passion. Without passion, a person will have very little influence as a leader. Passion provides an individual with the light of leadership and creates an undeniable drive to make a difference.

Leadership and inspiration are inseparable. Leaders create an inspiring culture within their organization. Great leaders inspire people to move worlds and change the world.

The heart of leadership is the willingness to assume responsibility, not just for the people at the top, which implies:

a. Personal responsibility: Individual responsibility for making sound and ethical decision that considers the interests of all stakeholders.

b. Organizational responsibility: Develop a sense of responsibility in your people

Great leaders accept responsibility, that is developed through accountability, courage, self-confidence and focus on the whole. Be responsible means be dependable, work hard, and show self control; have a sense of duty to fulfill willingly the tasks he or she has accepted or has been assigned. Taking responsibility means being accountable for your choices, not depending on others to establish controls for your behaviors.

Leadership is not possible without a strong sense of accountability. Leaders who are accountable do what needs to be done, no matter where in the organization they have to go. The emphasis on accountability is not primarily to facilitate the excuse of sanctions when something goes wrong.

Accountability means the organization can point to a single person or group who must be accountable for effective management, explaining deviation from the norm, and acting to implement corrective action when problems arise.

A leader takes a courageous decision; when other may not. Courageous means ability to control your fear in a difficult situation; and *have the courage to stand up for your beliefs.* Leaders have to give courage to others, while creating the illusion that they know exactly what they are doing.

Great leaders are admired for their courage. Courage contributes greatly to a leader's ability to inspire. Great leaders have the courage to do what is right and ethical.

Douglas Mac Arthur was a highly complex leader. He was a great thundering paradox of a man, noble and ignoble, inspiring and outrageous, arrogant and shy, the best of men and the worst of men, the most protean, most ridiculous, and most sublime.

Unquestionably he was the most gifted man-at-arms this nation has produced. He was also extraordinarily brave. His twenty-two medals-thirteen of them for heroism-probably exceeded those of any other figure in American history.

He seemed to seek death on battlefields. (David M. Boje, Douglas MacArthur, 2001)

Taking risks is difficult (whether for an individual or an organization) because it involves uncertainty. Leaders are risk takers. Risk taking can lead to great losses or great successes. It's good to take risks - if you manage them well. Great leaders are not afraid to take risks.

Leader must be able to attune to the proper timing. Sense of timing is an intuitive skill. Leaders demonstrate awareness that affect timely decision-making; what to do and where to go. Great leaders understand the importance of timing, specifically when it comes to making decisions.

Leaders who have a good sense of timing seem to be wired into their situations. Great leaders make and execute decisions in a timely fashion. It demands well-coordinated and timely execution of strategy from others

Leaders direct people to focus on the right strategic issues. They present a challenge that calls forth the best in people and brings them together around a shared sense of purpose. A challenge should provide appropriate opportunities, new perspective, space for inspiration, meet our personal interests, and benefiting the people and organization.

The great leaders also understand the importance of team purpose, challenge, camaraderie, responsibility, and growth, and focus much of their time on creating the conditions for these to exist.

Great leaders have several qualities, i.e. make tough decisions, etc. Leadership greatness can be measured in the decisions made and the demonstrated commitment to those choices made by an individual.

Great leaders are decisive, resourceful, have a deep sense of urgency, and maintain tough-minded accountability. They make timely decisions, which are intelligent and unwavering, means that in some instances, the outcome might be failure.

Confidence brings trust and respect from others, and demonstrates the degree of certainty in leaders' ability to successfully achieve their goals and the resiliency to withstand the challenges along the way. Sense of confidence can only be forged through strong leadership. We should base our confidence on our ability to offer great solutions rather than on the skill of drawing solutions out of others.

Leaders focus on the big picture think in terms of what's good for the entire organization. The leader will focus on the solution rather than on the problem.

Sense of entrepreneurship is shown by one's thought and action, reward people and be model of the behavior. Entrepreneurs are risks takers. They show tolerance to uncertainty and risk. Entrepreneurial people need leaders to share ideas with, to help translate those ideas into action, to acknowledge successes and to put failures into perspective.

Great leaders recognize that innovation and entrepreneurship can thrive only in a healthy environment. They make their people feel appreciated, successful and determined to achieve. They accept mistakes.

Leadership requires discipline. Great leaders inspire standards and a culture of discipline, instead of pure charisma, to motivate others. Great leaders subscribe to a set of standards on which they will not veer. Leaders are responsible for such things as a sense of quality in the organization, for whether or not the organization is open to influence and open to change. Great leaders manage themselves and others for maximum effectiveness.

Leaders who exert ethical influence relearn and reapply these principles as their experience, knowledge and responsibilities expand. Ethical influence flows from those who align their words and behavior. Greatness is not manifested by unlimited pragmatism. The leaders fully take responsibility on their code of ethics and values and take them into account in decision-making.

Great leader combines moral foundations with intellectual talents and serves a cause. Morals are not absolute; they are a code of conduct more or less haphazardly developed for group survival, and vary with the nature and circumstances of the group.

Morality is a critical factor in leadership that its absence could turn an otherwise powerful leadership model (i.e. transformational leadership) into a disastrous outcome.

Great leaders always have self-discipline. Leaders, whose organizations are in order, have a minimum of members' misbehavior. Discipline in organization means teaching the followers to acquire: the great virtues of sound judgment, a sense of responsibility, personal courage, self-control, and magnanimity.

Values are the qualities and things in your life that you think are important. Great leaders know what they stand for and what is important to them.

Leaders must have a commitment to personal and organization's core values. Shared values build trust, and trust is the glue that enhances performance.

Leadership is first of all service; to serve whom you are leading. Great leaders focus their followers on serving one specific core group. By serving this core group, the organization can better serve other groups as well.

Success depends on high standards of service: a skillful selected variety of goods; highly qualified staff; a pleasant atmosphere in which the customer feels welcome and valued; products which are refreshed, finest quality and innovative.

Crisis is a time of great danger or trouble. Urgency is needed to avert a crisis. A leader handles crisis by sense of urgency - inner drive and desire to get on with the job quickly and get it done fast. This inner drive is an impatience that motivates you to get going and to keep going.

A leader is a master in the art of communication. As communication is the core component and without it one can never be a great leader. They keep communicating the vision to create a strong field which then brings their vision into physical reality.

Leadership is based on a spiritual quality -- the power to inspire, the power to inspire others to follow. A leader brings unique and individual spirits to the organization and is highly motivated by the spiritual need to experience a sense of transcendence and sense of community in the organization.

A leader generates a type of commitment among his/her people based on personal trust and transcendent motivation. Leaders with transcendence are persons who rise above their ego to build bridges instead of creating polarities. Leaders bring people together in the spirit of some greater outcome.

Leaders continually demonstrate competence, impressive aptitude, shrewd thinking, resourcefulness and apparently limitless capacity. Great leaders have core competence for which everyone can totally respect. They have the competence and skill to succeed. Each inspires trust and understanding of the perils of reaching their goal.

Humor promotes teamwork and camaraderie and stimulates creativity. Humor is also a powerful form of persuasion. Great leaders have a charming sense of humor. They laugh at their failures and take their successes in stride. They take the light things seriously and the serious things lightly. They constantly have fun, finding the genuine humor in the tragedy of the situation.

Leadership advances a relationship. Leaders should accept that the value of connecting things with each other is when they are able to connect everything with each other. Connection inspires the people to believe, that they truly have a leader who cares about them. Leaders should show connectivity with their people, understand their needs, and create the environment they need to be successful, and with the organization.

To become a great leader, you must develop a great team. *Team-building* describes the ability to develop an atmosphere where different kinds of people with different skills, personalities, interests, and passions can support each other and work together with joy.

A community is a group of people who form relationships over time by interacting regularly around shared experiences. Sense of community will be able to increase well-being and commitment to the organization. It creates a strong sense of recognition where people want to be and appreciate the contributions of others.

Followership is an essential element of leadership. Leaders also function as followers; everyone spends a portion of their day following and another portion leading. A key leadership trait is the ability to inspire followership. Great leaders are followers too. The great leader is a great follower.

Leadership won't work when it's artificial, contrived, or insincere. Being authentic is central to trust, and without trust you cannot lead. Authentic in leadership means knowing you were born an original. The authenticity displays leaders' capability to relate to others in an authentic, courageous, and high integrity manner. Authenticity gives us congruence, a sense of harmony that aligns our thoughts, our words, and our emotions.

Leaders must show integrity - what drives us regardless of our situation or position. . This doesn't just mean not breaking the law. The leaders with integrity, respect the rights of other people, and follow their own bliss; and show themselves as they wish to be seen. Great leaders know how they cope with people when times are tough.

Great leaders in all walks of life comes a wealth of wisdom. Wisdom is not something a person is born with. It only comes from living, from making mistakes; from listening to others who have made mistakes and learned from them.

Thinking win-win is a frame of mind that seeks mutual benefit and is based on mutual respect. Win-win nurtures empathy. Leaders develop consensus building that create win-win situations that ensure all have been listened to and honored for their expertise and feelings.

Consensus does mean that people have agreed to cooperate in the implementation of a decision. They have accepted the final choice, even though they may not be completely satisfied with it.

Leaders may grow in self-knowledge and maturity. Their power is derived through past experiences of failure and success. They will be about being their best, asserting your strengths and growing your team. Leaders promote the maturity and responsibility of everyone in the organization. Great leadership requires great emotional maturity.

A leader has to find consistency in an inconsistent world. Leaders keep things simple and consistent. Great leadership must be having consistency; as consistency creates stability. It creates sustainability.

Great leaders have a profound sense of humility. The great leaders are those who encourage; humble; competent; and kind. Nobody should be humiliated.

Leaders provide motivation and drive towards excellence. The organization should encourage people's inclination to compete against their own sense of excellence. Leaders demand excellence, not perfection. They expect the members to work as hard as they are doing and to be as committed to the goal as they are. Excellence promotes individual effort and puts a premium on exceptional competence and skill.

A leader forms his/her identity by selecting values, beliefs, and concepts that better define our sense of self. Self encompasses one's feeling thought and sensation. Leadership is honoring the greatness, and uniqueness, in others. Each organization is unique, as same as individual within the organization.

Great leaders have willingness to accept others, which requires a tolerance for imperfection. Acceptance is the need to accept self and be accepted by others. This includes a feeling of belonging. Great leaders excel by understanding their ways may not always be the right way extends to others' acceptance of ideas.

Character describes the morals, ethics and judgment one shows in making ones decisions and taking actions. Character is your internal makeup, your personal DNA. Great leaders are reliable persons of character who are committed to compelling principles and purposes, while embodying both empathy and respect for others, as well as inner connectedness and respect for oneself.

The foundation for leadership is the ability to manage effectively. Having control provides us with a sense of achievement, strength and possibility. A person, who cannot control him/herself, can never control others. By managing their sense of control, leaders can achieve far greater actual control.

Organizations need great leaders in order to create the performance, future, and fulfillment that everyone desires. Sense of awareness is the leader's ability to gain respect of those who follow him. If they know the leader is always going to do the right thing, then it's easy to follow him to the destination. Leaders must be having more self-aware and reflective than others; they follow an inner sense of direction, and lead from the inside out.

Leaders have a broad sense of direction, a vision that others can share to unify their efforts. It represents a clear view of how the organizations for which a leader has responsibility to contribute in the strategy of the whole. Right direction gives followers an unmistakable clear sense of direction.

A leader is good with actions as well as words. A leader's ability to generate commitment shapes and is shaped by the broader culture of the organization. Commitment ignites action; the engine that generates implementation energy from others. It reflects the leader's ability to get others excited about and dedicated to turning the vision into a reality.

Great leaders not only see the world differently, they do things differently. Great leaders take charge and get things done. They take disciplined, organize action. A leader has the courage to act.

Leaders with presence assert themselves, offer a hand first, ask questions and appear interested. This has a great impact on the quality of your personal relationships. Leaders' presence and comportment affects how others follow them and whether they are open to their ideas.

Persons who are not trustworthy cannot be leaders. Leaders can demonstrate good order, discipline and accomplishment to the extent that their relationships with the followers are based upon mutual trust and respect. Believability is achieved through both honesty and consistency between both the leader's statements and actions.

Leaders build relationships of trust through both their character and competence and they also extend trust to others. they show others that they believe in their capacity to live up to certain expectations, to deliver on promises, and to achieve clarity on key goals

Honesty is characterized by truth and sincerity. Honesty denotes the quality of being upright in principle and action. A leader who is considered honest is one who displays integrity, is genuine and not deceptive or fraudulent. Honesty means display sincerity, integrity, and candor in all your actions. Honesty should also show fair treatment to all people. Great leaders are honest, the need to establish a strong reputation.

For an organization to be truly successful, it has to have credibility. Building up the credibility of the organization takes time and effort. Leaders create credibility that results from trust and knowledge.

Great leaders apply scientific and rational approaches towards presenting new innovative ideas and healing scars of internal divisions. The key of great leadership is having the capacity to generate intellectual capital. Leaders demonstrate sound knowledge as well as abilities such as being able to communicate with their followers.

As a thinker, the leader will always remain fresh and will be willing to try new and innovative ideas. The leaders must possess key critical thinking skills that steer organizational strategy and decision making. Critical thinking is a differentiator, and as such, it should play a prominent role in both the selection and the development of the people.

The greatest thing in life is to keep your mind updated. By applying what we learn, we can become better leaders. Leaders are more powerful role models when they learn than when they teach. They take time to learn. Leaders develop a field that encourages learning.

Everyone has a basic sense of fairness, since everyone can distinguish between equal or unequal returns, or at least thinks he/she can, and therefore is capable of distinguishing between fair or unfair actions.

Fairness implies an elimination of one's own feelings, prejudices, and desires so as to achieve a proper balance of conflicting interests; and treat equally and without prejudice or bias and in a timely manner. Leaders develop a personal sense of fairness and help others do the same.

People love to be recognized for their accomplishments, and this will instill a sense of pride in your employees. Recognition is important; it builds positive self-esteem. Giving people recognition generates energy within them. They will then direct that energy toward increased productivity.

Great leaders show recognition to other's achievements. They create environments where their followers are rewarded for their hard work and success.

Great leaders don't sit around telling others what to do. They are created through hard work, dedication and experience. They often inspire their followers to high levels of achievement by showing them how their work contributes to worthwhile ends. Being a great leader is hard work.

Leaders wisely take care of their organizations and their people first. The leaders must first display an unquestionable sense of loyalty before they can expect members of their unit to be loyal. Once a decision is made and the order is given to execute it, carry out that order willingly as if it were your own.

Leaders inspire a deep devotion in their followers. They consistently display a strong sense of devotion to duty. Success can only come to you by courageous devotion to the task. Leaders with outstanding personalities serve the organization in their respective spheres with a sense of devotion.

Great leaders would rather be respected than liked. Caring is the basis of leadership, the work upon which a good organization is built. Caring requires not only compassion and concern; it demands self-sacrifice and tough-mindedness and discipline. The leader fosters a sense of care for one another.

Empathy can be used to form strong relationships, pick up early warning signs, and recognize opportunities to influence. Leaders take care of their people. Empathetic leaders will be able to help followers identify the situation and then develop a plan to improve it.

Leadership is an active ability to inspire by example – to ardently motivate others to achieve with integrity and accountability their greatest potential. Great leaders lead by example. Example, the foundation of everything else, makes a truly great leader.

Listeners have a big leadership advantage over those who do all the talking. A leader listens emphatically. Active listening focuses entirely on what the other person is saying and confirms understanding of both the content of the message and the emotions and feelings underlying the message.

Regardless of the nature of the counseling, leaders should demonstrate the qualities of a counselor. Leaders mentor others and have a mentor(s). The leaders are valuing both giving and receiving feedback.

Leadership requires foresight; that is contingent on leader's ability to evaluate the current state, assess, and predict trends and act to prevent those actions that will lead to crisis. People sometimes even need to be protected from the damage they may do to themselves. Leaders are protecting their flock from harsh surroundings.

Simple indicates a condition which is not complicated; ordinary or common; humble in condition; composed of only one thing; easy of use; not guileful or deceitful; sincere to the user; free from vanity; not sophisticated. Leaders have a unique ability to make things simple.

The greatness of a leader is measured by the sacrifices he/she is willing to make for the good of the group. Leading means giving. They transmit energy to people, giving them a new sense of hope and confidence in achieving the vision.

Gandhi helped free the Indian people from British rule through nonviolent resistance, and is honored by his people as the father of the Indian Nation. The Indian people called Gandhi Mahatma, meaning Great Soul. (Robin Chew, Mahatma Gandhi, 2008)

Our ability to lead is directly proportional to our ability to forgive ourselves and risk failure again. Leaders must be able to forgive themselves. Failure must be forgiven and learned from. Without forgiveness, we would never commit ourselves to the interdependent relationships of our communities.

Encouragement grows confidence and plants the seeds of self-esteem in the people. Great leaders encourage their people by making them feel that they can successfully accomplish their job tasks. People will be able to do real work when they are under the stimulus of encouragement and enthusiasm and the approval of the people for whom they are working.

Harmony should be built on collaboration and trust. Harmony supports one to act from a place of authenticity and integrity; there is no fakeness or phoniness, no self-deception. Organizational structure should not be duplicative in nature and confusing in responsibility and accountability. It may create disharmony.

Harmonizing means negotiating or reliving tension when appropriate; suggesting ways of accommodating differing views; helping others explore their disagreements; seeking appropriate compromise solutions that split the difference or make some type of trade-off.

We need a sense of balance to deal with multiple interest groups, whilst also achieving our goals. We must first understand and communicate our own value systems, and must focus on balancing the interests and concerns of others, helped by understanding their value systems.

Organization *needs leaders with vision and integrity, who are balanced in their judgment and actions as well as balanced within themselves.*

Leaders are not necessarily liked. They are respected. The leaders treat people with respect, give support and challenge as appropriate. A leader must create an environment of trust and mutual respect for what each person contributes to the organization.

Hierarchy and equality are not necessarily incompatible, as hierarchy provides connections while equality makes hierarchy responsive and responsible. Leaders display equality in the relationship, a desire to give of what you know so others can move forward. Justice maintains fair and harmonious relations and should be treated so. Justice is what is right for everyone; it would be best applied by someone who is neutral, objective, unbiased, and detached from irrelevant considerations; and should be devoted to treating all equally and according to the facts.

Leaders never outgrow the need to change. Adaptive challenges require leadership. Leaders produce change by establishing a vision and a direction, and then by aligning, motivating, inspiring, and empowering people to collectively desire, seek, and attain the shared vision.

A leader, who is flexible and adaptable, should be able to learn new things, experience new situations and be prepared to have days that don't always turned out as you had planned. Great leaders are adaptable. When a coaching method does not provide fruit, they change the approach. When they are not connecting with the team members, they examine and modify their leadership style.

Ownership motivates members through the chance to build assets, to make their organizations more fulfilling places to work, and for all of us to have greater control over their own destinies. Ownership develops when members play a key role in formulating and implementing tasks and understand the benefits of participation.

A great leader is able to rally their people and give them hope and a sense of ownership.

Great leaders have many qualities. Some of these qualities include doing the right thing, acknowledging the potential of others, accepting personal responsibility, celebrating milestones, and empowering their team. Great leaders self-select greatness. They determine a path to greatness.

The great leaders show the paths that will lead to greatness. It's because great leaders know their followers are capable of greatness. They believe the best of their followers. They understand what the organization is capable of achieving. Great leaders know that greatness matters – mere mediocrity is never good enough; even excellence falls short of the mark.

Great leaders choose a path that will accomplish something great – and then determine the path to attain greatness. Leaders make people feel that they're at the very heart of things, not at the periphery. Everyone feels that he or she makes a difference to the success of the organization.

Great necessities call forth great leaders – ones who act with sense of greatness. The leaders demonstrate 'GREAT' attributes, which are **Growth, Responsibility, Entrepreneurship, Authenticity, and Trust.**

1ST

LEADERSHIP STYLES

Success in leadership comes when the leadership style is matched with the characteristics of the follower. Problems with leadership come when the leadership style does not fit the follower.

If you're not sure what kind of a leader you should be, consider the one person that comes to mind when you think about someone you respect as a competent leader. While the proper leadership style depends on the situation, there are other factors that also influence which leadership style to use, i.e.:

a. The leader's personal background: personality, knowledge, values, ethics, and experiences the leader has.

b. The followers being led: Followers are individuals with different personalities and backgrounds. The leadership style that a leader uses will vary depending upon the individual follower and what he/she will respond best to.

c. The organization: The traditions, values, philosophy, and concerns of the organization will influence how a leader acts.

Leading others is not simply a matter of style, or following some how-to guides or recipes. Ineffectiveness of leaders seldom results from a lack of know-how or how-to, nor typically due to inadequate managerial skills.

Leadership is even not only about creating a great vision. It is about creating conditions under which all the followers can perform independently and effectively toward a common objective.

The style that leaders use will be based on a combination of their beliefs, values and preferences, as well as the organizational culture and norms. Leadership styles are the manner and approach of providing direction, implementing plans, and motivating people. Those styles are consisting of:

COMPETENCE-BASED LEADERSHIP

Competence is simply labeled as intelligence and the ability to make intelligent, imaginative decisions. A leader should have good values. Values are the leaders' beliefs and emotional feelings that drive the inner self.

Competence-based leadership is a way of thinking about how organizations gain high performance for a significant period of time. There are situations from where a competence-based leader can be identified or nurtured:

a. Possess a certain skill set and has the ability to take up the leadership role

b. Lack or absence of proper leadership or a crisis situation brings out extraordinary leadership skills to handle the situation

c. Commitment to develop the required skill set.

Competence-based leader needs to focus on building the knowledge and skills needed in an organization.

Competence is often defined as a combination of awareness, skills, knowledge and attitude that enables an individual to perform a job to the standards required for successful job performance.

In other words, competence deals with 'what is expected in the workplace' with the emphasis on performing an actual job and not gaining knowledge or skills for their own sake.

VALUE-BASED LEADERSHIP

Value-based leadership is based on recognizing the strength of having the many differences amongst organization members. In valuing differences people can agree to disagree and learn from each others varying backgrounds and experiences.

Values-based leadership is a way of making decisions that builds the trust and commitment of followers. When a situation arises that we have to deal with, there are different ways we can arrive at a decision on what to use, i.e.:

a. Beliefs: Perceptions, judgments, and actions that create the outcomes they want.

b. Values: Where a leader stands, the guiding principles that determine leader behavior, which, in turn, motivates and inspires follower behavior.

c. Intuition: The capacity of the mind to discern or "see" particular self-evident truths.

A leader should have good values, which are the leaders' beliefs and emotional feelings that drive the inner self. Values include ambition, human awareness, and a commitment to ethical practices. Value-based leadership focuses on adding value to the entire process; which includes:

a. Survival and safety: Display results, financial stability, discipline, and member safety.

b. Relationships and communication: Exhibit conflict resolution, recognition, satisfaction and open communication.

c. Performance and best practice: Show results orientation, efficiency, productivity and quality.

d. Adaptability and member participation in decision-making: Display courage, innovation, teamwork, and accountability.

e. Shared values and vision: Display enthusiasm, fairness, trust and integrity.

f. Involvement and strategic alliances: Show stewardship, collaboration, member fulfillment and mentoring.

g. Ethics and responsibility: Display compassion, forgiveness, humility, and ease with uncertainty.

It is a leader's responsibility to add quality (value) to each service and product delivered to the customers; which represents their commitment on their vision for the organization, and their performance on that vision. In valuing differences we can agree to disagree and learn from each others varying backgrounds and experiences.

Value-based leadership focuses on adding value to the entire process. In some instances, this type may overlook the aspect of being the nice guy on the block and rather focus on adding value to the leadership process. It is an organization's responsibility to add quality (value) to each service and product delivered to its customers. People rate leaders on their vision for the organization and their final performance of that vision, or on their character or principles followed.

CHARACTER-BASED LEADERSHIP

Character is the critical measure of leadership excellence. The leadership crisis in ethics in many organizations partially stems from the crisis in character of our leaders. The character of the leader is grounded on such core values as integrity, trust, truth and human dignity, which influence the leader's vision, ethics and behavior.

The moral literacy of the leader and the essentials of an ethical culture are connected to his/her character.

Leadership is a developmental process of growing one's skills in leading others with an awareness and knowledge of our own honesty and integrity. The character of a leader is recognized in how he/she chooses to demonstrate his/her abilities within the organization.

Leaders need more than technical expertise and mental aptitude to succeed. They must possess the ability to effectively inspire and direct others. Such capacity is only achieved through the development and maintenance of strong relationships - strong relationships that come from a leader with good character.

Many people have heard about principle-centered leadership and servant leadership. Not so well known is character-based leadership. Character-based leaders operate with integrity and with a heart to help others. They lead with a genuine concern for the greater good of all. Although they care for their own needs, they are just as concerned for their employees, company, customers, community, etc.

Leaders of character are not doormats for followers to trample. Rather they are assertive and most importantly they develop the untapped potential and character qualities in their followers.

Character-based leadership is rooted in the belief that principles are not complete by themselves in leading people to greatness. Often principles kept for a long time becomes character. The chain of creating the future through character-based leadership methods goes something like this:

Thoughts (thinking on principles) leads to action, acting on principles leads to habits, habits lead to character, character then leads to creating your future or destiny.

Character refers to ones moral and ethical structure. However, the problem is that people tend to only briefly embrace principles and shortly thereafter return to their set behavior and character.

A moral and ethical character structure must become the essence and operating motive in every situation before a perfect moralistic and ethical leader could emerge. But it should be realized that being a great character-based leader is not insurance for effective performance.

Character-based leaders lead the people toward the achievement of great results, i.e.:

a. Display value system: Organization will encounter situations that will test its values. The organizational values should look balanced. All the members should be able to adjust and adapt quickly – to find balance – so their actions can always represent the organization's values.

   The whole essence of inculcating values and the whole essence of leadership is making sure the people are truly following you.

b. Form mission: Organization exists for a purpose. A mission. One of the biggest fears members have is that they might be part of something that is meaningless. To lead effectively, you will need to specifically identify the organization's meaning, its mission.

   Character-based leaders give their members a strong sense of meaningfulness in their work by forming a clear, easy to understand and memorable mission and making it the hub of all of their organization's actions.

c. Provide strategic vision: The direction that makes sure the organization is heading in the right track. Character-based leaders take an honest look to make sure their strategic-vision is not only producing their desired strategic objectives, but also supports their mission and values.

Leadership definitely involves creating a vision and sticking to it because of ones character. Character-based leadership is in the belief that principles are not complete in leading people to greatness. Often principles kept for a long time to become character.

A moral and ethical character structure must reflect the soul purpose and operating motive in every situation before a leader can become such. A character-based leader does not dictate superior performance.

Character-based leadership takes a leader right into the heart of the matter, challenging him/her to do the daily character work that allows him/her and the organization to hold and honor the legitimate, pulls of followers.

With character-based leadership, an organization has a road map to create energetic alignment between followers, leader's strategic vision, and the organization's structure and systems. Character-based leadership successfully impacts morale, productivity, and excellence.

CULTURE-BASED LEADERSHIP

Not all individuals can adapt to the leadership styles expected in a different culture; whether that culture is organizational or national. Culturally competent leaders need to understand their cultural history and contemporary status, as well as that of their members and organization. A culture-based leader should:

a. Understand how people learn, and the impact of race, power, legitimacy, cultural capital, poverty, disability, ethnicity, gender, age, language, and other factors on learning.

b. Understand patterns of discrimination and inequalities, injustice, and the benefits and liabilities associated with individual groups.

The leader possesses capacity to break down systems of practice that perpetuate inequalities, engages people from different cultures; acts as cultural broker; conducts situational audits; and creates a safe environment of cultural competence where people are held accountable; facilitates dialogue and mediates conflict

c. Able to articulate his/her own philosophy of education and use it to maintain the status quo or to empower others' active participation in their own transformation. The leader is effectively communicating a culturally competent vision and its goals; has capacity to catalyze change and deal with dissonance

d. Foster empathy/caring, commitment - heart, spirit, and energy, high expectations for all, role model, open to change and to differences, values cultural diversity, and comfortable sharing power.

Leaders also need to consider systemic patterns of discrimination and prejudice. As such, cultural competence requires that organizations to:

a. Define set of values and principles and demonstrate behaviors, attitudes, policies, and structures that enable them to work effectively cross-culturally.

b. Have the capacity to value diversity, conduct self-assessment, manage the dynamics of difference, acquire and institutionalize cultural knowledge, and adapt to diversity and the cultural contexts of the communities they serve.

c. Incorporate the aforementioned in all aspects of policymaking, administration, practice, and service delivery and involve stakeholders

A variety of skills can help leaders mitigate the negative effects of prejudice and cultural barriers, i.e. he/she is the ability to develop and model a positive vision of a culturally diverse organization and use it to strengthen organization; and simultaneously keep the focus on effective strategies for improving individual achievement and well-being.

COMMUNITY-BASED LEADERSHIP

Identifying leaders and supporting them is crucial. Efforts to develop leaders should be consistent with community-based approaches to strengthening community and neighborhood life. The efforts should include promoting strong role models, building capacity, and encouraging followers' participation.

Although leadership often focuses on individuals, the family unit provides another focus for building leadership within the community. Strong leadership is essential to community development, vigorous economies, strong organizations and healthy businesses.

Leaders should understand the social, economic, and political dimensions of changing local, state, national and global environments.

Community-based leadership combines a community orientation with empowerment; which develops greater responsibility and ownership of the organization by the community; and fosters succession planning for emergent leaders. There are four generally accepted models of leadership for community organizations:

a. Conventional leadership model: Inspire the fulfillment of individuals to their potential. The objective is to increase the capacities of individuals to mentor, and network. Conventional leadership is focused on individual leadership skills.

b. Leadership model for human services: Inspire hope and purpose in individuals who want to develop skills that improve the community. Objectives are focused more on the needs of the organization than those of the individual.

c. Community leadership model: Inspire hope and commitment in individuals who wish to become more involved in community issues. Although, individual objectives are secondary, the community leadership model identifies those who can champion community issues.

d. Family leadership model: Inspire hope and purpose in individuals who want to advocate for their families or important family issues. The primary focus is encouraging family member(s) to assume leadership roles.

Leaders in the community model are individuals who appoint themselves as leaders or who are encouraged by the community to participate. Community members should be familiar with the goal of each, and adopt the model that works best.

Community-based leader is a person in the front line on achieving positive community conditions, including: helping communities to become vision and mission driven, tailoring services to fit the community, developing preventative solutions, and emphasizing the shared value, collaborative use of resources, and the democratic formation of public policy. Taking a community based approach acknowledges that community is the key to the communities future.

Community based collaboration is the process in which community, agencies, organizations, and businesses make a sustained commitments to work together to accomplish a shared vision.

PRINCIPLE-CENTERED LEADERSHIP

Principal-centered leadership is focused on the principals rooted in the rules that govern people and organizational effectiveness. Breaking the principles cause harm to the organizational success.

Principle-centered leaders are persons of character who work on the basis of principles and build it into the center of their lives, relationships with others, agreements and contracts, management processes, and mission statements.

The key, to dealing with the challenges, is the recognition of a principle-centered core within the leaders, followers and the organizations. Principle-centered leadership presents a new way of thinking that is to help a leader to:

a. Get principles at the center of the activities: Promote learning, achievement, and excellence in people

b. Understand reciprocating principle: The only way you want to treat people is how you want them to treat you.

c. Competitiveness is learning source that keep you sharp and teach you where your weaknesses are

d. Your identity may not be threatened by others or by external conditions, if you have an anchor and a compass to stand: Maintain a sense of direction

e. Maintain perspective and judgment in turbulent change: Encourage the desire to change and improve without creating more pain from the gain. Look at individual weaknesses with genuine compassion and understanding rather than accusation and self-justification

f. Always empower from within: Get empowered and empower others with confidence and competence to solve problem and seize

33

opportunities. Know where to start, when and how to maintain momentum for learning, growing and improving.

Principle-centered leadership fosters to not just an understanding of how to increase quality and productivity, but also to appreciation of the importance of building personal and professional relationships.

SITUATIONAL LEADERSHIP

The situational leader bases the choice of a leadership style on the competence and commitment of the person being led rather than on the leader's usual or preferred style. Situational leaders are able to adapt their leadership style to fit their followers and situations in which they are working. The leaders analyze the needs of the situation, and then adopt the most appropriate leadership style.

Situational leadership will make conscious choices between their use of directive behavior and supportive behavior; being autocratic or democratic. The key for the successful situational leader is to know which of the styles to use in a particular situation with a particular person.

There are a few forces that lead to the leader's action: The forces in the situation, the forces in then follower and also forces in the leader. He/she should fully diagnoses the situation at hand, and chooses a leadership style to best fit the particular situation Situational leader is one who can quickly change leadership styles as the situation changes.

The key to being a situational leader is noticed when to use each style. The decision is primarily a function of two variables: the degree of difficultly of the task and the development level of the person doing the task. Factors that affect situational decisions include motivation and capability of followers. This is affected by factors within the particular situation.

The relationship of a leader with his/her team has evolved from a supervisory role to a multi-tasking role. The leader is a guide, mentor, motivator as well as a team member. Instead of moving ahead of the team, he/she has to move along with it. More than dependence, it is now a question of synergies and inter-dependence.

Leaders must be able to change their styles to increase performance. Successful leaders have good leadership characteristics and can adapt their behavior to followers' needs and the particular situation they are in.

CREATIVE LEADERSHIP

Innovation is the lifeblood of an organization. Knowing how to lead and work with creative people requires knowledge and action that often goes against the typical organizational structure. Leadership is not limited to the ability of a person to influence other people in getting things done, above their normal standard and quality, or does the society need a new breed of leaders who can evolve on a continuous basis, addressing new challenges.

Traditionally, leaders have been known to possess the ability to motivate people, identifying their strengths, nurturing them and making their team function in a synthesized manner, thereby delivering up to its true potential.

Creative leaders search for and discover opportunities, introduce positive change and make quantum leap forward in creating new products and process.

Individuals who are creative are able to bring out and visualize. Their role is not limited to merely guiding people in the right direction. They require creative leaders, who do not only limit their role to addressing problems through novel solutions, but by giving new viewpoints on how to resolve problems in the future as well; which includes:

a. Motivate people to become more creative and empower them to bring their ideas into life

b. Inspire and energize people to see problems as opportunities for innovation and failures as stepping stones to success

c. Encourage creative problem solving and creative entrepreneurship

d. Encourage ideas among the people and search for synergies

e. Make business fun for the people: Fun is associated with creativity

Whenever an organization demands for a creative leader, it should create a healthy environment, in which such a leader can be identified and groomed. Members should be encouraged to be flexible in terms of accepting new ideas.

Creative leaders are a critical resource needed to find answers to difficult problems. They are the ones who can navigate the future. They are able to embrace ambiguity and reframe problems as opportunities. They have competencies that include how to read and understand the environment, build alliances, recognize the importance of social responsibility, manage complexity, use information technology, and encourage creativity.

Creative leaders can be broadly segregated as re-definers and re-directors; who introduce a new dimension to existing ideas

NARCISSISTIC LEADERSHIP

•

Narcissism is especially prevalent in long-established organizations with a past track-record of success. They become so proud of their past, and so complacent about their prestige, that they no longer notice clear signs of pending problems and an obvious need for change.

Narcissistic organizations tend to have an unusually high proportion of narcissistic leaders fixated on issues of power, status, prestige, and superiority.

Narcissistic and bureaucratic dimensions are identified as being factors that impede leader's effectiveness while visionary and egalitarianism leadership enhance a leader. The narcissistic leader is the culmination and reification of his/her period, culture, and civilization. He/she is likely to rise to prominence in narcissistic organization.

The narcissistic leader fosters and encourages a personality cult with all the hallmarks of an institutional religion: Priesthood, rites, rituals, temples, worship, catechism, mythology. The leader supposes him/herself as a religion's ascetic saint. He/she monastically denies him/herself earthly pleasures (or so he/she claims) in order to be able to dedicate him/herself fully to his/her calling.

Narcissistic leadership is about theatre, not about life. To enjoy the spectacle (and be subsumed by it), the leader demands the suspension of judgment, depersonalization, and de-realization. Here are some clues of narcissistic organization:

a. The leaders are revered and accorded almost god-like status.

b. Followers treat the leader organizationally - Approved way of thinking or acting as Holy Writ.

c. No one ever admits to any mistakes. Problems are always blamed on someone else - Often people outside the organization.

d. People treat the bombastic, dictatorial behavior of certain leaders as justified by their exceptional status.

e. Questioning any aspect of the organization is strongly discouraged. Objections to policy or procedures from outsiders are met by an amused and superior smile.

f. Obtaining employment within the organization is seen as a life-changing achievement and a gift of immeasurable value, which must be repaid with unquestioning loyalty.

A narcissist who regards him/herself as the benefactor of the poor, a member of the common folk, the representative of the disenfranchised, and the champion of the dispossessed against the corrupt elite - is highly unlikely to use violence at first.

To the narcissist, things and people are either entirely bad (evil) or entirely good. He/she projects onto others his/her shortcomings and negative emotions, thus becoming a totally good object.

A narcissistic leader is likely to justify the butchering of his/her own people by claiming that they intended to kill him/her, undo the revolution, devastate the economy, or the country, etc.

Narcissistic leaders learn little from defeat. When setbacks occur, such leaders don't take any personal responsibility; instead, they scapegoat others in the organization, passing on the blame. Even when things are going well, they can be cruel and verbally abusive to their subordinates, and they are prone to outbursts of rage when things don't go their way.

The narcissist aspires to acquire authority by any means available to him/her. He/she may achieve this by making use of some outstanding traits or skills such as his/her intelligence, or through an asymmetry built into a relationship.

The narcissistic leader is the culmination and reification of his/her period, culture, and civilization. He/she is likely to rise to prominence in narcissistic organization He/she maintains a tenuous grasp on reality to start with and this is further exacerbated by the trappings of power.

Narcissistic leaders are not prepared to share power. On the contrary, as leaders they surround themselves with 'Yea-Sayers.' Unwilling to tolerate disagreement and dealing poorly with criticism, such leaders rarely consult with colleagues, preferring to make all decisions on their own. When they do consult with others, such consultation is little more than ritualistic. They use others as a kind of 'Greek chorus,' expecting followers to agree to whatever they suggest.

Narcissistic leaders typically show strong hostility to anyone who fails to give them the unquestioning loyalty to which they believe they are entitled; followers are faced with a stark choice: do what the leader wants or suffer consequences.

The leaders are deprived of truthful feedback. The self-satisfied blindness that results can lead to catastrophe, as leaders are deprived of sensible reality-testing and followers provide praise for personal gain.

SPIRITUAL LEADERSHIP

Spiritual leadership is focused on the primary need of values and spirit for meaningful personal and organizational growth. Spiritual leadership was supposed to be feasible when traditional command and control, centralized, standardized, and formalized fear-led.

Bureaucratic organizational paradigm cannot effectively respond to today's chaotic global environment. Members who work for organizations they consider being spiritual are less fearful, more ethical, and more committed. And there is mounting evidence that a more spiritual workplace is more productive, flexible and creative.

Spiritual leadership also requires integrity. People do not want to follow a person they do not respect. Spiritual leadership demands honesty. People are repulsed by a person they cannot trust to tell the truth. *Jesus, Buddha, Mohammed, Confucius, as an example, is the great prophet of the world.*

Many are called to become spiritual leaders, assisting others in their spiritual journey. Spiritual leaders - clergy or lay, paid or volunteer - seek to meet the needs of people in their own communities of faith. Maturing as spiritual leaders requires them to learn how to care for themselves - emotionally, physically, psychologically, and especially, spiritually. Spiritual leaders must be able to locate resources which help them continue to grow and learn along with their organizations.

Spiritual leadership insists on humility. Humility is the attitude that puts others ahead of you, that considers others more important than yourself. Spiritual leadership involves humbling yourself and doing the tasks that no one else wants to do.

Spiritual leadership comprises the values, attitudes, and behaviors required to intrinsically motivate one-self and others in order to have a sense of spiritual well-being through calling and membership, i.e. we and they experience meaning in their lives, have a sense of making a difference, and feel understood and appreciated.

The effect of spiritual leadership in establishing this sense of leader and follower spiritual well-being is to create value congruence across the strategic, empower team. Ultimately, this value congruence fosters higher levels of health, psychological and spiritual well-being, organizational commitment, productivity and, ultimately organizational performance.

Spiritual leaders seek continuous improvement for themselves, their co-workers, and all other people. They believe development and maintenance of a learning organization through spiritual leadership is the ultimate source of member well-being and, ultimately, profitability and growth. Both leaders and followers in this quest for spiritual well-being are surfacing from all areas.

Spiritual leadership, with a spirit of humility and service, will cause people to follow you because they want to, not because they have to. Genuine humility and spiritual leadership is attractive.

People want to follow a person who serves alongside them and sets an example for them. Thinking too highly of yourself prevents you from genuinely caring for others. Humility enables you to serve others wholeheartedly and thereby set an example that others will follow. Organizations, that commits to ethics, trust, vision and spirituality; attract the right people and give them a clear purpose when striving to achieve greatness.

VISIONARY LEADERSHIP

The word vision is used so frequently that it has become almost a cliché and thus, at times, a challenge to fully appreciate the concept. Visionary leader is effective in manifesting his or her vision because s/he creates specific, achievable goals, initiates action and enlists the participation of others.

Visionary leadership is based on a balanced expression of the spiritual, mental, emotional and physical dimensions. It requires core values, clear vision, empowering relationships, and innovative action. When one or more of these dimensions are missing, leadership cannot manifest a vision.

The leadership style focuses on how the leader defines the future for followers and moves them toward it. Visionary leadership increases efficiency by moving decision-making responsibility to the frontline.

Efficiency is achieved with limited supervision. To make frontline responsibility effective, leadership must give members opportunity to develop quality decision-making skills and learn to trust them.

Visionary leaders are the builders of a new dawn, working with imagination, insight, and boldness. They present a challenge that calls forth the best in people and brings them together around a shared sense of purpose. They work with the power of intentionality and alignment with a higher purpose. Their eyes are on the horizon, not just on the near at hand. They are social innovators and change agents, seeing the big picture and thinking strategically.

Leaders serve the good of the whole. They search for solutions that transcend the usual adversarial approaches and address the causal level of problems. They find a higher synthesis of the best of both sides of an issue and address the systemic root causes of problems to create real breakthroughs. A visionary leader possesses some of the following characteristics:

a. A commitment to values: Visionary leaders often have the ability to see higher spiritual forces at work behind the scenes of events, and they align with the vision of these redemptive forces. A visionary may dream wonderful visions of the future and articulate them with great inspiration. A visionary is good with words. But a visionary leader is good with actions as well as words, and so can bring his/her vision into being in the world, thus transforming it in some way. It requires leadership and heartfelt commitment.

A commitment to values is an outstanding characteristic of all visionary leaders. They embody a sense of personal integrity, and radiate a sense of energy, vitality and will.

b. Visionary and future focused: Spending most of their decision-making time looking forward.

c. Show a clear inspirational vision: Visionary leaders transmit energy to people, giving them a new sense of hope and confidence in achieving the vision. Visionaries who are successful at manifesting their visions base their leadership on an inspirational, positive picture of the future, as well as a clear sense of direction as to how to get there.

   Vision is a field that brings energy into form. Visionary leaders have the ability to sense the deeper spiritual needs of followers and link their demands to the need for purpose and meaning.

   Visionary leaders are emerging in all fields of human endeavor around the world, leading a quiet revolution energized by power of the soul. By appreciating and supporting those who lead from their core spiritual values, we strengthen those leadership qualities in ourselves.

d. Entrepreneurial spirit: Organizations (in business) operate in a fast changing marketplace seeking products and services to meet emerging customer needs.

e. Good communicators: Understand the importance of effective communication at all levels.

f. Keep respectful that empowering relationships: Good relationships are the heart of effective visionary leaders. They embody a deeply caring approach to people, seeing them as their greatest asset. Visionary leaders embody a receptive, as well as a dynamic energy. They know how to listen and learn from other points of view and have fine tuned their communications skills.

   Visionary leaders promote a partnership approach and create a shared sense of vision and meaning with others. They exhibit a greater respect for others and carefully develop team spirit and team learning. The most effective visionary leaders are responsive to the real needs of people and they develop participative strategies to include people in designing their own futures. Rather than confront or avoid conflict, the leaders have learned how to transform conflict into usable energy. They work to unite - rather than divide -people.

g. Systems thinkers: Seeking to understand the root causes and forces that shape the issues and challenges they will face.

Visionary leaders are innovative, and show courageous action. They are especially noted for transforming old mental maps or paradigms, and creating strategies that are outside the box of conventional thought. They embody a balance of right brain (rational) and left brain (intuitive) functions. Their thinking is broad and systemic, seeing the big picture, the whole system, and the pattern that connects. They then create innovative strategies for actualizing their vision.

Visionary leaders anticipate change and are proactive, rather than reactive to events.

Their focus is on opportunities, not on problems. They emphasize win/win - rather than adversarial win/lose - approaches. Visionary leader accomplishing great things, s/he is drawing on the resources of their soul and its remarkable capabilities.

They look for courses of action that will exert the highest possible leverage as they respond to those issues. In the new board, leaders also look for creative ways to connect their organizations to the world around them, exploring and imagining new forms of partnership and alliances that will support their missions and advance in their strategic plans.

The leaders also have a deep appreciation of the strength of diversity, understanding that diversity helps to assure a higher level of responsiveness to customers and also promotes creativity, innovation and organizational learning.

Visionary leadership is based on values, vision and vitality. Visionary leaders have a commitment to core spiritual values. Their leadership is based on an inspirational and practical vision of the future that invites others to participate as partners. They radiate a sense of vitality, energy and optimism that motivates others. And they are innovative, whole systems thinkers who go beyond the limits of conventional thought in their efforts to truly serve the common good.

A visionary leader builds a business that will lead the organization to future growth. He/she draws a fine balance between the past, present and future and build businesses that continue to grow over time. It takes commitment, passion and perseverance to make a visionary leader, which, if developed, can lead businesses to another level of growth.

STRATEGIC LEADERSHIP

A strategic leader is responsible for the organization strategy development and implementation the prime responsibility is to ensure that the organization is going in the right direction.

A strategic leader can provide vision and direction. They motivate the people through love and passion, and build a complementary team based on mutual respect if he or she is more effective-minded than efficiency-minded, more concerned with direction and results than with methods, systems, and procedures

Strategic leadership is guidance or direction that is essential to meeting intended objectives or successfully implementing a plan of action.

Strategic leaders are generally responsible for large organizations and may influence several thousand to hundreds of thousands of people. They establish organizational structure, allocate resources, and communicate strategic vision.

Strategic leaders work in an uncertain environment on highly complex problems that affect and are affected by events and organizations outside their own.

Strategic leaders apply many of the leadership skills and actions they mastered as direct and organizational leaders; however, strategic leadership requires others that are more complex and indirectly applied. Strategic leaders process information quickly; and assess alternatives based on incomplete data, make decisions, and generate support.

However, strategic leaders' decisions affect more people, commit more resources, and have wider-ranging consequences in both space and time than do decisions of organizational and direct leaders.

Strategic leaders often do not see their ideas come to fruition during their "watch" and their initiatives may take years to plan, prepare, and execute. In-process reviews (IPRs) might not even begin until after the leader has left the job. This has important implications for long-range planning. On the other hand, some strategic decisions may become a front-page headline of the next morning's newspaper.

Perhaps of paramount importance - because they exert influence primarily through subordinates - strategic leaders must develop strong skills in picking and developing good second-tier leaders.

The common usage of the term strategic is related to the concept of strategy - simply a plan of action for accomplishing a goal. One finds both broad and narrow senses of the adjective strategic.

Strategic leadership entails making decisions across different cultures, agencies, agendas, personalities, and desires. It requires the devising of plans that are feasible, desirable, and acceptable to one's organization and partners - whether joint, interagency, or multinational.

Strategic leadership demands the ability to make sound, reasoned decisions - specifically, consequential decisions with grave implications. Since the aim of strategy is to link ends, ways, and means, the aim of strategic leadership is to determine the ends, choose the best ways, and apply the most effective means.

The strategy is the plan; strategic leadership is the thinking and decision making required developing and affecting the plan. Skills for leading at the strategic level are more complex than those for leading at the tactical and operational levels, with skills blurring at the seams between those levels.

One may define strategic leadership as the ability of an experienced, a leader who has the wisdom and vision to create and execute plans and make consequential decisions in the volatile, uncertain, complex, and ambiguous strategic environment. It is practiced by the military services and many large corporations. It stresses the competitive nature of running an organization and being able to out fox and out wit the competition.

Strategic leadership provides the vision, direction, the purpose for growth, and context for the success of the corporation. It also initiates outside-the-box thinking to generate future growth. Strategic leadership is not about micromanaging business strategy. Rather, it provides the umbrella under which businesses devise appropriate strategies and create values.

Entrepreneurial Leadership

Entrepreneurial leadership displays an attitude that the leader is self-employed. It instill the confidence to think, behave and act with entrepreneurship in the interests of fully realizing the intended purpose of the organization and stakeholders involved. In the new era of rapid changes and knowledge-based enterprises, managerial work becomes increasingly a leadership task.

Leadership is the primary force behind successful change. Leaders empower followers to act on the vision. They execute through inspiration and develop implementation capacity networks through a complex web of aligned relationships.

One of the key elements of highly effective leadership is the refusal to believe that a business model, however sound and well crafted, is ever good to run on autopilot. Recognizing this, the most successful leaders continuously improve their models by engaging in a perpetual process of interactive learning.

Since every leader has a distinct style made up of combinations of these orientations, it's impossible to accurately predict your style without a thorough analysis.

As with most leaders, you'll tend to use different styles when faced with different situations. Each orientation presents two extremes between which leaders have to determine the right balance for themselves, based upon their personality and specific leadership challenges. Leaders as entrepreneurs:

a. Make a significant difference: Leaders have to do something different to get different results, influence on organizational outcomes. Great leaders not only see the world differently, they do things differently.

b. Creative and innovative: Demonstrate entrepreneurial creativity, search continuously for new opportunities and pursue them

c. Spot and exploit opportunities: Find the resources and competencies required to exploit opportunities

d. Team-builders and networkers: Work is performed by teams rather than solely by individuals. A good team brings a greater variety of skills and experiences to solve difficult problems compared to one person. Leaders must become team-builders to gain the greatest potential and superior accomplishment from their teams.

e.   Advance adversity and competition: Develop a deeper sense of what is essential to thrive and excel as leaders under conditions of adversity and uncertainty.

f.   Manage change and risk: Take risk, venture into new areas and provide strategic direction and inspiration to their people

g.   Control of the business: Take responsibility for the failures of their team, learn from these failures and use them as a step to ultimate success and strategic achievement.

h.   Put the customer first: Create a culture that's dedicated to service.

i.   Create capital: Create sustaining values which attract investment, i.e. quality, sense of urgency, efficiency, etc

Entrepreneurial leadership involves instilling the confidence to think, behave and act with entrepreneurship in the interests of fully realizing the intended purpose of the organization to the beneficial growth of all stakeholders involved. Entrepreneurial leadership is not a position, it is a process.

The entrepreneurial leader takes responsibility to assist the organization in creating such conditions so that, instead of being controlled, the organization generates its own order and responds creatively to the environment. This role is not only more productive for the organization, it is liberating for the leader as well. By helping to unleash the creative potential of their organizations, entrepreneurial leaders are unleashing their own.

AUTOCRATIC LEADERSHIP

Autocratic leadership is one in which a leader retains as much power and decision-making authority as possible. The leader does not consult followers, nor are they allowed to give any input. Followers are expected to obey orders without receiving any explanations. The motivation environment is produced by creating a structured set of rewards and punishments.

Autocratic leadership style involve the leader making all the decisions, wielding absolute power, assigning tasks to members of the group and maintaining a master-servant relationship with members of the group. Leadership style refers to a leader's manner of behavior in a work situation.

One's leadership style depends on one's personality and is therefore relatively fixed; which deals mainly with the manner in which the leader carries out his/her leadership functions or roles - the use of authority and power and the approach to the decision-making process.

Mohammed Reza Pahlavi was the king of Iran, known as the Shah. The Shah was a pro-western dictator. The Shah ran a brutally repressive regime, enforced by the notorious Savak secret police. Many Iranians were angered by his autocratic rule and the spectacle of rampant corruption throughout his government. (David Leigh and Rob Evans, Shah of Iran, 2007)

Authoritarian leaders provide clear expectations for what needs to be done, when it should be done, and how it should be done. Autocratic leadership is an extreme form of transactional leadership, where leader has absolute power over his or her followers or team. Followers and team members have little opportunity for making suggestions, even if these would be in the team or organization's interest.

Most people tend to resent being treated like this. Because of this, autocratic leadership usually leads to high levels of absenteeism and staff turnover. For some routine and unskilled jobs, the style can remain effective where the advantages of control outweigh the disadvantages.

People who get this rating are very much task oriented and are hard on their subordinates (autocratic). There is little or no allowance for cooperation or collaboration. Heavily task oriented people display these characteristics: they are very strong on schedules; they expect people to do what they are told without question or debate; when something goes wrong they tend to focus on who is to blame rather than concentrate on exactly what is wrong and how to prevent it; they are intolerant of what they see as dissent (it may just be someone's creativity), so it is difficult for their subordinates to contribute or develop.

Autocratic leaders may use an authoritarian style on a new member who is just learning the job. The leader is competent and a good coach. The member is motivated to learn a new skill. The leader has a low concern for people and uses such methods as threats and other fear-based methods to achieve conformance. There are 2 (two) characteristic of autocratic leadership styles, includes:

a. The leader solves the problem or makes the decision using information available to the leader at the time.

b. The leader obtains the necessity information from team members, than decides the solution. The leader may or may not tell team members what the problem is in getting information from them. The role played by team members in making the decision is one of providing the necessary information to the leader rather than generating or evaluating alternative solution.

The authoritarian leadership style is well suited for certain environments such as the military, a prison, etc. In those settings, in which the lives of people depend on others following orders, the authoritarian styles is ideal. Organizations with many autocratic leaders have higher turnover and absenteeism than other organizations.

Authoritarian leaders make decisions independently with little or no input from the rest of the group. However, organizations built on authoritarian lines have many problems. In authoritarian organizations it is orders which are passed down from above and the manager's role is to pass orders down the 'chain of command'. He/she is usually not expected to make decisions and so carries little responsibility.

Authoritarian organizations are effective in an emergency and perhaps the best known authoritarian organizations are the armed forces. Orders are passed down and mistakes readily result in critical appraisal and dismissal. Hence people avoid making decisions so that matters to be decided are either passed up for the decisions to be made at a higher level. An autocratic leader usually:

a. Rely on threats and punishment to influence members: Create a structured set of rewards and punishments

b. Do not trust members: Members only do what they have to for leaders, they do not trust

c. Do not allow for member input: Do not consult members, nor are they allowed to giving any input

The authoritarian leader who unilaterally controls situations and forces others to comply with his or her demands can't create the environment needed to sustain these changes. Authoritarian leadership saps the intrinsic motivation that is the lifeblood of creativity. Autocratic leadership is not all bad. Sometimes it is the most effective style to use. These situations can include:

a. New, untrained members who do not know which tasks to perform or which procedures to follow

b. Requirement of detailed orders and instructions: The instructions that provide greater detail and context to the order, to ensure an appropriate level of understanding.

c. No response to any other leadership style: No one best style of leadership exists, therefore use the style of leadership necessary in any situation you face. It might be autocratic style

d. Need high productivity: Leaders should realize that obtaining high performance requires the total team to be productive. They must be brave and smart enough to implement a leadership style

e. Time limitation to make a decision: When time available for decision making is limited; team participation might not be required. The leader makes final decision, and team is not part of decision

f. A leader's power is challenged by member: Autocratic leadership was characterized by the greatest incidence of hostility and aggressiveness among members or by the greatest apathy. Leader retains all authority and responsibility

g. The area was poorly managed: This leadership style is good for followers that need close supervision to perform certain tasks. Unfortunately, when the autocratic group leaders were absent, the group tended to fall apart

h. Work needs to be strictly coordinated with another group or organization: Leaders define the way that fosters the ability of everyone in the group to collaborate with other group, maximize diversity and foster cultures of inclusion. Organization needs better leadership, more coordination and a more professional attitude

Autocrats primary are concerned with tasks for which they're responsible. They believe the key is to focus less on followers and their needs and more on the work related issue. In doing so, they use their position to prescribe solutions and direct others to comply. This type of leader usually has more followers with low level of job satisfaction. The autocratic leadership style should not be used when members:

a. Become tense, fearful, or resentful: They need a leader who understands them and their point of view; and involve his/herself in other people's problems

b. Expect to have their opinions heard: A leader must be ready to lend their ears to people who just want to be listened and understood

c. Depend on their leader to make all their decisions: Leaders might be forced to make quick decisions; therefore they must have this skill

d. Show low morale, high turnover and absenteeism and work stoppage: Leaders should show a high degree of confidence that the followers will assume their capability to do something in effective manner

An authoritarian leadership style thus well suited in a very structured environment, where the lives of people are stake, or the level of professionalism need is high.

The authoritarian leadership style is characterized by a leader who makes all the decisions and passes the directives to subordinates who are expected to carry these out under very close supervision. Any follower's attempt at questioning the directives given is discouraged.

There is little or no opportunity for subordinates to develop initiative and creativity. Employee behavior is closely controlled through such means as punishment, reward, arbitrary rules, and task orientation.

The authoritarian leadership style is based upon the assumption that the leader knows everything and knows what is best for the organization. They tend to be arrogant, hostile, boastful, and egotistical.

BUREAUCRATIC LEADERSHIP

Bureaucracy is the structure, and set of regulations in place to control activity, usually in large organizations. It is represented by standardized procedure (rule-following), formal division of powers, hierarchy, and relationships.

Bureaucratic leaders work by the book. They ensure that their members follow procedures exactly. This is a very appropriate style for work involving serious safety risks (such as working with machinery, with toxic substances or at heights) or where large sums of money are involved (such as cash-handling). A bureaucracy needs:

a. Well-defined division: Define area and responsibility appropriately

b. System: Require to prevent conflict between persons within group, and between groups within organization.

c. Hierarchy: The authority and status are differentially distributed among group members

d. Networks that connect one to another through flows of information and cooperation.

Everything must be done according to procedure or policy. If it isn't covered, the leader refers to the next level above him or her. This leader is really more of a police officer who enforces the rules. This style can be effective when:

a. Members perform routine tasks over and over: Leadership a first stage and central to getting day-to-day routines carried out. It doesn't stimulate improvement.

b. Members need to understand certain standards or procedures: Members work with dangerous or delicate equipment that requires a definite set of procedures to operate. Work needs highly safety or security. Leaders ensure that all the steps have been followed prior to sending it to the next level of authority.

c. Members perform tasks that require handling cash: Leaders in the organizations to decrease corruption.

Bureaucracy applies a system of promotion based upon seniority or achievement (dependent on judgment of superiors); rules that regulate the conduct of an organization are clearly defined. Therefore, administrative acts, decisions, and rules are formulated and recorded in writing.

People, who demonstrate adequate technical training qualification, can be selected to the higher level; and the hierarchy is dominated by the principle of appointment. This style is ineffective when:

a. Work habits form that they are hard to break, especially if they are no longer useful.

b. Members lose their interest in their jobs and in their co-workers.

c. Members do only what is expected of them and no more.

This style of leadership follows a close set of standards. Everything is done in an exact, specific way to ensure safety and/or accuracy. You will often find this leadership role in a situation where the work environment is dangerous and specific sets of procedures are necessary to ensure safety.

The bureaucratic leader is subject to strict and systematic discipline and control in the conduct of the office; to obedience based on rational values and rules and established by agreement (or imposition). The office holder is restricted to impersonal official obligations and commands.

There is a clearly defined hierarchy of offices. Persons exercise the authority of their office and are subject to an impersonal order; officials, not persons exercise authority. They have the necessary authority to carry out their specialized functions.

In a business, people are remunerated by fixed salaries, in money and in pensions. Salary scales are graded according to rank in the hierarchy. A bureaucratic leader will tend to create detailed instructions for other members of a group. This type of leader would also be very successful working in organization role.

CHARISMATIC LEADERSHIP

Fundamentally, the leadership adopted is the one with which the person is most comfortable; which is dependent on the person's values, personality, and how comfortable it is to allow subordinates to participate in the decision-making process.

A charismatic leadership style can appear similar to a transformational leadership style, in that the leader injects huge doses of enthusiasm into his or her team, and is very energetic in driving others forward.

Martin Luther King Jr. was a charismatic, persuasive leader with spiritual energy that grabbed the attention of his audience and his persuasion led people to make changes. Martin Luther King believed in freedom for his people, which affected the way he gave many of his speeches and the way he lived his life.

A charismatic leader tends to believe more in him/herself than in their team. This can create a risk that a project, or even an entire organization, might collapse if the leader were to leave. In the eyes of their followers, success is tied up with the presence of the charismatic leader. As such, charismatic leadership carries great responsibility, and needs long-term commitment from the leader.

Charisma describes quality that inspires loyalty and enthusiasm in others; a spiritual power or personal quality that gives an individual influence or authority over large numbers of people. The trait approach to charisma looks at qualities such as being visionary, energetic, unconventional, and exemplary. Charismatic leaders are also thought to possess outstanding rhetorical ability.

Charisma is your key to become attractive, confident and successful person; quickly and easily. Charisma actually comes from working on yourself. It comes from liking and accepting yourself unconditionally as you do and say the specific things that develop within you a powerful, charismatic personality. Charismatic leaders show transformational viewpoint, i.e.:

a. Vision and articulation: Leadership is the ability to articulate a vision, to embrace the values of that vision, and nurture an environment where everyone can reach the organizations goals and their own personal needs.

b. Sensitivity to the environment: Leaders are able to learn and adapt.

c. Sensitivity to member needs: Leaders are self-aware to best meet the needs of their followers. The leaders should find out a sure way to experience an increase in their organization's giving.

d. Personal risk taking: Risk taking is a major component of leadership. They understand the worthiness of the personal sacrifices and effort.

e. Perform unconventional behavior: Leaders demonstrate behavior that is unconventional. They express the vision not just verbally but through the leader's behavior.

The charismatic leader and the transformational leader can have many similarities, i.e. the transformational leader may be charismatic. The transformational leader has a basic focus of transforming the organization and, quite possibly, their followers, but the charismatic leader may not want to change anything.

Charismatic leaders use a wide range of methods to manage their image and, if they are not naturally charismatic, may practice assiduously at developing their skills. They may engender trust through visible self-sacrifice and taking personal risks in the name of their beliefs. They will show great confidence in their followers. They are very persuasive and make very effective use of body language as well as verbal language.

Deliberate charisma is played out in a theatrical sense, where the leader is 'playing to the house' to create a desired effect. They also make effective use of storytelling, including the use of symbolism and metaphor. Main components of charisma include

a. Message - Unconsciously send out signals to others

b. Persuasive talent - No idea, however great, ever gets anywhere until it's adopted. Charismatic persons can distill complex ideas into simple messages

c. Ability to speak – Able to communicate his goals to the people, understand of how to deal with people, ability to command the follower, and capability to interact with people

d. Listening skill - Rarely taught and infrequently practiced, listening is nonetheless a key to communicating and making others feel special in your presence;

e. Utilize space and time - Use of spatial and temporal territories can make or break relationships

A charismatic person has generally these attributes, i.e. ability to control emotions; induce them in others; be impervious to the influences of other charismatic people. Charismatic leadership is an impression process enacted in acts of:

a. Framing - Communication that causes others to accept one meaning over another; describes frames as being conceptual views of particular situations; presenting the organization's purpose and mission in ways the energizes followers; framing vision, charismatic leaders choose words that amplify audience values, stress importance and efficacy, and if necessary, will denigrate their opponents; and strategic encounters in which one is attempting to sell a particular self-image.

b. Scripting - Set of directions that outlines expected behavior; and supply the definition of the situation. Scripting is what leaders do before a performance. Scripts are to integrate activities in a very repetitive and integrated way, with few spaces for improvements.

The charismatic leader cast themselves in the role of the visionary leading the assembled characters in pursuit of their vision, while not falling into victim to the trickery and schemes of their antagonists.

The charismatic leadership can save the day, and rescue people from antagonists. It will evolve dialog that is verbal and non-verbal exchanges to express character. Directing that includes rehearsals to give desired impressions; deal with the changed expectations of followers, who wanted a confident and dynamic, and using props in speeches.

c. Staging - Charismatic leaders manage their performances; not just passion for a cause, commitment, vision, energy, courage; they all have dramatic stage-effect and performing - show time. The charismatic leader takes the stage to enact scripted dialog and set up the frame to construct their charismatic character; exemplifying trustworthiness and moral responsibility; to be examples to their followers of the non-violent characters they expected followers to imitate; self-sacrifice and discipline.

Charismatic leaders engage in self-promotion to appear competent, powerful, determined, innovative, etc. They may also perform in ways that promotes their vision of the future, and promote the organization or the cause of why they lead/serve/embody; includes face-work that can be the defensive protection of self-image, as in saving-face; giving accounts that control the damaging of scandals; it can also be the personalization of a cause.

Charismatic leaders, who are building a group, whether it is a political party, a cult or a business team, will often focus strongly on making the group very clear and distinct, separating it from other groups. They will then build the image of the group, in particular in the minds of their followers, as being far superior to all others.

Charismatic leaders voiced overarching goals, communicated high performance expectations to followers, and exhibited confidences in follower ability to meet those high expectations. In their charismatic character roles, actors were coached to use nonverbal cues such as extended eye contact, using vocal variety, speaking in a relaxed posture, and using animated facial expression.

The values of the charismatic leader are highly significant. If they are well-intentioned towards others, they can elevate and transform an entire organization. If they are selfish and Machiavellian; they can create cults and effectively rape the minds (and potentially the bodies) of the followers. Their self-belief is so high, they can easily believe that they are infallible, and hence lead their followers into an abyss, even when they have received adequate warning from others.

The self-belief can also lead them into psychotic narcissism, where their self-absorption or need for admiration and worship can lead to their followers questioning their leadership. They may also be intolerant of challengers and their non-replace-ability (intentional or otherwise) can mean that there are no successors when they leave.

Delegating Leadership or Laissez-Faire Leadership

The laissez-faire leadership style involves non-interference policy, allows complete freedom to all workers and has no particular way of attaining goals. Leaders allow followers to make the decision.

However, the leader is still responsible for the decisions that are made. Also known as lais…sez faire (or lais…ser faire), which is the noninterference in the affairs of others. This French phrase means leave it be and is used to describe a leader who leaves his or her colleagues to get on with their work. It can be effective if the leader monitors what is being achieved and communicates this back to his or her team regularly.

Most often, laissez-faire leadership works for teams in which the individuals are very experienced and skilled self-starters. Unfortunately, it can also refer to situations where leaders are not exerting sufficient control.

The style is largely a hands off view that tends to minimize the amount of direction and face time required. This style works well if you have highly trained and highly motivated direct reports. Delegating leadership is characterized by the following behaviors:

a.   Give freedom: Leaders give members the power to accomplish their responsibilities. They give them the creative space and freedom to do their job.

b. Non-intervention: Interventions are contentious, challenging and potentially capable of negative and unintended consequences. Non-intervention can encourage true acceptance.

c. Non-judgmental: Leaders help a member or team to work together in a collaborative way by focusing on the process, which enable the followers themselves to come up with their own answers and solutions.

d. Accept: A leader is willing to accept the responsibilities, learn to accept criticism, and accept mistake and failure.

The "laissez-faire" style is essentially non-influential. It tends to leave people alone to do as they see fit. This is used when members are able to analyze the situation and determine what needs to be done and how to do it. As a leader, you cannot do everything. You must set priorities and delegate certain tasks. On other hand, this is not a style to use so that you can blame others when things go wrong, rather this is a style to be used when you have the full trust and confidence in the people below you. This is an effective style to use when:

a. Members are highly skilled, experienced, and educated.

b. Members have pride in their work and the drive to do it successfully on their own.

c. Outside experts, such as specialists or consultants are being used

d. Members are trustworthy and experienced.

Delegating leaders offer little or no guidance to group members and leave decision-making up to group members. While this style can be effective in situations where group members are highly qualified in an area of expertise, it often leads to poorly defined roles and a lack of motivation. This style should not be used when:

a. Members feel insecure at the unavailability of a leader.

b. The leader cannot provide regular feedback to let members know how well they are doing.

c. Leaders are unable to thank employees for their good work.

d. The leader doesn't understand his or her responsibilities and is hoping the members can cover for him or her.

The laissez-faire leadership style is also known as the hands-off style. It is one in which the leader provides little or no direction and gives members as much freedom as possible. All authority or power is given to the members and they must determine goals, make decisions, and resolve problems on their own.

A Laissez-faire leader will let his/her people do whatever they need to do to get the job done, because the people will act in their the best interest of the organization and themselves. The leaders are still involved in decisions and problem solving, but control is with the follower. The follower decides when and how the leader will be involved.

PEOPLE-ORIENTED LEADERSHIP OR RELATIONS-ORIENTED LEADERSHIP

When there is the absence of leadership and every one is free to do as it pleases; usually, with no goals or direction. There is a state of confusion, and lack of confidence in leadership. If the members also often doubt their own ability to accomplish the task at hand, thus productivity is usually very low.

The people-oriented leadership is the opposite of task-oriented leadership. The leader is totally focused on organizing, supporting and developing the people in the group/organization.

This leadership is a participative style; it tends to lead to good teamwork and creative collaboration. In practice, most leaders use both task-oriented style and people-oriented style of leadership. People-oriented leadership is characterized by:

a. Focus is on people: He or she motivates, provides incentives, delegates the authority, empower, consults, and involves others.

b. Efforts focus on selecting, developing, building, and guiding the staff and co-opting them to achieve the goals of the organization.

c. The leader motivates members to seek self-fulfillment, sets challenging goals, and encourages self-development.

d. The leader develops tools, mechanisms, methods, and technologies for problem solving and conflict resolution

This type of leadership style would also be appropriate when there is nothing significant at stake. Leaders who set relationships as a priority recognize the synergistic effects of attending to the human side of work. If you want people working with you; focus on them first, i.e. understand their needs and motivations, support them, work together to fill the gaps in skills and knowledge.

The leaders are concerned about the human needs of their followers. They build teamwork, help members with their problems, and provide support. They're sensitive toward their feelings, needs and goals. Before making decisions, they seek suggestions from subordinates and consider what effects these decisions will have on the team. They enjoy being the center of attention, and that often bothers followers.

While people oriented leaders are strong relationally, they may struggle at accomplishing necessary leadership tasks and may prove to be weak at administration.

SERVANT LEADERSHIP

Servant-leadership emphasizes the leader's role as steward of the resources provided by the organization. Servant leadership is different from servant-hood. It encourages leaders to serve others while staying focused on achieving results in line with the organization's values and integrity.

Some leaders have put the needs of their followers first. So that, the people served grow as individuals, becoming 'healthier, wiser, more autonomous and more likely themselves to become servants. This term describes a leader who is often not formally recognized as such.

When someone, at any level within an organization, leads simply by virtue of meeting the needs of his or her team, he or she is described as a servant leader. In many ways, servant leadership is a form of democratic leadership, as the whole team tends to be involved in decision-making.

Supporters of the servant leadership model suggest it is an important way ahead in a world where values are increasingly important, in which servant leaders achieve power on the basis of their values and ideals. The servant leader serves others, rather than others serving the leader. Serving others thus comes by helping them to achieve and improve. Principles of servant leadership are:

   a. Service: Leadership enables environments that empower and encourage service; serve others

b. Empathy: Treating everyone in the organization with empathy helps leaders earn trust.

Empathy is an important leadership attribute that directly impacts your ability to relate well to others. When it comes to leading others, empathy is a clear difference maker. Those who lead others in an empathetic way are seen as caring and in touch with their followers.

c. Listen: Leadership needs to listen, and feel the pulse of the workforce. The leaders listen and earn respect.

d. Trust: Trusting relationships as a basic platform for collaboration and service

e. Awareness: Awareness is a continuous process of understanding related to capacity, abilities, potential and results. A high degree of organizational awareness improves organizational analysis, hiring and staffing decisions, team building, communication, and culture and leadership style.

Awareness fosters insight that transforms good results to great results. Awareness identifies needs and creates urgency for change by measuring realities, environment, effectiveness, opportunities for growth in people

f. Persuasion: As a good leader, persuasion is vital to meet the group's goal or objective. You must have the instinct of incessantly finding yourself seeking fulfillment through directing others to success. The persuasion consists of the drive to succeed, preservation of the group, and attainment of a common goal.

Leaders have to influence others to follow in order to meet the team's need of achievement. Persuasion strategies also leads the group to attain a common goal as you may try to show the process, the end results, and the rewards of accomplishment to encourage them that their efforts will not be in vain.

g. Conceptualization: The leaders dare to dream great dreams. They value the ability to think beyond day-to-day reality. They nurture others' ability to work outside their usual frame of thinking. They encourage creative ideas and innovation.

h. Stewardship: Leaders demonstrate a sense of responsibility to the larger entities. They take ownership for the outcomes of their acts, including successes and setbacks.

i. Growth: Leaders are committed to fostering personal and professional growth of all people, encourage worker involvement, responsibility, expression of talents, and input in decision-making. They give credit when it's due, appreciate effort and success, and help others grow in strength, awareness and maturity.

j. Community: Community building as a way to create environments in which people can trust each other and work together

k. Foresight: The leaders strive to understand lessons from the past, appreciate present realities, and strive to foresee possible consequences of their decisions.

l. Healing: Leaders appreciate each person's inherent worth, talents, efforts and contributions, and express their appreciation. They strive to act in ways that are positive, caring and considerate.

Servant leadership instead emphasizes collaboration, trust, empathy, and the ethical use of power. The leadership is dedicated to the growth and development of others.

Servant leaders are committed to building value-based organizations that contribute to creating a sustainable, just, and caring society. The servant leader serves the people, he/she leads, which implies that they are an end in themselves rather than a means to an organizational purpose or bottom line.

TASK-ORIENTED LEADERSHIP

A highly task-oriented leader focuses only on getting the job done, and can be quite autocratic. He or she will actively define the work and the role required, put structures in place, plan, organize and monitor.

Leaders believe that they get results by consistently keeping people busy and urging them to produce. They may identify poor performers and demand more of them, therefore the leaders need to:

a. Take responsibility for the group and guiding the group toward its goals: Setting group goals is basically a process of generating a number of alternative concerns the group might pursue and then selecting a few top priority concerns the group feels it can address.

Leadership is required to create an atmosphere in which the quality of opinions is not judged and in which all members feel free to participate.

b.   Determine how the group will achieve the goals: A strategy is a plan of action to achieve a goal and the goal of the organization.

Your strategy consists of specific steps and milestones. The milestones are periodic measurements to determine that you are on the path to achieve your goal. Check in on your strategy and compare your progress at predefined intervals. Allow some flexibility in between those scheduled intervals, but challenge yourself to remain on schedule as each milestone date arrives.

The leaders should be visionaries and most set goals for their ministries and regularly challenge people to accomplish those goals. They focus on tasks: most of their daily initiatives occur simply to facilitate achievement of work-related goals. Characteristic of task-oriented leadership style is, at least, i.e.:

a.   Place emphasis on achieving organization goals: Take the organizational structure and internal work procedures into account.

b.   Give emphasis to the roles of planning, coordination, administrative communication, budgeting and decision making.

c.   Authoritative, centralized: No delegation of authority and no involvement of organization members in decision making.

d.   Demonstrate tight control and supervision closely linked to processes and outcomes.

e.   Not tolerate deviations from the rules and processes that regulate the life of the organization. The leader displays very low tolerance for ambiguity.

Task orientation means a leader has foremost in mind the job that must get done. Without seeking input from members, the leaders structure the work, define the goals, allocate resources, and focus on achieving production quotas or delivery of services.

TRANSACTIONAL LEADERSHIP

Transactional leadership as being when one person takes the initiative in making contact with others for the purpose of an exchange of valued things. The exchange could be economic or political or psychological in nature: A swap of goods or one good for money; a trading of votes between candidate and citizen or between legislators; hospitality to another person in exchange for willingness to listen to one's troubles.

Task-oriented leaders often struggle with the relational side of leadership. They have to resist the temptation to take control of a ministry and to work around rather than with a ministry team. A few leaders rely on their official designated power or on their ability to be persuasive to get people to do what needs to be done. Most managers and leaders utilize transactional leadership techniques.

Transactional leadership makes clear to members the reward or compensation for completing the task or requirements. This leadership starts with the idea that team members agree to obey their leader totally when they take on a job.

The transaction is (usually) that the organization pays the team members in return for their effort and compliance. The leaders have a right to punish the team members if their work doesn't meet the pre-determined standard. The approach emphasizes getting things done within the umbrella of the status quo; almost in opposition to the goals of the transformational leadership.

It's considered to be a by the book approach in which the person works within the rules. As such, it's commonly seen in large, bureaucratic organizations.

When things go wrong, then the subordinate is considered to be personally at fault, and is punished for their failure (just as they are rewarded for succeeding). Team members can do little to improve their job satisfaction under transactional leadership. The leader could give team members some control of their income/reward by using incentives that encourage even higher standards or greater productivity.

Alternatively a transactional leader could practice management by exception, whereby, rather than rewarding better work, he or she would take corrective action if the required standards were not met.

Transactional leadership is really just a way of managing rather a true leadership style as the focus is on short-term tasks. It has serious limitations for knowledge-based or creative work, but remains a common style in many organizations.

TRANSFORMATIONAL LEADERSHIP

Transformational leaders are always visible and will stand up to be counted rather than hide behind their people. They show by their attitudes and actions how everyone else should behave. They also make continued efforts to motivate and rally their followers, constantly doing the rounds, listening, soothing and enthusing.

Transformational leadership augments the effects of transactional leadership on the efforts, satisfaction, and effectiveness of subordinates.

Transformational leadership starts with the development of a vision, a view of the future that will excite and convert potential followers. The leader is to constantly sell the vision, which this takes energy and commitment. A person with this leadership style is a true leader who inspires his or her team constantly with a shared vision of the future.

Transformational leaders are highly visible, and spend a lot of time communicating. They don't necessarily lead from the front, as they tend to delegate responsibility amongst their team. While their enthusiasm is often infectious, they generally need to be supported by details people.

Management styles have began to shift and superior leaders are developing who elevate the interests of their followers, ensure the group is aware of the collective mission and purpose and motivate followers to strive for the good of the group rather than self-interest. To do this, the leaders utilized a few different approaches collectively called transformational leadership.

Transformational leadership occurs through a leader's charismatic personality, inspiring followers to improve; through meeting the needs of the followers or through intellectually stimulating them. Managers who utilize transformational techniques are more likely to be viewed as effective leaders by their own management and by their workforce.

Organizations that develop their members in a transformational style experience a vast improvement in growth and development. The primary focus of this leadership style is to make change happen in oneself, others, groups, and organizations

Many organizations need both transactional and transformational leadership. The transactional leaders ensure that routine work is done reliably, while the transformational leaders look after initiatives that add value. Transformational leader is called on to support and facilitate others in the process of change.

Transformational leaders ask themselves to lead and support large scale changes. This high level of change almost certainly elicits whatever strengths and weaknesses the leader has. At the core each transformational leader must commit to personal development.

A leader sees how they examine their own beliefs, cultivates positive and effective communication, and contributes to effective team functioning are key to their credibility with others. Transformational leader also uses to sustain motivation in the use of ceremonies, rituals and other cultural symbolism. Transformation leadership approach is often highly effective, as it exhibits:

a. Charisma: Personal attribute that arouse fervent popular devotion and enthusiasm.

b. Inspirational: Able to do just that inspire their members and others around them.

c. Intellectual stimulation: Stimulate others regardless of the people's intellectual capabilities.

d. Individual consideration: Have a high degree of empathy for others and their belongings.

e. Proactive and prospective: Leaders have to be proactive about "knowing what they don't know," especially about themselves. Managers have a short-term perspective, leaders have a longer-term perspective.

f. Passionate about quality: have the management skill, be capable, and have a solid commitment to progressive values.

g. Show good stewards of resources: accompany and support members in meetings with organization's objective, and give stewards the skills, knowledge and resources to make them effective people.

h. Catalysts for creativity and innovation: Leadership can and does create a climate that encourages creativity and innovation. They stimulate the creativity and innovation processes within the organization.

i. Contemplative: Demonstrates the connection between beliefs held and the integration of those beliefs into leadership practice.

j. Facilitators and team players: Leadership involves being a good team player. A person who performs the role of team leadership also functions as a team member and team player. Leaders need to build effective teams and teams need to practice the art of teamwork and build leadership skills. The leaders, as facilitators, enhance their effectiveness.

k. Open communication: Communication between leaders and followers is essential, not only for getting individual and organizational needs met, but also for developing significant interpersonal relationships and for assuring the adequate functioning of the people in the organization.

    Open, honest communication builds leaders and grows businesses. Open communication and strong leadership are the keys to managing organizational change successfully.

l. Place the well being of others and the organization above personal endeavors

m. Have integrity: Integrity is the cement that binds organizations together, the cornerstone of mission accomplishment. Leaders must always display the highest standards of integrity.

n. Respect and empower others: Leaders are able to motivate, to energize and to empower others. When people are excited and empowered in this sense, it affects both their task initiation and task persistence. Empowered people get more involved, take on more difficult situations, and act more confidently. They expend more effort on a given task and are more persistent in their efforts.

    With leadership comes respect. With respect comes communication. Leadership shares and communicates a unified vision to the entire group or organization, and ensures that those individuals are guided properly.

o. Care for individuals and the organization: Leadership that fosters care would bring clarity to the issue of roles and responsibilities; accountability, and improve satisfaction.

Transformational leaders pursue personal awareness through reflection, planning, and action. They are aware of their own interpersonal strengths and weaknesses and use that awareness to build positive relationships. Transformational leadership is about aligning personal, organizational goals to create a new, redesigned organization. It needs to turning:

a. Relationships into partnerships: Internal partnerships are actually relationship between leaders, followers and other stakeholders within the organization. The deeper the relationship with all your vendors, the more value you will receive from them. One way to derive value for any relationship is to take advantage of your contacts' expertise, knowledge, and connections. You can "buy" more influence with relationships.

   Relationship building is a great way to maximize your influence within and outside an organization. Partners share authority, responsibility and risks, jointly contribute resources and funding and benefit mutually from the goods and services provided.

   At the least, such partnerships require common objectives, active partners, interdependent and complementary contributions from the partners, and a commitment to open relationships under the criteria of equity and mutually agreed upon rules of the game.

b. Plans into actions: Having dreams and passion is not enough. Action is the key. You can be the most talented person in the world or have the best ideas, yet still if you do not take action you will achieve nothing. Set goal and take action.

c. Opportunities into achievements: There are many paths to achievement and many opportunities for involvement. Leadership develops from opportunities to be in decision making situations and taking an active part in all phases of the business.

Transformational leadership is hard work, especially in the context of the practical realities of leading change. Transformational leader has to be very careful in creating trust, and their personal integrity. They are people-oriented and believe that success comes first and last through deep and sustained commitment.

DEMOCRATIC LEADERSHIP OR PARTICIPATIVE LEADERSHIP

An organization built on participative basis showing the spirit through decision making, including setting of targets, takes place at all levels of the organization. The position where an organization is placed thus depends on the balance of authority between rulers and ruled, between owner and worker, between the establishment and the population.

Leaders would require a detailed knowledge in each case of management and of organization effectiveness. In a participative organization, involvement in decision-making improves the understanding of the issues involved by those who must carry out the decisions; people are more committed to actions where they have involved in the relevant decision-making; people are less competitive and more collaborative when they are working on joint goals; when people make decisions together, the social commitment to one another is greater and thus increases their commitment to the decision; and several people deciding together make better decisions than one person alone.

The democratic leader acts to value inputs and commitment via participation, listening to both the bad and the good news. The leader makes maximum use of participative methods, engaging people lower down the organization in decision-making.

Although a democratic leader will make the final decision, he or she invites other members of the team to contribute to the decision-making process. Members feel in control of their own destiny, such as the promotion they desire, and so are motivated to work hard by more than just a financial reward. As participation takes time, this approach can lead to things happening more slowly, but often the end result is better.

Democratic leadership style involves the use of consultative approach, encourages group participation in decision making and maintaining a master-master relationship with group members. Participative (democratic) leadership is an effective leadership style.

Democratic leaders offer guidance to group members, but they also participate in the group and allow input from other group members. Both leader and members are participating in group decision making by giving input and seeking clarity.

Participative leaders encourage group members to participate, but retain the final say over the decision-making process. Group members feel engaged in the process and are more motivated and creative.

This leadership style is characterized by a structured but cooperative approach to decision making. It focuses on group relationships and sensitivity to the people in the organization. This type of leadership style fosters professional competence. Supervision is minimal as individuals take the responsibility for their behavior. Members are encouraged to express their ideas and make suggestions. However, shared decisions are not likely to occur in all aspects of the organizational operations. Democratic leaders sell ideas. They tend to be warm, confident, and friendly.

The democratic leadership style encourages people participation and professional growth. It is well suited in environments where people have a very high level of expertise such as software engineers, lawyers, doctors, mature teachers, etc. The democratic leadership style promotes greater job satisfaction and improved morale.

A leader is not expected to know everything - this is why he/she employs knowledgeable and skillful people. Using this style is of mutual benefit - it allows people to become part of the team and allows the leader to make better decisions. The leader facilitates and takes part in decisions, but control is with the follower.

Partnership is a sound strategic approach, it is not the only one, and is a complement to the others. Because partnership is a relationship between two or more persons who join to carry on shared goals; encourage teamwork; and believe that an active and well-informed team member is necessary to ensure the highest standards. In a partnership the partners share equal responsibility for the duty, benefits, risks and liabilities.

By using a participative style of leadership, a leader doesn't relinquish the responsibility to get the job done, but gives members the authority to help arrive at the right decision to get the job done correctly. Participation is particularly effective in less structured or rapidly changing work environments.

In democratic leadership style, members share common goals, solve common problems, and cooperate for the common good of each other; they share expertise, resources, and responsibility to reduce inefficiency and duplication of effort while fulfilling their own responsibilities; accomplish their tasks to the best of their abilities, both individually and collectively.

Partnership is midway between consensus and conflict. It will adopt methods of negotiation, dialogue and decision making. Partnership should not generate exclusiveness, but involve all the resources, reduce an individual's isolation and the social exclusion of individuals, work in closer co-operation, share other's values, striving to find the general interest, and create synergies.

Participation can occur when the leader either delegates total responsibility for tasks or allows subordinates to participate in problem-solving and decision-making processes.

At the heart of Churchill's politics was a deeply felt dedication to and confidence in the people he led.

A scarred veteran of democracy, Churchill scorned those who loved the word but rejected free elections. "Democracy is not some harlot in the street," he said in condemning the Greek Communists in the closing weeks of World War II, "to be picked up by some man with a Tommy gun. Democracy is based on reason, a sense of fair play, and freedom and a respect for the rights of other people."

Churchill is the democratic hero of our age. (Christopher Matthews, Churchill's Greatness: The Very Model of a Democratic Statesman)

On the other hand, collaboration is the basis for bringing together the knowledge, experience and skills of multiple team members to contribute to the achievements more effectively. Work can be done by consolidating and sharing your knowledge, experience and skill with others.

Collaboration enables people get involved in a common task to achieve their goals, unites a group or community with different culture and cross-cultural communication in a common commitment.

In collaboration people gain efficiently-achieved results meeting objectives; savings in time and cost; innovative, extraordinary, breakthrough results, and collective accomplishment; enabling the emergence of shared understanding and realization of shared visions in complex environments and system.

In collaboration, members should understand and appreciate different perspectives through a dialogue with their peers, show ability to work effectively with peers, groups and community.

Democratic leadership can produce high quality and high quantity work for long periods of time. Many followers like the trust they receive and respond with cooperation, team spirit, and high morale. Typically the democratic leader:

a. Develop plans to help members evaluate their own performance: Leaders regularly encourage his/her members to evaluate their performance. The members and you as leader - will soon make ongoing performance improvement a natural part of each day.

b. Allow members to establish goals: Members determine their own goals; the leader guides them how it fulfills the organization's mission and then allowing the flexibility in how work gets done so as to best meet organizational goals.

c. Encourage members to grow: Leaders encourage members to participate in training sessions, form relationships with one another, and utilize their abilities to grow.

d. Recognize and encourage achievement: Leaders encourage members to act, individually and in group, to move forward to reach their full potential.

The democratic style is not always appropriate. It is most successful when used with highly skilled or experienced employees or when implementing operational changes or resolving individual or group problems. The democratic leadership style is most effective when:

a. Keep members informed about matters that affect them.

b. Share in decision-making and problem-solving duties.

c. Develop a high sense of personal growth and job satisfaction.

d. Problem requires lots of input to solve.

e. Encourage team building and participation.

Leaders use participative style with group who knows their job. The leader knows the problem, but does not have all the information. The members know their jobs and want to become part of the team. Democratic leadership should not be used when:

a. Time is not appropriate to get everyone's input: Leadership demand time commitment. Often time is not sufficient to discuss and get feed back from the concerns. Leaders should take decision based on their own considerations and calculated risks.

71

b. Easier to make the decision: Give yourself time to brainstorm and make a list of each decision you presently face. But, if it's easier to make decision without involving others, you may do it yourself.

c. Safety is a critical concern: To achieve - and sustain - high-level safety performance, it is critical to elevate personal motivation, communications, and leadership.

   The primary responsibility of leaders is to provide for the safety of people and operations. The ability of organizations to change and improve their safety performance is to a great extent dependent on leadership.

Democratic leaders focus on their followers because they feel the welfare of their team is of great importance. They tend to be easily approachable, relationship-oriented and considerate of others' feelings. They prefer to lead their members by collaboration and empowerment. They're convinced that tasks will be better accomplished if they consider their others' needs. There is no one right way to lead an organization that suits all situations. To choose the most effective approach for you, you must consider:

a. The skill levels and experience of your team

b. The work involved: Routine or new and creative

c. The organizational environment: Stable or radically changing, conservative or adventurous

d. You own preferred or natural style.

A leader will find him or herself switching instinctively between styles according to the people and work they are dealing with. This is often referred to as situational leadership. Using this style is not a sign of weakness rather it is a sign of strength that members will respect. The best leaders concern themselves both with people relationships and the tasks for which they are responsible because tasks usually are accomplished more effectively when human factors are considered. The degree of integration of task and relationship varies considerably with each leader; the exact mix partly depends upon task urgency, members' work performance and ability, organizational climate, and the leader's natural inclination toward one orientation or the other.

Leaders have to make adaptations in their leadership pattern - whether they are autocratic, democratic-participatory, charismatic, task-oriented, or person oriented, etc - if they which to be effective and achieve their goals. A leader needs to have and to display traits, or inherent personal qualities, in order to gain peoples' trust so that they will willingly follow, accept change and improve to achieve goals which are the right thing to do for themselves, the organization and those whom the organization supports.

Democratic leaders have the difficult task of both guiding the people and seeming to respond to the popular will. Autocrats are obviously freer to exercise leadership, but among them the most successful have been aware of the need to be loved and admired as well as feared, just as many of the best democratic leaders have been natural autocrats, restrained only by conscience and realism.

There are many other leadership styles, i.e. purpose-centered leadership, authentic leadership, action-centered leadership, etc, which could not be explained one by one in this book. None of the styles are inherently good or bad. Each is effective when appropriately matched to the situation.

Leadership styles, which are applied to a specific work situation or job, create the climate in which people work. The climate, which in reality is the atmosphere or perceptions of a workplace, includes the clarity with which people understand their roles and how they relate to the organization's objectives.

2ND

LEADERSHIP GREATNESS

Leadership is like beauty: difficult to define, but most people will recognize it when they see it. Being a leader is no longer denoted by a position of authority, technical skill, or one's I.Q. There is a profound yearning in both people and organizations to matter, to make a difference, to find greatness.

Leadership is communicating people's worth and potential so clearly that they are inspired to see it in themselves. We do not have to be born leaders.

Leadership is the ability to facilitate action and guide change. To lead is to direct, supervise, encourage, inspire, and co-ordinate. A leader develops personal leadership skills and encourages and trains new leaders who will follow. A leader who is aspiring to reach great heights can succeed through effective leadership training and executive coaching programs.

Leadership can be learned, practiced, and developed by training, by choice and by strength of character, people become leaders. Being a leader requires hard work, sacrifice, commitment and a willingness to grow ourselves. Usually we only get to see great people after they've achieved success. We see them after the race, not during the rigors of training.

Leaders are followed because people trust and respect them, not for the skills they possess. Leaders are sensitive. The leaders evince a high level of sensitivity to others. This sensitivity often manifest in responses to needs of others.

Leaders are present, not aloof or detached. When in conversations with others, be highly attentive to the other people involved. Listen carefully to the words and to the feelings being expressed. And they will respond with a higher level of openness and genuine communication.

74

For a comparison between an iceberg and a person's leadership; the visible 10 (ten) percent (the tip of the iceberg) represents leadership skill-the practices, attitudes and behaviors that people see. The other 90 (ninety) percent represents leadership character - those defining qualities that represent who we are but can't be seen from the outside. *(John C. Maxwell, Look Out Below, 2005)*

When our character is weak - when we are in any way lacking in self-discipline, core values, a strong sense of identity and emotional security - it will eventually hurt our capacity to lead.

Leadership is about behavior; when a self-disciplined, emotionally secure leader has a healthy sense of identity and operates under a good set of core values - in other words, when the unseen portion of his/her leadership is on solid ground.

As a leader, we must have the same sensitivity to our organizations; to the people and the systems in our organizations. When something isn't running right, the leader often identifies that something's not right.

Diagnosing humans or systems running off-kilter is more difficult than picking up a machinery problem, and often more difficult to fix. To be a great leader, build your sensitivity in your environment so you can detect when something is amiss. Then you can go find it and fix it. That's a special part of leadership.

Sensitivity to the needs and expectations of others will strengthen your authority and inspire loyalty from your followers. Sensitive leadership does not reflect weakness or a reduction in power or authority. In fact, it's just the opposite - a thoughtful and empathetic management style leads to the wise use of power. Leaders who exhibit sensitivity in the appropriate sense will find their authority.

Great leaders demonstrate actions that indicate sensitivity to and regard for the feelings and needs of others and an awareness of the impact of one's own behavior on them; being supportive of and fair with others.

Sensitivity is critical as it involves the strongest emotion of all, believing in the worth of the individual human being. We need to know people's hopes and fears, aspirations and doubts. We need responses from others as we simply can't do it alone. We learn to be responsive by concerning ourselves with others.

In Aristotelian terms, the good leader must have ethos, pathos and logos. The ethos is his moral character, the source of his ability to persuade. The pathos is his ability to touch feelings, to move people emotionally. The logos is his ability to give solid reasons for an action, to move people intellectually.

By this definition, Pericles of Athens was a great leader. Winston Churchill, Thomas Jefferson, or almost any of the founding fathers - Adams, Madison, Washington. Perhaps Lincoln, Franklin D. Roosevelt and Woodrow Wilson as well. (HP-TIME.COM,, Who Were History's Great Leaders?, 1974)

Anybody can be a leader, but it's not easy to be a great leader.

GREATNESS

No person who is a leader actually has a goal of becoming a leader. They have no interest in proving themselves but a great interest in expressing themselves. Greatness is nobleness of character. It describes superiority of a person.

Greatness can be, but is not necessarily achieving something that puts you in the history books, makes you a celebrity, or you are simply considered great in the eyes of others.

Greatness is dependent on a person's perspective. Greatness is a state of mind that one embraces and exudes that reaches into depths beyond oneself. By their passion, conviction, and continual giving to others you can recognize greatness in a person.

Greatness displays a fascinating perspective on one's character. It also reflects the optimism and compassion that is the hallmark of his/her work. Greatness emphasizes perceived superiority of a person or thing. It something meriting the highest praise or regard.

People who achieve enduring fame are those who dare to be different. Great achievers truly were different, when comparing their personality traits. We also noted many reoccurring characteristics such as courage, risk-taking, a passion for their work, and a strong determination.

One must know not only what is good for oneself but also what is good for others. One must have moral virtue, judgment, and public spirit in a fine balanced, and these traits must be equally matched to the particular circumstances of time and place.

Great organizations need great leaders; ones who act with sense of greatness. They create positive energy and generate ideas and approaches for organizational effectiveness. Leaders aren't necessarily born; leaders are often shaped by opportunity. Some men are born great, some achieve greatness, and some have greatness thrust upon them. It's not necessarily coming by genetic. There's no hard evidence to support that assumption, it dooms every one of us to accept our limitations as our destiny.

Born great has two possible meanings: either being born to a great position, such as that of a hereditary monarch, or possessing natural talents and/or virtues of an exceptional kind. Clearly not everyone born to a great position is worthy of it and relatively few people may have the qualities of great leaders. But the greatness indicates a person has qualities out of the ordinary. There is a greatness gene but there is also a string of extraordinary qualities.

Dalai Lama, the spiritual and political leader of Tibet is believed to be the Living Buddha by his followers and devotees. He is not elected but discovered on the manifestation of certain characteristics as a child.

There was a gap of leadership when the 13th Dalai Lama died in 1933 without an immediate successor. He was born in Takster, a small Tibetan village, to a peasant family on 6th July 1935. The two-year old child was said to be the reincarnation of the 13th Dalai Lama. Dalai Lama was awarded the Nobel Peace Prize in 1989 for his patient peaceful struggle for Tibet. (Dalai Lama - The Born Leader)

Some great leaders become so by being great followers. Some great leaders are perceived as great leaders because they have great followers. Some great leaders are automatically thought to be great because they have a well-known name. Some great leaders are thought to be great leaders because they were in the right place at the right time. Some great leaders realize they're really followers with a lot of work to get done.

Greatness, however, by very definition implies a great, an expanded view. It transcends intelligence and merely technical competence. It implies an ability to see the lesser in relation to the greater; the immediate in relation to the long term; the need for victory in relation to needs that will arise once victory has been achieved.

A leader is best when people barely recognize that they are being led and when they succeed can all say: "we did this by ourselves".

Success lies in being who we are and in the choices we are willing to make for ourselves, not in the fear of what you should do or be. A leader is someone who helps others do and become more than they ever thought possible.

Leadership is about unlocking potential, whether individual potential or that of a group, company, or organization. It is not about telling people what to do, but inspiring them to see what they are capable of, then, helping them getting there.

The qualities of great leaders - self-knowledge, commitment, willingness to look to others for support, being open to change, and a desire to go the extra mile - can determine whether anyone chooses to follow.

An important measure of a leader's own success is success of his or her followers. The strength of a leader is measured by the ability to facilitate the self-leadership of others. The first critical step towards this goal is to master self-leadership. If leaders want to lead somebody, they must first lead themselves.

Greatness merely refuses to change in the face of bad actions against one – and a truly great leader cares his fellows because he/she understands them. Greatness is simply the best of what one has to offer. Greatness does what has not been done before and inspires the same courage that it requires.

When we see it in others, we know it, and when we trust its presence in ourselves, we embody it. Greatness and leadership are so closely akin that the words give us a useful point of departure.

All of us have greatness within us. The Great Wall of China is truly great. They call it the Great Wall - because it is great, in size, and in power. It's so impressive structure that even the crass commercialization doesn't stop you from feeling its greatness. If you have a sense of personal wholeness, meaning, and connection in your work; your personal greatness will shine through your work if you do.

One way to follow your path for greatness is to focus on your spiritual growth through work. We spend most of our waking hours at work. Thus it is essential we find ways to bring spirituality to our work so we grow to our fullest potential.

Once we define the qualities of greatness, our next task was to identify the ways we work to develop these characteristics at the organization, which includes:

78

a. Promote core values; i.e. spirit, discipline, purpose, pride, etc.

b. Provide appropriate challenges: Commit to develop challenges that stretch members while allowing them to succeed; provide direction and room for innovation.

c. Expose people to great leaders: Allow people to work directly with a great leader and continue to lead with greatness in their organization. Role modeling is critical.

d. Reinforce values: Encourage practicing the organization's values for pulling meaning and learning from the day's experiences.

e. Develop core competencies: Develop the necessary skills; everyone has the ability to develop competencies with appropriate training.

f. Provide resources and support for growth: Leaders effectively lead their people towards positive change and growth.

Nothing can stop you from feeling great. Greatness describes extraordinary qualities that most clearly reveal what is good by revealing more clearly the limits of what is possible. Everyone can dream big, but not everyone takes those dreams and makes them true.

LEADERSHIP GREATNESS

Some men are born great, some achieve greatness, and some have greatness thrust upon them. Born great means either being born to a great position, such as that of a hereditary monarch, or possessing natural talents and/or virtues of an exceptional kind.

Not everyone born to a great position is worthy of it, and relatively few having the qualities of a great leader. Some achieve greatness denotes those whose greatness is self-made, achiever.

Leaders unleash their leadership potential and the leadership potential of the entire organization. Leadership is crucial to achieving organizational greatness. Greatness in leadership can be a catalyst for bringing out greatness throughout an organization.

Greatness comes from persistent quality - even in the most mundane actions. Leadership greatness describes the extraordinary qualities of one's leadership, in which the person brings out greatness throughout the organization. He/she leads others to and through greatness that keeps them feeling great.

A great leader demonstrate ability to set a strategic vision; ability to be an innovator or pioneer, impact on the way the organization evolves or functions, impact on community, results/performance, and development of others. A great leader is also trustworthy, loyal, helpful, friendly, courteous, kind, obedient, cheerful, thrifty, brave, clean and reverent.

George Washington was one such "great person" whose life and character helped to bring grand ideas about people and governments to earth at the core of a new nation.

During the American War of Independence, General Washington showed a keen sense of martial leadership. He was acutely conscious of the strategic importance of mobility and strived to keep his ill-equipped army from being pinned down in defending fixed positions against the more powerful British forces.

More impressive still was his leadership in simply keeping together an army that usually lost on the battlefield, and whose soldiers were anxious for an excuse to return to their families, farms, or other occupations. (Vontz, Thomas S. - Nixon, William A., Teaching about George Washington, 1998)

The price of greatness is responsibility; an attitude, a re-deciding every day not to do what's easiest, but to do what's right. Greatness is born during tough times and unexpected circumstances. Organizations can realize their greatest potential by exploring and understanding the values inherent in their people and purpose.

SENSE OF GREATNESS

Leadership is a key factor in organizational greatness, and today leadership is big business - organizations and individuals spend millions of dollars a year are spent on leadership courses, aimed at unleashing the greatness within seemingly ordinary people.

Leaders don't have to be perfect but to be great. It is one thing to want to be a great leader; it is another to be a great leader. Greatness is a way of life; it is the way a person lives relationships both professional and personal. They live consistently with integrity, commitment, and respect for others.

Great necessities call out great virtues. Great need gives rise to great leadership. Great need, i.e. a time when so many are focused on the individual good, instead of the common good; a time when the disparity between those with resources and those without continues to grow; a time when many are struggling to define what really matters and to live their lives accordingly; a time when violence - in the form of shootings in offices and schools - has taken on a whole new level of intensity. It is a time that calls for great leadership.

Sense is one's capacity for displaying a perception. It implies the faculty of thinking, reasoning, and acquiring and applying knowledge. It demonstrates the condition of being aware; capacity to make judgment and sensible decisions.

Sense of greatness makes people want to do more than what they are currently doing. Most often it stimulates them to think about doing things for other people, rather than directing toward self gratification.

It is really amazing the way the human mind works when the right stimulus is applied. It will switch them out for something slightly different; i.e. get up, get out and do something great. They are thinking about doing something great, and accomplishing greatness. They set up stimuli in their life that pushes them to go above and beyond their normal thought process to accomplish all that they dream of.

Everyone has the ability to dream; therefore everyone has the ability to become great.

The world needs leaders who lead with moral, ethical and values. We need leaders who do not only say they support such values, but demonstrate the sincerity of those values with positive action. We need leaders who are honest and accept responsibility for their actions. We need leaders who encourage independent thinking and action for bettering the world and the environment.

Transforming into a great leader does not occur overnight. It is a journey that is built up and torn down through circumstances, and has no finish line.

Leadership greatness must not be recognized only for its organizational accomplishments. They believe that the core of legendary leadership consists of human influence, as well as organizational accomplishment.

Attitude is the defining factor that separates leadership-mediocrity and leadership-greatness. Learn how small changes in your attitude can help you lift the spirit and motivation of your entire organization.

Great organizations are created by great leaders - leaders who can unleash the highest and best contributions of their team toward their organization's most critical strategic priorities. Every organization - and every leader - aspires to greatness. Leadership greatness takes a mind set, skill set, and tools set approach.

Great leaders act with sense of greatness. A leader is a sense-maker; displays how makes sense of the circumstances so he/she can act meaningfully in it. Becoming clear, making sense, creating meaning, is the most powerful driver the leader has working for us in leading people and organizations.

Leaders, as sense-makers, know that the way they view, review; reframe and build on past experiences - how they make sense of things - influences how successful they will be in setting positive, realistic expectations and successful outcomes. They are more rational during turmoil, inherently motivated, focused, effective and productive. Sense of greatness includes, but not limited to:

1. Sense of Growth

    i.   Development

    ii. Empowerment (Challenge, delegation, etc)

    iii. Purpose (Success, accomplishment, etc)

    iv. Vision (Hope, passion, inspiration, etc)

2. Sense of Responsibility

    i.   Accountability

    ii. Courage (Risk taking, timing, challenge, hero, decisiveness, etc)

    iii. Confidence

    iv. Focus

3. Sense of Entrepreneurship

i. Standard (Quality, ethics, morality, complying, principle, value, excellence, etc)

ii. Service (Urgency, response, communication, etc)

iii. Spirituality (Transcendence – honesty, beauty, goodness, unity)

iv. Competence (Humor, etc)

v. Connectivity (Team work, partnership, community, followership, etc)

4. Sense of Authenticity

i. Integrity

ii. Wisdom (Win-win, etc)

iii. Maturity (Consistency, humility, self-worth, belonging, expectation, responsibility, accountability, equality, etc)

iv. Excellence

v. Identity (Acceptance, character, etc)

vi. Control (Discipline, awareness, direction, etc)

vii. Commitment (Action, presence, etc)

5. Sense of Trust

i. Credibility

a. Honesty

b. Competence (Intellect, knowledge, thought, learning, etc)

ii. Fairness (Openness, etc)

iii. Sincerity (Recognition, hard work, loyalty, duty, devotion, seriousness, care, empathy, example, listening, counsel, protecting, simplicity, giving, forgiveness, encouragement, harmony, balance, ownership, etc)

iv.   Respect (Equality, etc)

v.   Courage (Change, creativity, flexibility, adaptability, etc)

Leading others to and through greatness keeps people feeling great. We are all born with the potential for greatness.

Leaders create a culture of greatness. Understanding greatness and applying greatness are completely different. Others won't understand your greatness until you lead them to greatness. Therefore, to become a leader with true sense of greatness, you have to demonstrate 'GREAT - Growth, Responsibility, Authenticity, Entrepreneurship, and Trust'.

GREATNESS-CORED LEADERSHIP: 'GREAT' CONCEPT

Core indicates the central or the basic or most important part; or the essence. Greatness-cored leadership is a set of subjects; this book describes it five sense of greatness that makes up great leader. Greatness is the core of leadership. For great organizations, sense of greatness is the core of actions.

Greatness-cored leadership is a leadership style that implies the leader, followers and the organization to truly act with sense of greatness. It consists of at least five attributes, i.e. growth, responsibility, entrepreneurship, authenticity, and trust. To becoming a great leader, you have to put sense of greatness as a guidance to lead people.

Leadership is influence – use words to move others to acting; attitude – display equality in words and actions; and example – stand before the followers and organization that creates trust and confidence. Leadership is the art of engaging the hearts and minds of ordinary people to achieve extraordinary results.

Leadership is the key to outperforming the competition. Through leadership seminars, coaching, tools, and comprehensive growth system, you will develop great leadership behaviors. Leadership focuses on the needs and growth of those being led, not the needs of those who are leading.

Leadership means greatness in all one does. A leader displays ability to take charge of his/her own life and the consequences of his/her decisions.

Leadership is rooted in one's free will, which underpins both responsibility and accountability. Just having authority does not turn anyone into a true leader.

Leaders can be made. They are ones who rise to the highest levels of greatness. At the heart of extraordinary organizations are leaders who inspire greatness that stirs passion and determination; make the impossible, possible; and produces extraordinary results.

Leaders have a clear sense of purpose, exhibit discipline and determination, elicit trust, display courage and through their example inspire those around them to overcome obstacles and achieve greatness.

Entrepreneurship cannot happen without great leaders in the organization. The role of leadership in business is indisputable. Great leaders create great businesses, as they possess traits which will help them motivate others and lead them in new directions. The leaders also have a strong sense of ethics and work to build integrity in their organizations.

A leader, who is authentic, is a person who demonstrates a passion for their purpose, practices their values consistently, and leads with their hearts as well as their heads. Authenticity is the catalyst that leverages all of the positive leadership attributes and brings them to bear more quickly and effectively on the organization. You must be genuine. Don't pretend to be someone you're not.

Leadership requires congruence, honesty and authenticity. Authenticity is a pathway to greatness. Being authentic means being present, in the moment free of any embellishment, falseness, etc. Leaders must be authentic and therefore they can be trusted. Authenticity is an important investment in greatness.

Leadership and greatness begin with a commitment to the journey of greatness. Leaders cannot lead without trust. Trust is not something that comes automatically, and establishing it requires effort, particularly in an environment of declining trust.

Mutual trust is the key to overcoming the greatest challenge of organizational development. It implies followers to respect and trust leadership, as well as leader believes in people. The most precious and intangible quality of leadership is trust.

People trust leaders who are honest, transparent, are accountable and have integrity. When leaders communicate to people that their work is meaningful and that they are important to the success of the organization, the people are likely see themselves as valued members of a team who have been entrusted with something that makes a difference. This kind of trust tends to breed more trust and good will inside the organization. It builds ownership. When people trust you, they help you win.

'GREAT' (Growth, Responsibility, Entrepreneurship, Authenticity and Trust) are traits, in which a leader, who displays great leadership and greatness within the organization, is called **The Great** by his/her followers, and the others. Great leaders are mostly demonstrating 'GREAT' attributes.

3RD

SENSE OF GROWTH

Leaders are learners and in the same time are teachers. Greatness would shine through your work if you did. One way to follow your path for greatness is to focus on your growth through work. We spend most of our waking hours at work. Thus it is essential we find ways grow to our fullest potential.

Leaders learn from mistakes - the ones you make and those made by others. Don't let failure paralyze you. Within those failures are the seeds for improvement. Look at them as opportunities for constructive growth. And develop ways to improve and develop yourself and those around you appropriately.

DEVELOPMENT

Development is to produce confident, knowledgeable and courageous leaders and others. Leadership entails a personal touch that must be personally developed. Any growing organization needs a greater amount of leaders available to lead the organization.

The leader who disciplines him/herself to be a coach will most likely not have to worry about where that leadership will come from. The power of knowledge works when each person takes responsibility for what he/she knows, who he/she knows and what he/she know.

Leaders understand that there is an invisible structure of the personal and networks within their organization that define the true roles, influence and interdependencies. When a key person left the organization without sharing his/her understanding of how to get things done; unshared knowledge loses value.

An individual, who shares his/her knowledge, earns trust and a solid reputation, which increases his/her value in the organization.

Success is not an individual matter; it depends upon our relationships with others. Connection and coordination with others matter. The manner in which you are connected matters. Increasing one's social capital is all about sharing knowledge and adding value to the organization.

Sharing knowledge in one-on-one or group discussions (through stories, analogies and metaphors) is the pathway to agreement about what something means and increased insight.

Process improvement is important; but ultimately, the long-term effectiveness of any organization lies in its people improvement. If people are committed to personal quality, innovation and continuous improvement, they are more likely to contribute their maximum potential to organizational quality objectives. Leaders make developing and challenging others a priority.

Great leaders balance personal development and organizational development. Successful organizations have leaders who develop other leaders throughout the organization with the ideas, values, energy, and edge needed to make decisions.

Develop means help others learn through teaching, training, and coaching, which includes:

a. Skill development and knowledge acquisition: Facilitate the doing of leadership - knowing what to do as a leader.

b. Personal insights: Self awareness that facilitates the "being" of leadership - being comfortable enough with your sense of self so you can truly be an effective leader.

Development creates an exciting place to work and learn. Never miss an opportunity to teach or learn something new yourself. Coaching suggests someone who cares enough to get involved by encouraging and developing others who are less experienced. Members who work for developers know that they can take risks, learn by making mistakes, and winning in the end.

Leaders must value continual learning; have the ability to grasp the essence of new information, master new technical and knowledge, recognize own strengths and weaknesses and pursue self-development.

Leaders see beyond the current problems and limitations to help others recognize their own potential. This process becomes the key to their growth and development. Leaders develop themselves while they're fostering growth in others. When you show people that you really do care whether they learn, it can greatly improve the morale and performance of your organization. Success is related to real teaching where there's a transformational experience.

A great leader has willingness to develop people to the point that they eventually surpass him or her in knowledge and ability. The leader learns from mistakes, the ones you make and those made by others. Don't let failure paralyze you. Within those failures are the seeds for improvement. Look at them as opportunities for constructive growth. And develop ways to improve and develop yourself and those around you appropriately.

A leader guides a team, not rules a team. He or she charts a course, gives direction and develops the people. The leader provides an atmosphere where others can learn and grow. The leader must give some responsibility to the group and have the courage to foster independence.

Leaders also move their followers to become leaders in their own right. Leaders are interested in self-improvement. However, when it comes to improving others, they are compassionate, not demanding. They realize people have flaws and make allowances for them. Nevertheless, since they wish to uplift others, they point out the correct path and offer encouragement.

Leaders create a culture of coaching. Just as all leaders are not born, neither are all good performers. All of us need nurturing if we are to achieve our potential.

A good way to bring out the best in people is to coach them: provide them advice, counsel, and constructive criticism. Coaching cultures are contagious. When members see a leader coaching or mentoring, they may emulate the behavior. In this way, leaders not only coach individuals they create an entire organization of coaches. Such an environment encourages people to do their best, maybe even take risks, which may in the long run benefit the organization.

Great leadership means lead by exceeding your potential. Leaders must change our relationships by disengaging from the people we've outgrown. Disengaging is painful because you care about them; they may not understand why you've drifted away from them; but remember unless you are willing to endure these pains, your own growth as a leader will be limited. Leaders only grow to the threshold of their pain.

Leaders are also responsible for future leadership. They need to identify, develop, and nurture future leaders. Great leaders are often scholars in their field and are intelligent. Like all great scholars, they aren't know-it-alls, they feel there is always more to learn and have a willingness to admit mistakes. Leaders make decisions based on facts, and apply common sense and simplicity to complex tasks.

You must select the right strategy for the right situation, even when the pressure is overwhelming. They are well organized, detail-oriented and, due to their thorough preparation, rarely caught off guard. Their great knowledge allows them to be great educators and motivators. They are also smart enough to know that many times they will have to alter what they originally planned due to changing circumstances, so flexibility and having an open mind are crucial to leadership.

Great leaders tap the full potential and contribution of each individual, respecting all the dimensions of the whole person.

EMPOWERMENT

Empowerment exists when members have the authority to make decisions and take appropriate actions without first seeking approval from others. Empowerment allows a member to act quickly, improving satisfaction and boosting morale.

Sense of empowerment and connectedness is the key to creating positive change in the organization. Empowerment means recognizing that people already have power through their knowledge, experience and motivation, and then creating an environment that encourages letting that power out.

Organizations should create a steady succession of leaders capable of moving through every layer of the organization. A leader cannot micromanage the execution of a decision; he/she needs people throughout the organization to be capable of making adjustments and trade-offs as obstacles arise; shared understanding promotes that type of coordinated, independent action.

Leaders demonstrate the willingness to develop and encourage the gifts and skills of others, even when to do so is costly. Empowerment displays positive characteristics, i.e.:

a. Inspire commitment, instill a vision and excite people: When you inspire trust and share a common purpose with aligned systems, you empower people. The leaders are well trusted and their followers feel confidence in them.

b. Consider needs for growth and development: Treat people as if they were what they ought to be, and you help them become what they are capable of being. The greatest ability of a leader may be the ability to recognize ability in others and encourage it.

c. Raise peoples' awareness of issues and problems: Help people become aware of their own thoughts, imagination, beliefs and values.

Leaders are motivated by the wish to empower others. They want to bring out the best in others. The main role of delegation is not efficiency, but empowerment; for the main role of a leader is to create more leaders. Leaders are able to motivate, to energize and to empower others. When people are excited and empowered in this sense, it affects both their task initiation and task persistence. That is, empowered people get more involved, take on more difficult situations, and act more confidently.

Empowered people expend more effort on a given task and are more persistent in their efforts. If you don't empower people, you aren't raising up people to be independent. Now you may think that if you are creating independent people you are creating people that may rise up against your own leadership. However, most of the time, the opposite is actually true. If you treat people with respect and empower them to do great things, they will honor and respect you for that.

The secret is to treat the unit manager as a CEO in his or her own right. Don't impose targets, for a start, but let them tell you what they are going to achieve and how. Second, don't have a fixed idea of how long people (or yourself, for that matter) should stay running an operation. If they are happy and doing an excellent job, only move them if you both feel they are not living up to their full potential: or you have another, more important post for which they are ideal.

You should always have a reservoir of able internal candidates for any such promotion. Characteristically, Buffett (Rank 1 on The World's Billionaires 2008 – Forbes) delegates this aspect of his responsibility, too. Thus, his top managers were asked to 'send me a letter updating your recommendations as to who should take over tomorrow if you became incapacitated tonight. Anything you send me will be confidential'. (Robert Heller, Management styles & leadership styles of Warren Buffet & Bill Gates, 2007)

Surround yourself with people who have the skills you lack but that share your passion and vision. Then challenge them to live up to their capabilities. When people sense that you expect great things from them, they tend to be challenged by that expectation and work hard to live up to it. Load your people with responsibility (and the authority), provide them with the resources to do the job, and stand behind them when they make mistakes.

Leaders are motivated by the wish to empower others. They want to bring out the best in others. The main role of delegation is not efficiency, but empowerment, for the main role of a leader is to create more leaders.

Empowering people to succeed will create an incredible team of people around you that will be able to do anything that is thrown at them. If you don't empower people and help them reach their full potential, you are actually falling very short of maximizing your own potential as a leader. If you empower people you are also empowering yourself.

When leaders focus on developing conditions of empowerment, they will cultivate a quality culture of effective, productive, interdependent relationships. Such an environment can release within members the power to contribute their maximum potential to achieving the mission and strategic goals of their organizations.

Developing a leadership within the organization does not only require learning to delegate. It requires a conscious strategy for identifying leaders (opportunities for leaders to emerge), recruiting leaders (opportunities for leadership to be earned), and developing leaders (opportunities for leaders to grow).

Leaders are responsible for effectiveness. Efficiency is doing the thing right, but effectiveness is doing the right thing. Leaders can delegate efficiency, but they must deal personally with effectiveness, which enable others to reach their potential - both their personal potential and their corporate or institutional potential.

Empowerment means inspiring others to be more than they think; and giving others the power to be successful. The ability to empower another individual is an important leadership skill. It represents the fact that you have acquired skills that help you solve problems and allow you to pass the knowledge on to other people to help them solve problems. It allows your circle of influence to increase and allows you to help more people than you could with your own limited resources.

Great organizations have strong leaders. To be successful, great organizations learn to empower their leaders to be great leaders.

Load your people with responsibility (and the authority), provide them with the resources to do the job, and stand behind them when they make mistakes. Having leaders at every level, or encouraging self-actualization of the work force, greatly enhances the possibility that initiative, creativity and dedication will flourish throughout an organization; the accompanying positive impact on productivity and continual improvement is obvious.

Leaders owe people space or freedom, which enabling one's gifts to be exercised. People need to give each other the space to grow, to be themselves, and to exercise their diversity; so that they may both give and receive such things as ideas, openness, dignity, joy, healing, and inclusion.

Leaders should provide an environment that enables people to achieve great things and one common trait will become apparent - getting the best performance from the people. By delegating and empowering members wisely, leaders create a committed and proactive member that will produce exceptional results.

Leaders learn that their real power comes from others. It is by unleashing the individual talents and skills of other people that they can achieve their intended results. The release of this collective energy can occur only if the leader grants people the responsibility and authority to act.

Empowerment becomes a powerful motivational tool because it puts people in control of their own destinies. One of your greatest calls as a leader is to empower others. The greatest leaders that this world has seen had the ability to find untapped potential in people and then empower them to do great things. If you want to be a great success as a leader than you will have to adopt the empowerment principle into your life.

A great leader helps others become great leaders. They come from a position of service and they are always thinking about how they can help the other person to become a great leader as well. They offer everyone with whom they come in contact the chance to join them in becoming a great leader.

A leader is great, not because of his/her power, but because of his/her ability to empower others. Great leaders develop and empower the people around, so that they can watch the accomplishments of those around them and be available when they need help. The leader is not there to dictate every little move others make, but there to help them see the big picture and priorities.

CHALLENGE

People like to be challenged. Leaders who tap into this need can achieve powerful goals because they will be linking those goals with the fulfillment of desires. The hard part of crafting a challenge is to focus on what is attainable in ways that energize and exciting and play upon people's imagination and creativity. Appropriate response to challenge is the basis for the rise of organization. The first challenge of leadership is to know who you are (authenticity).

Leaders are sometimes called to greatness because of the way they respond to challenges. A leader's value to others is to lead them through difficult challenges by providing hope and bestowing courage.

Challenge is the opportunity for greatness. People do their best when there is an opportunity to change how things currently stand. Maintaining the status quo facilitates mediocrity.

Leadership is the challenge to be something more than average. When others run from the challenge before them, leaders rise to the challenge before them. They are willing to encourage, correct and challenge them to greatness. By opening the challenge to them, he created a sense of empowerment. Those who lead others to greatness seek and accept challenge.

Great leaders create work environments that provide a sense of challenge and meaningfulness for followers. By galvanizing people with a clear vision and strong values, the leaders are able to challenge their teams to achieve significant organization's goals.

Leadership is the ability to seize opportunities and lead people and organizations to greatness. Leaders do when they set the right example, communicate clearly, and challenge appropriately. You may start being a leadership mentor to someone today. Helping others grow into great leaders also comes with its set of challenges and frustrations.

Surround yourself with people who have the skills you lack but that share your passion and vision. Then challenge them to live up to their capabilities.

When people sense that you expect great things from them, they tend to be challenged by that expectation and work hard to live up to it. Load your people with responsibility (and the authority), provide them with the resources to do the job, and stand behind them when they make mistakes.

Leaders create followers. Great leaders create other leaders. Your leadership style is, therefore, the key to creating empowerment.

DELEGATION

A leader is an empowerer. Empowerers help others become competent and capable persons who in turn will empower others. The goal of leadership is partly to create autonomous individuals who can complete tasks with confidence, making their own decisions and taking responsibility for their own successes and failures.

Empowering is the affirmation of the individuals' ability to learn and to grow and to become all that they were meant to be. Leaders are motivated by the wish to empower others. They want to bring out the best in others. The main role of delegation is not efficiency, but empowerment, for the main role of a leader is to create more leaders.

Leaders empower their followers to get things done by delegating tasks. The most critical element of leadership is delegation. Delegation must assist the leader with the performance of required duties and challenge members by providing added responsibility and/or greater proficiencies.

Leaders motivate others to greatness. A leader is only as powerful as his/her team. As a leader, you will want to surround yourself with a powerful team by assisting others in recognizing and utilizing their strengths, gifts, and potential.

Motivating others to their own greatness will improve the group energy, increase the vitality of your projects, and move you forward toward achieving your goals and vision. It is crucial as a leader that you not try to do everything yourself; delegate anything that you can delegate. True delegation will help people embrace the greatness.

Great leaders begin in the capacity of followers. Delegation is one of the most important tasks as a leader. Delegation frees up your time and can develop your people. It also increases productivity, morale and commitment.

Delegation builds trust, develops skills in those to whom the tasks have been delegated and frees the leader to work on other things. Delegation should involve both authority and responsibility.

Delegation of authority requires confidence in the individual, since the leader is relinquishing some control over team activities. Yet without the necessary authority and room for decision making, people are not empowered to complete the tasks they have been given. Meanwhile delegation of the responsibility to complete a task is relatively easy.

In business organization, mostly executives (the director, manager or supervisor) are leaders by delegation of power.

PURPOSE

Leaders have a clear sense of purpose. From your sense of purpose, you can set goals and align them with that purpose - goals that serve as a blueprint to others. Your drive to achieve something will help you develop a certain amount of focus to attain your set goals. Passion and determination is essential to help you gain focus on things that you want to do.

Money should not be the sole measure for evaluating and rewarding the effectiveness of a leader. Have a strong sense of purpose makes it easier to make decisions because our inner conversation is simplified. Sense of purpose includes:

    a. Personal purpose: Whatever your purpose, it must be rooted in your most cherished personal values.

    b. Organizational purpose: Your organizational and personal values align with your purpose.

Having a purpose is the difference between making a living and making a life. Few of us clearly know our life purpose. But if we watch how our lives unfold, and if we know what questions to ask ourselves, we can begin to understand why we are here. To be successfully living a life of purpose, you should:

a. Define your purpose - Your purpose is your reason for existing.

b. Commitment to the purpose - Commitment demands action; it cannot be divorced from responsibility. It possesses spirit, have within them, full of faith, and affect others.

c. Act intentionally on purpose - A purpose gives you meaning and direction.

d. Harmonize your thoughts, feelings, words and deeds with your purpose.

If a leader promotes a sense of purpose that is not embodied, he/she is sensed as inauthentic. He/she will not be trusted. Leaders require trust. Assessing our purpose reflects:

a. What we naturally do best - The gifts, talents and skills our personality has to offer.

b. How we aspire to be - The qualities of our authentic self.

Leaders make people feel that they're at the very heart of things, not at the periphery. Everyone feels that he or she makes a difference to the success of the organization. When it happens, people feel centered and that gives their work meaning. Leaders should also look at their ability to forge new meaning and purpose for an organization and its members.

Great leaders work effectively with others to create a clear and compelling purpose that is focused on customer needs - strategically aligned and financially viable.

Organization should inspire people to live and lead by a clearly defined sense of purpose. A person's self esteem and confidence is strongly linked to a sense of purpose. People are persuaded by reason, but moved by emotion; the leader must both persuade them and move them. A leader brings followers together around a shared sense of purpose and meaning.

SUCCESS

Great leaders build in time to think and reflect. In particular, they reflect on what causes success and they think about excellence. Leadership is lifting a person's vision to higher sights, the raising of a person's performance to a higher standard, the building of a personality beyond its normal limitations. No person can be a great leader unless he/she takes genuine joy in the successes of those under him/her.

Leadership is very much about performance. It is about doing the right things. And in many ways, the followers may care less what principles you follow or if you are moral and ethical in leading the organization. What they care about is your performance.

Leadership is a key to member engagement, innovation and success. To create a successful organization, a leader should be investing in building his/her leadership ability, includes:

a. Demonstrate enthusiasm: Have an abundance of passion for what you do. You cannot inspire unless you're inspired yourself.

b. Articulate actions: The power of a vision set everything in motion

c. Sell the benefit: You need to sell your vision that beneficial for everybody constantly throughout a presentation, meeting, pitch, or any situation where persuasion takes place.

d. Invite participation: Bring others into the process of building the organization.

Great leaders must be regarded as achievers, whatever their advantages of birth and training. The great leaders always make sure that you surround yourself with great people. You cannot learn how to be great from people who are not great themselves. If you want to become great, or a great leader, you have to surround yourself with people that will motivate you to be great by their example.

ACCOMPLISHMENT

Enjoying great success does not depend on having a great ego. In fact, the opposite is almost always true; those who think the most of themselves are usually respected little by others. Great leadership begets great results. In today's world there are countless opportunities to make a difference. And more than ever there is a need for people of all ages, from all backgrounds, with all types of life experience to seize those opportunities that lead to greatness. More than ever there is a need for leaders to inspire us to dream, to participate, and to persevere.

People who display greatness rely upon others who are able to see as they do, to listen, encourage, and support. Without those people who recognize greatness and move in to support it, even the greatest ideas, works of art, and political movements would remain unborn. Great leadership begets great results.

Leadership is the act of making a difference. It's the ability to achieve results - through people. Great leaders maintain competitive preeminence. They must create vision and direction, organize operations so that the vision is profitably attainable, inspire and retain their workforces, and develop tomorrow's leaders.

Leaders use to transform values into actions, visions into realities, obstacles into innovations, separateness into solidarity, and risks into rewards. It's about a climate in which people turn challenging opportunities into remarkable successes. Leaders offer visionary, authentic, and high achievement leadership.

The leaders encourage a focus on achieving end results that are at once purposeful and strategic, and the creative use of power and effective decision-making. Leadership is not taking a group where the leader wants to go, but in seeing that every member of the group has a sense of accomplishment and feels his or her objectives have been met.

A leader obtains a sense of accomplishment from group, not only individual. The leader demonstrates winning attitude. Develop and stick to a routine that fosters an environment of security and productivity. Look for ways to create small victories that will lead to other, more important victories. Create a sense of accomplishment.

Great leaders inspire their followers to believe, to expend more effort, and to accomplish great things that otherwise would not get done. Great leaders expect a lot from their people. If you expect a lot you'll get a lot. Expect little, and you may get even less.

VISION

More, better, faster is noted as an outline for the future of leadership. A visionary sees an opportunity, or an opening, and then shares this vision with others who help to realize that opportunity. Vision has always been considered an important component in leadership, which refers to the ability leaders have to form a plan for the future and to get others excited about their plan.

Often, leaders have less a plan, but more of a simple picture of a possible future, and let people sort out the action steps toward that more general picture.

Visioning is the first step in strategic planning. A vision shared by all the members of an organization can help all members set goals to advance the organization. A vision can also motivate and empower members.

Visioning skills are used by leaders to pull people toward themselves and their ideas through the creation and communication of a vision. Without a strong vision, strategic plans cannot be properly delineated since there is no guiding principle or ideal to plan.

Leadership starts with having a vision, then developing a plan to achieve it. A vision of the future is the key to getting started as a leader. A vision that is likely to come true has to take account of the culture of the organization. Great leaders have vision and the ability to take people toward that vision.

Visionary in leadership moves people towards a shared vision, telling them where to go but not how to get there - thus motivating them to struggle forwards. They openly share information, hence giving knowledge power to others.

Great leaders talk more about where we must go to create a viable future. Look for a leader who, instead of majoring in the blame game, paints a positive vision for the future of the organization. The biggest difference between a vision and a hallucination are the number of people who can see it.

Leaders with vision are especially noted for transforming old mental maps or paradigms, and creating strategies that are outside the box of conventional thought. They then create innovative strategies for actualizing their vision.

As a leader, you have to learn to communicate your vision or the vision of your organization to the people you want to follow you. An important aspect of vision is the notion of "shared vision."

A person who is said to possess greatness stands apart from others in some way, usually by the size or originality of their vision and their ability to manifest that vision. A leader is someone who touches another's future. The leader has a clear idea of what he or she wants to do and the strength to persist in the face of setbacks, even failures. Vision describes clear picture of the future which is communicated in such a way that others can participate in making it happen.

A vision is simply an aspiration or a description of a desirable world that exists within the imagination that can inspire people, bring meaning to their work, mobilize them to action, and help them decide what to do and what not to do in the course of their work.

An effective vision strikes a chord in people, motivates them by tapping their competitive drive, arouses desire for greatness or interest in doing the right thing, tantalizes them with personal gain, or appeals to their need to make a difference in the organization.

A visionary may dream wonderful visions of the future and articulate them with great inspiration. Great leader has a vision of what is important for future direction, communicates this with urgency in meaningful ways, and can persuade others to align their efforts to drive for results.

The great leaders think about the kinds of situations they might face. They plan for them. They imagine the situations in detail. And they run through them in their mind - a kind of mental practice. Great leaders rehearse the long term future and they rehearse individual encounters. They play what-if in their head.

The great leaders also keep the future in mind. They remain aware of the future consequences of their decisions. They think farther ahead than most of their peers.

A vision is an idealized picture of the future organization and it expresses the organization's reason for existence. The peoples of leading organizations have always had a strong sense of vision. Vision reflects the leader's sense of external opportunities, ways in which internal resources can be mobilized to capitalize on them and the leader's personal role (self) in that process.

Visions grab people and then bring them into the fold. When a leader's vision is effective and strong, members get caught up in what they are doing, absorb the vision, and commit themselves to the goals and the values of the leaders.

With leaders, the future calls to them in a voice they can't drown out. The future is more real than the present; it compels them to act. Leaders know that nothing drives an organization like an attractive, worthwhile, achievable vision for the future.

A leader is a symbol of the unity of an organization. They can express the values that hold an organization together. Most important, they can conceive and articulate goals that lift people up, carry them above conflict and unite them in pursuit of objectives worthy of their best efforts.

A leader is manifesting his or her vision because s/he creates specific, achievable goals, initiates action and enlists the participation of others. Leaders need the skills to create and communicate a positive view of the future which is in harmony with their organization.

A leader's vision needs to be shared by those who will be involved in the realization of the vision. Vision comes alive only when it is shared. Whether the vision of an organization is developed collaboratively or initiated by the leader and agreed to by the followers, it becomes the common ground, the shared vision that compels all involved. The real advantage of scenario planning is that it helps you recognize changing future situations.

Great leaders pay attention to the future, because it's their job to choose the path for their organization in an unfamiliar environment. Without mental rehearsal and thinking about the future, leaders are forced to rely on precedents to deal with new situations.

In today's rapidly changing environment, that doesn't work. When you set clear goals and become determined and purposeful, backing those goals with unshakable self-confidence, you develop charisma. When you are enthusiastic and excited about what you are doing, when you are totally committed to achieving something worthwhile, you radiate charisma.

When you take the time to study and become an expert at what you do, and then prepare thoroughly for any opportunity to use your knowledge, skill or experience, the perception that others have of you go straight up.

Leaders who operate with a sense of vision demonstrate to others an orientation to marketplace trends, an understanding of how to get things done effectively within the organization and how to get the most out of the capabilities of the organization. They also demonstrate an excitement and determination about achieving the broader mission of the business. They ensure that daily activities are pursued and that decisions are made in the context of the broader goals.

Leader understands the past scans current trends and helps point people toward a meaningful future. The visionary leader always asks the question: where we are going. Leaders are the builders of a new dawn, working with imagination, insight, and boldness. Their eyes are on the horizon, not just on the near at hand. They are social innovators and change agents, seeing the big picture and thinking strategically.

It is critical that there be an ability to define, communicate and inspire a practical, relevant and easily digestible vision, and to update and adapt it as circumstances change.

Leaders must be able to think about the future and how they will propel, guide and adapt their businesses in the face of uncertainty and unfamiliarity. By not stretching organization's resources, offerings and capabilities, there won't be much of anything long-term, least of all the expanded intellectual capabilities of the members. We expect our leaders to have a sense of direction and a concern for the future of the organization.

Leaders must know where they are going. They must have a destination in mind when asking us to join them on a journey into the unknown. Constituents ask that a leader have a well-defined orientation toward the future. We want to know what the organization will look like, feel like, and be like when it arrives at its goal in future. We each need to challenge ourselves to develop greater leadership skills - and to develop a clearer vision.

Leaders inspire people with a vision, but they also take charge and make things happen. They are courageous in presenting the big picture, but also in providing a sense of meaning for others. They express passion, commitment, and responsibility. Future is characterized by something or expected condition that will happen in time to come; chance of success, growth or advancement.

Thinking of future involves imagination - situation without observing it, therefore mitigating risks, logical - predict inevitable consequences of actions and situations, and induction - adjust action based upon specific experience and draws inferences.

Future also implies a forecast that might be speculative. We can create our own futures through our intentions, thoughts, words and actions. Leaders have vision; they are not just for themselves, they set a common goal and give direction to their followers.

Success requires a strong future orientation and a commitment to both improvement and change. Increasingly, this requires creating an environment for learning and innovation, as well as the means for rapid and effective application of knowledge.

Future plan is to see and to make your success happens. You have to prepare your way for how and why you should be success in life. Future should be created and planned before and use it as a guide. The plan should help you shape a vision towards reaching a future destination and remind you that success does not happen by chance.

The one quality that all leaders have in common is that they have a clear and exciting vision for the future. This is something that only the leader can do. Only the leader can think about the future and plan for the future each day. Leaders, who are charismatic and visionary, can inspire followers to transcend their own self-interest for the good of the organization.

A great leader is someone who has a clear vision and can turn that vision into a vivid picture that others can see. When you speak about your vision, it should be with a passion you feel in your heart, a passion that creates so much enthusiasm that your team will want to jump on board.

A successful vision excites people to pull together and work toward a goal that is possible, but does not currently exist. It aligns people from a wide variety of backgrounds and organizational levels. It is clearly understood by everyone. The ability to turn their vision of the organization into a realistic, credible, attractive future that allows people to feel pride and satisfaction is critical.

The leader has a clear idea of what he/she wants to do professionally and personally - and the strength to persist in the face of setbacks, even failure. Vision is to accomplish a dream.

A great leader is a person of vision: necessarily so, for only with vision can he/she inspire his/her people to heroic action; only with vision can he/she make them desire victory as ardently as he/she does. He/she persuades them not by angry commands, but by the power of his/her conviction. He/she involves others in his/her vision, and inspires them also to be visionaries.

Vision also describes the desired future to which you aspire, i.e. struggling to find a means of accurately understanding the availability and performance of the fundamental pillars of organization's resources, finance and time; provide management information based on time and capability (both resources and skills).

If a leader cannot transfer personal loyalty to his/her vision, he/she has failed one of the critical tests of leadership.

Leaders always look ahead and develop a compelling vision of the future. Live for today, but be guided by your vision of what you want to accomplish.

Great leaders can tell you where they are going, what they plan to do along the way and who will share the adventure. Real vision arises from the deepest parts of yourself, your inner system of beliefs.

HOPE

Great leaders hold great power. A sense of hope gives organization and members the impetus to keep moving ahead. The first task of the leader is to keep hope alive. When the leader is free from fear; their people can live and work in hope.

Leaders are dealers in hope. It's important for leaders to give people hope. If we're going to make a positive change in the world, hope is a prerequisite. And that sense of hope can be either fed or depleted by what you choose. Hope is one of a leader's greatest possessions, without it a leader ceases to lead. Leaders with hope are characterized by at least:

a. Self-motivated: Know how to get the ticker to tick, are willing and able to pick themselves up and carry on

b. Self-assurance: Especially during the tight spots and tough times, they are able to assure themselves in spite of the criticism, discouragement, etc.

c. Persistent: Understand that victory is not to the swift, it's to the persistent.

d. Adaptable: Though they never give up their vision, they are able to survive because they are flexible enough to seek, discover, and find multiple ways to reach their goals.

e. Ability to incrementalize goals: They know when they have to break down larger goals into smaller goals so that they can still reach their goal, incrementally, if necessary. When one can't possibly think they can hold on for the long-haul, they break the long-haul down into smaller increments of time.

f. Willingness to mourn: They will face lots of tears, hurts, and reasons for loneliness. To be a shepherd is to care; to have to let go is almost always painful and sometimes almost unbearable.

Without purpose, virtue, and truth, it is difficult to experience hope. An absence of virtues and the presence of deceit do not create the conditions necessary for hope to survive. For leadership to endure, it must be intertwined with hope in the sense of looking forward to the future with expectation.

If leadership has a future, leaders must be able to articulate, find, and live out their own sense of hope. Hope grows dim as people deviate from their core values and grows stronger and becomes contagious in the context of shared hope within organization.

Leaders inspire. They give people a sense of hope. Great leaders tend to be optimists and purveyors of hope. Great leaders are dealers in hope.

PASSION

Leaders are inspiring, motivating, hard working people who give their jobs their all. They are able to do this because they are working at something they feel passionate about. Passion is the emotion that drives leaders to excel, achieve and produce. Great leaders have made the decision to be great leaders. They are determined and committed to be great leaders. Even when the going gets tough they are still great leaders and they do not falter.

Passion is the present where others as well as ourselves see and feel our emotional responses. There is no greatness without a passion to be great. Leaders' passion inspired people to take on new and risky challenges.

Leaders must have passion. Leaders combine a personal humility with a passion for the welfare of the larger organization. Your followers want passion. Leaders' passion inspired them to take on new and very dangerous challenges. Passion is such a key part of being a great leader. If you don't have it, you simply can't be a great leader.

Nothing is ever achieved without passion. Passion is infectious; when you talk about your vision for the organization, let your passion for your vision shine through. Others will feel it and want to get on board with you. If you don't have passion for your vision, you need to recreate your vision or reframe your description of your vision so it's connected to your passion.

Passion can give you courage, which can help you act on your beliefs. Passion - The drive and desire to do something extraordinary and powerfully well. To inspire passion in others is impossible without passion in yourself. Passion is the great energizer.

Leaders possess passion because they fully understand themselves and believe strongly in what they stand for. They know who they are, what they want to do, exactly where they want to go and why. Their passion is structured on three elements:

a. Sense of hope: Leaders demonstrate their passion through desires, hopes and the ability to dream. They know without hopes and dreams, no future gain is possible. For leaders, a sense of passion is useless unless they can pass it along to give hope and inspiration to everyone under their charge.

b. Sense of giving: Transmit energy to people, giving them a new sense of hope and confidence in achieving the vision. Leading is giving.

c. Sense of purpose: Passion is based upon the understanding of a selected course of direction and purpose. Leaders feel that an example is set by addressing, discussing and emphasizing their visions, goals and selected courses of direction as often as possible. In the process they are able to influence others and keep themselves on target.

Great leaders understand the difference between passion for excellence and passion for power. Passion is the critical partner to purpose and performance. Leadership is passion. Without passion, a person will have very little influence as a leader. Passion provides an individual with the light of leadership and creates an undeniable drive to make a difference.

INSPIRATION

Sense of inspiration is a fundamental motivating force. Leadership is found in the inspiration of others. Leaders can articulate their vision and ideals to others, convincing them of the value of their ideas. They can inspire people to work toward common goals and to achieve things they never thought they could do. Leaders, who inspire people, must create environment in which people sense a power beyond others, i.e.:

a. Demonstrate enthusiasm: One of leadership purpose is to spread enthusiasm, inspire confidence, and demonstrate integrity, i.e. create a sense of urgency, lend them your energy, make things fun, etc.

b. Display course of action: Leaders generate decision making that show ability to choose a course of action based on available information.

c. Show the benefit: A person with great leadership will show people that he/she is responsible and has proven himself or herself to do the right thing and people will do whatever he or she asks. People will follow the leaders because they are showing the benefit of the leadership.

d. Invite participation: Leaders create the environment that invite participation and shared responsibility from everyone

e. Encourage potential: Leaders encourage awareness of members for their abilities and potential

Leadership and inspiration are inseparable. Leaders create an inspiring culture within their organization. Great leaders inspire people to move worlds and change the world. Great leaders are people of great character. Great character enables vision and empathy.

Great leaders are reliable persons of character who are committed to compelling principles and purposes, as well as inner connectedness and respect for oneself.

Leaders develop daily, not in a day. The growth factor - long-term commitment to personal development - made the difference. Growth is the great separator between those who succeed and those who do not, in which a person is beginning to separate themselves from the pack, it's almost always due to personal growth. Growth equals change. To develop, we must step away from comfort and welcome fresh and challenging experiences. A leader encourages responsibility and growth. It is the capacity to develop and improve their skills that distinguishes leaders from followers. Without additional support, growth is a much more challenging endeavor.

Great leaders of learning create leaders of learners. The great leaders nurture the spirit of curiosity and are perpetual hunters of insight. They learn all of the time. Great leaders continually question employees' learning needs. A culture that values curiosity is inventive and exciting. Great leaders demonstrate their passion for learning by constantly asking questions of the others' experience.

Growth takes time, and only time can reveal certain lessons to us. Reflective thinking is required to turn experience into insight. A great leader looks for every opportunity to learn and communicate to members through their actions that searching for what's unknown is as important and valuable as acting on what is known.

Great leaders set a powerful tone when they show they're willing and able to learn out loud, as well as to encourage others in never-ending discovery. Members are more devoted to organizations that pass the gift of growth to them.

The more we grow, the more we know we need to grow; when you start developing yourself, instead of feeling wise, you'll be struck by how much you don't know.

A leader is responsible for the development and growth of the followers. Only persistence may have value in difficult times. But there are a few other qualities that inspire people, get an organization through challenges, and return it to a path of growth. These qualities lead to sustained greatness, not just a flash during good times. People who become great leaders commit themselves to that lead them to greatness. They commit themselves to growth.

Leaders are lifelong learners. Great leaders develop through a process of discipline, hard work, and more. Growth is not automatic. Growth doesn't happen by itself; it requires an active investment of time. If you are a person without a wealth of personal experience, borrow the experience. Ask questions, listen, and learn from a successful leader that has gone before you.

4TH

SENSE OF RESPONSIBILITY

Leadership is an interactive conversation that pulls people toward becoming comfortable with the language of personal responsibility and commitment. Leadership is not just for people at the top. Everyone can learn to lead by discovering the power that lies within each one of us to make a difference and practicing the law of reciprocity.

The heart of leadership is the willingness to assume responsibility, which implies:

a. Personal responsibility: Individual responsibility for making sound and ethical decision that considers the interests of all stakeholders. Seek responsibility and take responsibility for your actions.

b. Organizational responsibility: Develop a sense of responsibility in your people - Help to develop good character traits that will help them carry out their responsibilities. The responsible leader must recognize that he/she is responsible for the decisions made by him/her and therefore he/she should analyze the structure of how decisions are made within the organization.

Leaders accept the responsibility when things go wrong and learn from it so they and their team can grow and enhance performance. When you take full responsibility, your greatness will manifest.

As leaders, we have to make significant changes to increase our impact then we must be willing to shoulder progressively greater loads. Although added responsibility gives us a greater opportunity to exercise leadership, it also magnifies the consequences of our mistakes. To be a change agent, a leader must be willing to take ownership of pivotal decisions.

A responsible person is one who is able to act without guidance or supervision, because he or she is accountable and answerable for his or her behavior. Such a person can be trusted or depended upon to do things on his or her own. Such a person will follow though on obligations. Being a responsible person means you have good character.

A leader should look up to and respect for all he/she does. There is wariness for finger-pointing and for assignment of blame. Leaders take responsibility for decisions they have made or participated in, regardless of whether the outcomes are successful.

Leaders accept responsibility for their actions. Leaders are a little bolder, a little more courageous than others. Leaders make the decisions, take the risks, and accept the responsibility when things go wrong.

Responsibility is developed through accountability, courage, self-confidence and focus on the whole. Be responsible means be dependable, work hard, and show self control; have a sense of duty to fulfill willingly the tasks he or she has accepted or has been assigned. All work is conscientiously performed; and accept responsibility for their behavior.

Responsibility often implies the satisfactory performance of duties or the trustworthy care for or disposition of possessions, i.e.

a. When you agree to do something, do it. Because when you follow through on your commitments, people take you seriously. Otherwise they'll stop believing you.

b. Be accountable for your own actions. Don't make excuses or blame others for what you do.

c. Don not put things off. Doing things on time helps you take control of your life and shows that you can manage your own affairs.

The reality of leadership involves the heavy burden of responsibility. Missteps by a leader can affect people's livelihoods or an organization's sustainability. The fear of getting it wrong can paralyze a leader.

As a leader, you are responsible for your own life; identifying and fulfilling your own needs, wants and desires; living according to your own values and standards; setting your own priorities and for achieving your own goals;

your own decisions, and their outcome. Learning to be responsible includes learning to show respect and compassion for others, practice honesty, show courage by standing up for what we believe, develop self-control out of consideration for others, maintain self-respect.

Taking responsibility means being accountable for your choices, not depending on others to establish controls for your behaviors. Responsibility can only reside in the individual and cannot be disclaimed or diminished through delegation or shared duties.

Responsibility means not placing blame on others and proactively taking ownership to resolve problems in the interest of serving others above yourself.

Great leaders accept responsibility. They keenly seek the role of leadership because it carries with it the awesome burden of responsibility. They are not drawn to power nor do they shrink from it. They see it as an incidental by-product of the leadership role. They always hold themselves accountable and never blame outside factors.

People who are irresponsible often go against the rules - often by impulse - without thinking are caring of the possible consequences. Leader should accept responsibility for his/her piece of the mess, model the type of behavior needed through the change process, and be willing to accept casualties.

Leaders are responsible for effectiveness. Efficiency is doing things right. Effectiveness is doing the right thing. An action is good not because it has good results, or because it is wise, but because it is done in obedience to this inner sense of duty. The price of greatness is responsibility.

As a leader, your shoulders must be broad. Take responsibility for your actions. Don't make excuses. Accept the responsibility when things go wrong and learn from it so you and your team can grow and enhance performance. The price of greatness is responsibility. A leader is endowed with a mix of great responsibility and great power.

ACCOUNTABILITY

Leadership is not possible without a strong sense of accountability. While the organization as a whole is accountable for results, within the organization the issue of accountability is directly linked to a person, an individual who is charged with and accepts responsibility for the success or failure of strategies.

Accountability is a personal attribute. Leaders who are accountable do what needs to be done, no matter where in the organization they have to go. They hold themselves 100% accountable for making relationships work.

Great leaders don't think in terms of rewards and discipline that they deliver. More commonly they see such things as the natural result of a subordinate's performance.

Great leaders manage the systems of consequences so that it's in the best interest of the member to do what's in the organization's best interest. This starts with clear expectations. A person with the core quality of accountability implies:

    a. Take the initiative to get things done: Leaders don't wait for everything to be perfect before they move forward. Leaders take initiative. Once you take the first step and start moving forward, everything becomes clearer and easier.

    b. Not afraid to hold others accountable: An accountable-workplace produces better results and more satisfied followers. Good leadership is a key. Failure to hold followers accountable for their behavior and the results they create erodes leadership credibility and effectiveness.

    c. Cross departmental boundaries to help: Boundaries help you stay clear in your relationships and in your tasks. Staying healthy and productive in leadership requires very clearly defined boundaries.

    d. Take personal responsibility for organizational success: Leaders take responsibility for success, hold themselves accountable. Leaders create micro-climates of responsibility and performance.

The leaders believe that success of the organization is their responsibility, no matter what their job titles are. They don't have to do all the work themselves, but they have to make it possible for everyone else to succeed.

Great leaders spend a lot of time making sure that their people understand exactly what they expect and what the consequences of behavior are. They do this by spending time with individuals and groups, practicing active listening and repeating key points again and again.

Great leaders seem to understand the power of frequent communication better then their peers. They make sure they model the behavior they want. They practice leadership by example.

The emphasis on accountability is not primarily to facilitate the excuse of sanctions should something go wrong. Accountability means the organization can point to a single person or group that is accountable for effective management, explaining deviation from the norm, and acting to implement corrective action when problems arise.

The concept of accountability should not imply a gotcha mentality. It emphasizes a sense of control, the ability to explain performance deviations, and the need to stop or mitigate issues that constrain performance as soon as they are understood.

A kind of organization's value is accountability. Leaders should not be accountable for demonstrating a particular set of behaviors but rather should be held accountable for desired outcomes.

Accountability is a concept in ethics that involves either the expectation or assumption of account-giving behavior; willingness to stand up and be counted; as part of a process; reflecting personal choice and willingness to contribute to an expressed or implied outcome.

Being responsible implies a different relationship than being accountable. Accountability implies:

i.   The willingness to acknowledge responsibility to others, and the willingness to fully accept responsibility for one's actions and their implications

ii. Practice in a sound and sustainable manner, maintain accountability for their practices and are held accountable for any deficiencies in their activities

iii. Apply the positive dynamics of focused feedback to help themselves and others move away from excuse making and blame shifting

iv. Develop a clear understanding of how ownership and accountability drive organizational results

v.   Best practices that create a culture of accountability. Accountability is being answerable or responsible for something. All successful people are moving toward more empowerment, enlightenment - and creating a culture of accountability. With accountability comes a measure of discipline. Accountability is the opposite of permissiveness. Holding people accountable is really about the distribution of power and choice. When people have more choice, they are more responsible. When they become more responsible, they can have more freedom.

Accountability with responsibility equals authority. Accountability remains with the leader, and only responsibility may be delegated. Accountability accepts personal responsibility to see that objectives are adequately pursued and achieved. A leader is ultimately accountable to others – however, unlikely that seems in some settings.

So every leader must see their leadership role as a matter of trust. The leader holds responsibilities over others on behalf of the greater good of the organization. The leader must consider the path they have taken. They must ask whether their path and their actions align with the requirements of value-centered accountability.

Accountable means decisions and actions are clear - reasonable and open to examination; committed accountability results, and quality; serve and protect the long-term interests of all; challenge - taking on big challenges and seeing them through continuous improvement.

Leaders do not shift the responsibility for their circumstances to other people. They accept accountability of their actions, consequences, and experiences. They are proactive; instead of waiting for breaks. They identify and fine-tune their attitudes, beliefs, and actions. They search for ways to do more of what they enjoy. They proactively meet challenges head on and affirm that they will achieve the desires of their heart. They are life-long learners, seeking to increase their skills. They welcome change, and they change with the times. They communicate with others clearly and live with a spirit of cooperation.

Accountability suggests an outside-in relationship, in which others regulate and hold them accountable. Responsibility comes from within. Responsibility carries with a level of trust that might be absent when the focus is on accountability. It is possible to be held accountable, but at the same time not to be responsible. Accountability measures, such as large-scale external assessment, put the focus entirely on assessment.

Leadership is a group activity. There is an implied interdependence; that is recognition of the mutual interdependence of all members.

Great leaders stay focused on performance. You don't hear them talking much about somebody's attitude. They don't spend a lot of time on the internals. Instead they concentrate on the performance they want from subordinates and on the things they can control. They try to eliminate any excuses and then make the consequences of performance (good or bad) as inevitable as nature. This is perhaps the one ingredient in leadership that becomes the pivotal trait between being a great leader and a poor leader.

The great leader is accountable, and accepts that accountability without equivocation. A leader steps down fully accepting the consequences of accountability in leadership. This is the ultimate in the buck stops here leadership.

Accountability is always held by the leader. Responsibilities may be delegated, but accountability remains at the top. It takes courage to accept this kind of accountability. Leaders have that courage.

COURAGE

Courage does not come just by wishing - it only happens as a consequence of one's level of consciousness, one's inner experience, one's self identity. Leaders with courage assert themselves and take risks. We gain strength, and courage, and confidence by each experience in which we really stop to look fear in the face; we must do that which we think we cannot.

Courageous people trust their intuition. Courage is to stand by one's heart or to stand by one's core. People with courage tend to be restless, vivacious, and brazen.

Olof Palme was one Western leader who had consistently and effectively demonstrated his solidarity with the oppressed people, in words and in action. When Olof Palme became Prime Minister in 1969, the situation in southern Africa was cause for serious concern.

The white minority in Southern Rhodesia had declared unilateral independence and South African forces had moved into that country in open defiance of the colonial Power, the United Kingdom. Wars between colonial and racist authorities and liberation movements were taking place in Angola, Mozambique, Rhodesia and Namibia.

The repression of the African people had increased. The "unholy alliance" of the minority regimes in South Africa and Rhodesia, and the Portuguese fascist regime, posed a challenge to the world. (E.S. Reddy, World Leaders against Apartheid, New York, June 1989). Olof Palme, the Social Democratic Party leader was assassinated on his way home from a visit to the cinema in Stockholm late Friday evening on February 28, 1986.

Great leaders find what is shared among all members of a group and capitalize on it; they are optimists who rally people to a better future. They turn fear into confidence by providing great clarity regarding who the organization serves, what its core strengths are, how the organization will keep score (with focus on one specific measure) and what actions can be taken immediately.

The leaders don't always have the right answers, but they are confident and decisive in rallying followers with a clear vision and direction.

Courageous is characterized by courage; braveness; valiant. Courageous means ability to control your fear in a dangerous or difficult situation; and have the courage to stand up for your beliefs. Do the right thing for yourself and others. Have the determination to do the right thing, even when others do not.

A leader will take a courageous decision; when other not. The key to courageous and conscious action is how one responds to what arises on the path, rather than whether individual circumstances are defined as great, good, bad or just plain ugly.

Every situation or circumstance; i.e. success or failure, barrier or doorway; is simply another opportunity for greater creativity, mastery, and fulfillment of higher potential. The benefits of courageous leadership include the potential for:

Powerful acts of courage have such a high potential for "rocking the status quo," and would demand that we walk our talk about values, mission and purpose.

Of all the qualities needed for leadership, only one is indispensable – courage. Without it, all the others are more or less useless. Courage has been shown by all who we recognize as true leaders. A leader must have the ability to take hard decisions and calculated risks. Leaders have to give courage to others, while creating the illusion that they know exactly what they are doing.

Leaders are courageous by nature. They help inspire and guide others toward new vistas, through tough times and over seemingly insurmountable hurdles. Courage requires facing and moving through fear.

Great leaders take risks. They are willing, even excited, about entering unchartered waters. They face their own fears, their own demons, the doubts of naysayers around them, the very real structural and financial hurdles before them - and they go forth anyway. That takes planning and discipline, to be sure, but most of all it takes courage. Powerful acts of courage, i.e.:

a. Provide honest input and counsel: Leaders have the ability to listen to multiple points of view, including those who typically do not agree with them.

The leaders will have more complete input, thus making better decisions. To do this, a leader must be able to capture the key kernels of information. They have to be able to maintain bridges between people and create an atmosphere where people share information with each other.

The key to courageous leadership is how one responds to what arises during the journey, rather than whether individual circumstances are defined as good, bad, or indifferent.

b. Choose not to lay people off simply for a short-term boost: Leadership: It's not something you do to people; it's something you do with people. When you are too quick to lay blame on others, you risk misdiagnosing the situation.

Leaders accept share of the responsibility and face the problem together. They do not blame others for their shortcomings or failures and hold themselves 100% accountable.

c. Present outside-the-norm ideas: Courageousness in leadership addresses the necessity to step outside the box and take chances to help the organization establish appropriate and defensible goals. It also clearly places those who are leaders in a position to confront adversity.

d. Share an alternative viewpoint: Leaders develop an alternative, display openness to all viewpoints, and provide objective criticism. Courageousness in leadership is willing to identify issues that may affect the team and acts to address these issues quickly. Does not hesitate to provide useful feedback to move the group forward.

e. Speak up, rather than being complicit in silence: Courage in leadership involves having the courage to speak up when things are going wrong, and the courage to do the right thing for the right reasons.

Courageous leaders are persons who have shown courage to act authentically and speak up when silence means colluding with the problem.

f. Not fall prey to the perception that 'working longer hours equals increased productivity': Leaders concern with doing what is right and effective, rather than how they are viewed by others.

g. Advocate for a potential new hire without much direct experience: A new hire requires more supervision than an experienced follower. Leaders share information and help new hires understand how they contribute to achieving key business objectives.

h. Not settle for the status quo: For courageous leaders, settling is not an option. They exercise their courageous voice by challenging the status quo when they feel uncomfortable.

Courageous people are bright and creative, which might be rocking the status quo, and would demand that we walk our talk about values, mission and purpose. Great courage is about being present. Nearly everyone can see where changes need to be made; raise uncommon thought, willing to take the initiative; or to do something.

Leadership is not always seen in the brightest or the most talented, but it is always found in the courageous. Following steps may develop courage, includes:

a. Face the fear: The acute fear of failure can paralyze you into inaction. A decision always entails the possibility of error or risk. Without fear, there is no courage. Leaders overcome fears.

b. Explore vulnerability: Explore and develop your capacity for embracing power and vulnerability as a leader. When we admit our vulnerabilities we expose our True Selves - without apology.

c. Lean toward the risk: Great leaders are willing to take risks. They understand that only by taking risks will they reach new heights. Taking risks enables them to understand what other leaders experience and to help their developing leaders become comfortable taking risks as well.

d. Learn failures: Using mistakes to advantage unleashes our potency. Many entrepreneurs have admitted that their early failures held more learning.

    e.   Take action: Courage and will of an organization are cultivated by a leader's own thoughts and acts.

Sense of courage must be based on the notion that we are part of something bigger than ourselves. We develop courage by facing our fears; by tackling the big questions. The step in harnessing courage is to develop a vision that represents your authentic self and goals, and aligning that vision with the business and its goals.

Leaders, who have a strong vision, are backed up by a strong sense of courage. Courageous leadership spawns from a true sense of vision, and a commitment to that vision that transcends the inevitable rollercoaster ride that we call business.

Courage - not complacency - is our need today. People can learn to be more courageous and the organization can instill a sense of courage in followers. Leaders infuse sense of courage, hope and dedication in followers. Sense of courage in leadership includes:

    a.   Personal courage: Leaders are courageous; they get the job done by challenging the status quo, even at great personal risk

    b.   Organizational courage: Organizational courage and will are the essential requirements for the design of strategic processes that convert dreams into reality.

Great leaders are admired for their courage. A great leader overcomes the fear of rejection because not all right decisions are popular or appreciated at the time. Another hallmark of great leaders is their desire to seize the initiative.

A leader does not watch things happen; a leader makes things happen. Courage contributes greatly to a leader's ability to inspire. Great leaders spend considerable time on the front line and in the trenches.

Great leaders have character, integrity, and courage. Great leaders stand up for what they believe in and have the courage to defend their principles and their people. They are not afraid to challenge lies and falsehoods, take action to deal with incompetence and evil, and defend those who are doing what's right and needed for the long-term benefit of their organization and their followers.

Great leaders have the courage to do what is right and ethical.

RISK TAKING

Leaders are risk takers. They develop highly innovative approaches to problems. They are not afraid to challenge established practices. Risk taking is strongly influenced by sense of control. Individuals are more willing to take risks when they feel they can control the outcome of a situation.

Organization and personal profitability and financial integrity are at risk whenever leaders work in a world of uncertainty, volatility, and incomplete information. A leader is one who often takes risk. He/she is also a failure tolerant leader.

Leader's job is to control-information, people, risk, and the future. The leader is in charge of everything that's going on, both inside and outside the organization.

The leader's job is also to ensure that people in the organization obey the rules, and people in the organization look to the leader to keep them safe. Taking risks is difficult (whether for an individual or an organization) because it involves uncertainty. Sense of risk taking evolves:

a. Tolerate failure: Leader is one who not only allows, but even encourages subordinates to fail; and encourage their followers to soar.

b. Courage to take risk: Calculated risk-taking is an indispensable component of success. Ultimate success is forged through the inspired reworking of the remnants of failure. Where there is risk, there is an equal potential for failure. Examine the worst case scenario; if necessary call for brainstorming.

Leadership support is necessary in order to create an environment that encourages risk-taking. To do so, leaders at all levels of the organization need to reflect on their own risk-taking and facilitative behaviors; only through self-understanding can one clearly explain the desired behaviors and design structures and systems that support those behaviors.

Leaders' risk-taking needs to be accompanied by genuine support of others' risks. The keys to bold, but sound, risk-taking are:

a. Ensure that the risks we take are deliberate, ethical and considerate of all stakeholders

121

    b.   Understand the risks that surround us; and to build resilient organizations than can withstand these risks.

The winners are often those leaders who are willing to try, dare, even make fools of themselves. Leaders are always taking risks. The leaders who do the tried and true - who are risk-averse - will let the world pass them by establishing personal relationships built on mutual trust and respect.

Leaders show an appropriate level of comfort with others; and build lasting relationships and connections. We take risks to:

    a.   Try out new ideas, new strategies, and to experiment

    b.   Keep ourselves fresh and growing.

    c.   Train ourselves and others.

We do so to remain competitive because we recognize that simply maintaining the status quo isn't a viable position in the environment.

We take risks to advance our position, leverage our past gains, to move forward. Making the right decisions in work and in life can be very difficult. Executing the right strategies can prove even more elusive. Providing great leadership, however, should not be as rare as it seems to be in most organizations.

Leaders openly demonstrate the importance of taking risks. Risk taking allows individuals to experiment and try new approaches without any attached limitations. Leaders emphasize that risk taking builds character and instills a desire to persist. It allows them, and everyone under their charge, to overcome obstacles that most others find extremely difficult to surmount.

For leaders, mistakes are to be embraced and used as reference points for growth. Limiting one's risk taking does little else other than to hinder personal achievement.

Leaders attempt to redefine failure for their teams, allowing them to see, and allows an opportunity to learn and use the insights acquired through it to move onward and upward - it can infuse new life into an organization.

Napoleon was a great Leader. He balanced the budget, and established the Bank of France. He controlled prices, started public works to put people to work, and encouraged new industry. Order, security, and efficiency replaced liberty, equality, and fraternity as the slogans of the new regime.

Napoleon won many victories, and had several huge losses. He valued rapid movements and made effective use of large armies. He developed new plans for each battle, so the enemy could never figure out what was going to happen next. (Sedivy, The Life of Napoleon Bonaparte, 2002)

Risk taking can lead to great losses or great successes. It's good to take risks - if you manage them well. Great leaders are not afraid to take risks.

Great leaders are dissatisfied with the status quo and business as usual. They encourage team members to seek out new solutions, to consider alternatives to the norm, and to embrace the potential of change.

TIMING

Self-leadership means knowing your mostly unused potential and committing yourself to liberating the other 90% of your hidden capacity; knowing that every day you have the same number of minutes. *(Robert K. Cooper, Uncommon Reminders for Bringing Out the Best in Others and Ourselves, 2002)*

In this internet-savvy world, your competitors can figure out your business development plan almost as soon as you do. Leader must be able to attune to the proper timing. Sense of timing is an intuitive skill, timing is intangible.

Leaders demonstrate awareness that affect timely decision-making; what to do and where to go. Awareness powers a leader's internal clock so that you can exercise the right timing in decision-making, includes:

a.   Needs around you: Leaders interact in an environment abounding with needs. Customers, partners, and co-workers all have needs. Needs are all around you, but they are also within you. Leaders are able to look beyond their own needs to sense and respond to the needs of others.

b.   Reality before you: Decisions have consequences - positive and negative, intended and unintended. Leaders with a flair for timing are able to foresee the implications of their courses of action.

c.   Influencers behind you: Every organization has key influences that must be on board in order for pivotal decisions to be made. To excel at the art of timing, leaders must court the support of the influencers.

If your timing is off your communication becomes garbled. Your decision will not make a clear connection between a particular problem and the response you expect. To develop a good sense of timing, you first have to understand the sequence of decision making process. Being anywhere and anytime will extend our sense of timing. We will feel more in tune with everything that's happening.

Our minds will be more capable of wondering when to do something and what's going to happen next. It will become routine to experience what you now call uncanny timing: Being in the right place at the right time, happening along with fortuitous timing, experiencing synchronicities. You'll usually be prepared when the time comes. You'll consistently spend the right amount of time in time to make a timely comeback. Your sense of timing will be more powerful, reliable and important in your lives. A good sense of timing is a key to success.

Great leaders understand the importance of timing, specifically when it comes to making decisions. There are right times to consider issues and right times to make moves. Sometimes the leader is ready to make a decision, but other people need time to catch up. Conversely, even the right issue tackled at the wrong time faces certain defeat. There is no formula for great timing. It is part instinct, part intuition, part paying attention to surroundings, etc. Leaders who have a good sense of timing seem to be wired into their situations. Leaders with great timing know how to test the water, sniff the wind, and commit just enough to gauge reaction.

Great leaders make and execute decisions in a timely fashion. It demands well-coordinated and timely execution of strategy from others, their sense of timing in getting things done when they need to be done, so follow-up regularly. They have great sense of timing. They know when to act, and probably just as importantly, when not to act.

CHALLENGE

One of the greatest challenges confronting any leader is bridging the gap between strategy and getting people to execute. Leaders direct people to focus on the right strategic issues. They present a challenge that calls forth the best in people and brings them together around a shared sense of purpose. They work with the power of intentionality and alignment with a higher purpose.

Leaders learn how to think critically and go beyond the status quo to form meaningful new ideas. It gives them the ability to see the big picture, reframe questions to see different perspectives, create innovative solutions to problems, attend to detail, manage and reconcile diverse and complex interests and relationships. Sense of challenge demonstrates:

    a. Personal challenge: The biggest challenge is to be your best self; that requires recognizing and eliminating or improving our vices and weaknesses.

        Leaders should truly makes an impact on those within the leader's sphere of influence, i.e. building others up so they may reach their potential; have a clear sense of direction, continually working and studying to improve their leadership skills; they are not resting on their laurels, etc.

    b. Organization challenge: i.e. coping with change in organization culture, use the full capabilities of your organization by developing a team spirit, you will be able to employ your organization, department, section, etc. to its fullest capabilities.

Strong challenge is commonly connected with strong results. Sure you can get lucky every once in a while and find an easy path to success. Challenge means call to compete, stimulate to make demands, dare to do something or an interesting or difficult task. The purpose of challenge is to result a wide range of objectives that can be achieved in more rational and effective ways.

In business, challenge means finding balance between efficiency and innovation. For success, we should encourage and equip ourselves with vision, skills, knowledge, and character. Do something that will satisfy life purpose.

A challenge should provide appropriate opportunities, new perspective, space for inspiration, meet our personal interests, and benefiting both you and challenger. Those that take up the challenge are usually attracted by a new sense of meaning and purposefulness.

Leaders are comfortable with change. They prepare themselves for what someday may be open to them. They ask questions, listen to others and seek advice. When they are given or invent a challenge, they are ready to take it on with a full commitment.

Great leaders are not always popular. The great leaders also understand the importance of team purpose, challenge, camaraderie, responsibility, and growth, and focus much of their time on creating the conditions for these to exist.

The challenge for leaders then, is how to focus their attention and energy in the right ways to create and sustain a working culture where excellence is inevitable.

People will then want to work there because they know they will continue to learn to be successful and to develop their personal equity value. It is a working environment in which people are constantly seeking and finding ways to innovate and learn and where leaders are providing inspiring vision and direction, together with solid values and principles which drive organization priorities.

HERO

Great leaders have always been heroes. Heroes and greatness is a symptom of desire and loss: a desire for identifiable and objective standards, and nostalgia for hierarchy, whether of rank or merit.

Leaders inspire commitment toward a common goal within others. Often such commitment is self-sacrificial in character and requires no small degree of risk-taking by those being led. This risk and self-sacrifice requires an unusually high degree of credibility between a leader and his or her followers. Leaders create heroes all around them.

DECISIVENESS

Decisiveness means make decisions promptly and communicate them in a clear and concise manner. Leaders are required to make decisions that support the fair and ethical treatment of people, and act in ways that are perceived as ethical and responsible. Great leaders have several qualities. One is making tough decisions.

Leadership greatness can be measured in the decisions made and the demonstrated commitment to those choices made by an individual. You must learn to be a great decision maker. Indeed, you don't want to be one of those leaders who consults no one before making a decision, announces the change the next day and then gets frustrated when no one follows it.

Decision making should consider following points, which help making good decision, i.e.:

a. Timing: Be quick but not hasty.

b. Commitment: Be committed to your decision but not rigid.

c. Conduct analysis: Be analytical, but don't over-analyze. Too much analysis can cause paralysis.

d. Thoughtfulness: Be thoughtful about all concerned, but don't be obsessive.

Great leaders are decisive, resourceful, have a deep sense of urgency, and maintain tough-minded accountability. They make timely decisions, which are intelligent and unwavering, means that in some instances, the outcome might be failure. This is acceptable - almost expected - by followers. More important than the outcome is the decision making.

Leaders, by virtue of having made these leaps (successfully, or not), become better skilled at ensuring successful outcomes, thereby instilling ongoing confidence.

Leaders who desire improvements to their organizations using a strategy that focuses on sound judgment and a just and responsible outcome.

Decisiveness demonstrates how leaders can learn from failures and then change the process of decision that they employ in the future. They understand that failure is the process by which we succeed. They know that a certain number of failures must accompany every success. They have got to learn to fail faster in order to keep up in the changing environment.

Great leaders aren't concerned about what others think about them. Therefore a good decision should:

a. Determine the composition of the decision-making body. The selection should be based on access to expertise, implementation needs, the role of personal confidant, and the effect of demographic differences.

b. Shape the context in which deliberations will take place. Define norms and ground rules that will govern the discussions.

   c. Determine how communication will take place among the participants. In which people enable to exchange ideas and information, as well as generate and evaluate alternatives.

   d. Determine the extent and manner in which they will control the process and content of the decision. The leader should determine his/her role to play.

A tackling attitude is necessary for leader's success. Decisiveness is essential for the leaders, regardless of the problems they are facing. As a leader, every choice made can have introvert and extrovert influences.

Introvert choices influence subsequent decisions made by a leader and demonstrate his/her ethics. These choices then telegraph externally to a leader's direct reports the variances of choices, which they can make, that are expected and which will be tolerated.

To take decisive action, great leaders are always searching for the truth. As a leader, your job is to make people more confident about the future you're dragging them into. To that end, you need to tell them why they're going to win. The more clearly you can communicate to the people, the more confident you will be, and therefore the more resilient, the more persistent, and the more creative.

Greatness in leadership is acquired by people who have a strong sense of vision, have passion and are able to get people to commit 100% and take the necessary action to see that vision become a reality.

Great leaders are decisive at times when they need to be; they make decisions and they are consistent. They make decisions and then live with the consequences. They are well aware of the fact that indecision is, in fact, decision. They don't want critical decisions being left to fate, time, circumstances or default. They want the right to decide, even if they fail.

Followers will feel empowered and in control of events when they are able to make or influence decisions that they consider important. These choices and decisions need to be appropriate for their capacities, and for the organization's values. They know themselves unusually well and have become aware of their blind sides, their tendencies for avoiding or over-doing, and they are accomplished objective problem solvers.

Great leadership encompasses confidence, assertiveness and mutual respect. Great leaders take calculated risks and are innovative and confident in their decisions to do so. They realize that being timid will not get them where they want to go. This confidence and assertiveness will usually trickle down to the team members.

The quality and effectiveness of a great leader will often show itself by way of the team's effort as a whole.

CONFIDENCE

Confidence brings trust and respect from others. Everyone wants to feel confident. Leaders, who are confident of their abilities, attain positive outcome, convince others that they should follow their lead. Self-confidence is also infectious and imparts a degree of enthusiasm and optimism into the situation.

Leaders can be wrong. They can't be confusing. If people are going to follow you into the future, they need to know precisely whom they are trying to please. It's a scary thing to please all of the people all of the time. So to calm our fear, they need you to narrow our focus. Tell them who will be judging their success. When you do this with clarity, you give them confidence - confidence in their judgment, in their decisions, and ultimately in their ability to know where to look to determine if they have fulfilled their mission.

Confidence is the degree of certainty in your ability to successfully achieve your goals and the resiliency to withstand the challenges along the way. Leaders display self-confidence by expressing a sense of achievement. Sense of confidence can only be forged through great leadership. Sense of confidence implies:

a. Self-confidence: A sense of faith in one's ability to make decisions, appropriately act and/or react and survive and persevere. Matter of whether one can respect and appreciate one's own strengths and skills. The first step in creating confidence is to act confidently. Self-confidence is the fundamental basis from which leadership grows. Great leader begins to take him/herself seriously.

b. Confident on others: The degree of trust on the people. Give followers a chance to show what they are capable of doing. Allow them to take on tasks without being checked on all the time. This shows trust on your part, a sort of "letting go" with a sense of faith. A great leader inspires them to have confidence in themselves. If you have confidence in yourself your people will have confidence in you.

Leader in reality must instill confidence in their final decision by putting on the line their own integrity and sense of purpose. A sense of self-esteem, confidence and excitement is generated by ongoing learning and knowledge development.

When you are confident you know you will handle whatever comes up in the best way you can and move on. They believe in themselves and their abilities. Self-doubt and low self-esteem are stumbling blocks. Rallying people requires that leaders have innate optimism. Great leaders are not unrealistic; in fact they are grounded in reality. They are able to create a vision of this future and rally others to support it.

Confidence comes from the ability to make decisions or offer solutions when it should be on drawing solutions out of others. We should base our confidence on our ability to offer great solutions rather than on the skill of drawing solutions out of others. You feel confident whenever you have a lot of certainty.

Any actions you take to increase your level of certainty slides you over a little more toward confidence. Your confidence is characterized by

a. Believe in yourself: Have faith in your abilities, serve sort of purpose which figure out who you are or who you want to become.

b. Accept responsibility: Take total responsibility for what you are thinking. Control your thoughts, keep them positive. Be responsible for your actions: Any action has a reaction. If you do not control your actions then you have no control over the reaction. Be responsible for the results.

c. Have flexibility: Adjust rapidly to new situations warranting attention and resolution. Effectively deals with others and morale issues that may arise. Be receptive to new information, ideas, or strategies

d. Evaluate yourself: Evaluate how your decision may lead your action, and how you expect the outcome

e. Be assertive: Stand up for your rights and not being taken advantage of.

f. Be straight: Be clear and straight to the point.

g.   Influence situations: The more people you affect, the more likely it is that your actions will impact people who have power and influence over situations.

Great leaders are great. By showing up a lot, great leaders get the opportunity to share their ideas about the direction and purpose of the organization. That's where they learn what communication style each subordinate likes, what matters to them and what kind of problems each one is having. They get to lead by example too, showing people what's important, by what they pay attention to.

There's another, more subtle benefit, too. Because they're around a lot their people are more comfortable with them. Face it, if the leader only shows up to dump on folks or to pontificate, that's what folks will expect, and it's not a confidence building expectation. The confidence you exhibit will provide you with objectivity of the present, and formulation for the future.

A great leader can balance confidence in his/her abilities & that of his/her team with the fuzzy information available to him/her. He/she can take good decisions in a timely manner, adapting his/her decisions according to the level of information available and the confidence level.

The great leader inspires people to have confidence in themselves. People feel better when they're around a great leader. People have confidence they can solve any problem because the leader has confidence in them.

FOCUS

Success is no longer measured by simply getting things done. It's the people who know how to focus energy and enthusiasm on the most important goals that move their organizations forward.

Leaders focus on the big picture think in terms of what's good for the entire organization, not in terms of what's good for their own team or organization. They have an understanding of and enthusiasm for the organization as well as an understanding of their tasks. They consider the implications of entire jobs and commit to outcomes. A person with the core quality of focus demonstrates:

a. Realize he or she represents the organization.

b. Understand how work in individual areas affects the entire works and the whole organization.

c. Gather information from all stakeholders when making decisions.

d. Share information throughout the organization and understands the value of a knowledgeable workforce.

A great leader will focus on the solution rather than on the problem and will allow no obstacle to overcome the mission that he/she is serving. He/she can display his/her courage in many different ways.

Leaders develop people into highly effective contributors who take responsibility for their decisions and actions, and work interdependently. Responsibility is the price of greatness. People are looking for leaders who are willing to give it all they have and they will follow - for a while; however, when the going gets tough, when pleasure and comfort compete with responsibility and long hours, followers will drop away. That is when you have to be sure that what you are doing is right so that you will keep going. As leaders, we have to be responsible, no matter how painful it is. Running away is not an option. Facing problems and dealing with them by making good decisions is the difference between a leader and a follower. Great leaders do not blame their business conditions on others. They recognize how their behavior affects the corporate vision and how their leadership can affect the bottom line. They do not wait for things to improve, but act to improve things.

Great leaders surround themselves with greatness. They understand that their own success and the success of their organizations depend mostly on hiring and promoting the best qualified, ethical, skilled, responsible, mature, and productive people and giving them the proper resources, authority, and freedom to do what's needed for the long-term benefit of their organizations.

Great leaders accept failure. Leadership is not a license, it is a responsibility. Conversely, those who consider themselves not leaders escape responsibility. Leaders take responsibility and take blame rather than blaming others or finding excuses. They will take remedial measures to fix the deviations or corrections required due to stimuli created by external factors.

5TH

SENSE OF ENTREPRENEURSHIP

Entrepreneur is a French word meaning take an opening. Entrepreneurial leaders create a compelling vision of where the organization is headed. They also continuously communicate how to proceed, and energetically guide the development of the organization to advance that vision. Entrepreneurial start-ups exist in an environment where almost everything is new and many things have not been done before.

Sense of entrepreneurship shows one's ability to define importance, thought and urgency, action, and reward people, as well as be model of good behavior. It takes leadership to ensure and cultivate sense of entrepreneurship. Leaders understand that they, and the organizations they serve, are all parts of interacting relationships.

Entrepreneurial action must be based on a clear, simple system of values. These values must be lived, creating loyalty. The continuity of shared cultural values will become more important to organizations. When you have disciplined people, you don't need hierarchy. When you have disciplined thought, you don't need bureaucracy. When you have disciplined action, you don't need excessive controls. When you combine a culture of discipline with an ethic of entrepreneurship, you get the magical alchemy of great performance.

Today marks the last working day for Bill Gates at Microsoft. Bill Gates has demonstrated over nearly thirty years the importance of clarity of thought and execution. Along with focus, the ability to dream big and pursue that with single-minded determination sets Gates apart from other entrepreneurs. This is particularly true of entrepreneurs from emerging economies like India where an ultra-conservative attitude has stifled growth.

Entrepreneurs need to develop confidence in themselves and their team that they can take on the world and come out winners. There cannot be many role models better than Bill Gates. The last thirty years have seen the emergence of an entrepreneur par excellence. (B. V. Krishnamurthy, Bill Gates: Entrepreneur, Manager, and Leader, 2007)

Entrepreneurship emphasizes leadership abilities that can be used to motivate people in a growing business environment. Leaders constantly seek to perform at their best. They are open to feedback, are goal oriented, seek to be unique, and strive for accomplishments based on their own efforts; and risks.

Leaders take moderate risk means you have the ability to influence events, but don't have complete control. Entrepreneurs are risks takers. They show tolerance to uncertainty and risk.

Leaders screen incoming information to constantly seek new growth opportunities; separate the useful from the useless. The entrepreneur focuses on innovation entrepreneur knows that differentiation is at least as important as innovation.

While innovation focuses upon the offering, differentiation focuses on the value. Leaders with entrepreneurship typically shows a high internal locus of control; which likely to experience success. When someone perceives events as under the control of others, fate, luck, the system, their boss, etc. They have an external locus of control. If they assume that any success they experience is due to their personal efforts and that they have the ability to influence events. People with internal also assume failure was also their fault.

Entrepreneurial leadership is a boundless font of optimism that never seems to end. When faced with a problem, they view it as a challenge. When faced with a setback, they view it as a new direction. The leaders realize that their follower does not work for them, but with them in their joint and unified pursuit of common goals.

The leaders will seek to lead an organization which reflects the substance, style and structure consistent with each one's own visions and values.

The field of entrepreneurship is one that relies heavily on the ability to change and exploit new opportunities. Entrepreneurship relies on creativity, self-initiative and long-term vision. Innovation and entrepreneurship are vital to any organization. They recognize that innovation and entrepreneurship are the essential counterbalances to efficiency and productivity.

Entrepreneurial people need leaders to share ideas with, to help translate those ideas into action, to acknowledge successes and to put failures into perspective. Great leaders know that innovation and entrepreneurship can thrive only in a healthy environment. They make their people feel appreciated, successful and determined to achieve. They accept mistakes.

A leader might be born through a personal entrepreneurship. Entrepreneurs in some ways resemble great leaders. Some are born entrepreneurs. Entrepreneurship should not be something in the air. Leaders must do sense a gathering of forces that create the possibility for a new opportunity. An entrepreneurial leader's genius lies in bringing things together in a combination that no one has ever seen before.

STANDARD

Leadership requires discipline. The leaders discipline themselves in order to accomplish the tasks at hand. Leadership must set a standard that reflects loyalty to the organization's goals and the courage to stand accountable for all our actions. The standard includes:

a. Personal standard: Leaders are standard bearers, who establish the ethical framework within an organization. It demands a commitment to live and defend the climate and culture that you want to permeate your organization. What you set as an example will soon become the rule as unlike knowledge. And in fast moving situations, examples become certainty. Being a standard bearer creates trust and openness in your members, who in turn, fulfill your visions.

b. Organizational standard: Comprise the attitudes, behaviors, beliefs, ethics and values of the organization. These are values and norms that are shared by people and groups in an organization and that control the way they interact with each other and with stakeholders outside the organization. Leaders should make sure that these standards are communicated clearly to each individual member.

Complying means leaders act in ways that are overly conservative, cautious, and/or polite. It measures the extent to which leaders get a sense of self-worth and security by complying with the expectations of others rather than acting on what they intend and want. Great leadership is both highly practical and deeply inspirational because it mixes logical leadership skills with creativity and personality.

The great leaders inspire standards and a culture of discipline, instead of pure charisma, to motivate others. Great leaders subscribe to a set of standards on which they will not veer.

QUALITY

One of the greatest attributes of an organization is quality service. Finding a way to manage people to produce and maintain quality is probably one of the greatest dilemmas leaders face. People don't want to be managed. They want to be led. Manage things. Lead people.

Leadership is the defining quality of successful organization management. The best measure of leadership quality is how quickly people will follow you to a place they would not otherwise go by themselves. If leadership and quality are not flip sides of the same coin, they were at least struck in the same mint.

Without leadership, a quality effort inevitably transforms itself into a by-the-numbers productivity effort. Leaders with sense of quality display efficiency, energy, sympathy resolution, courage, tenacity and personality.

Leadership is the creation of an environment in which others can self-actualize in the process of completing the task. Everyone can function at their best, in an atmosphere both rational (i.e., task-oriented) and emotional (personality-specific).

Quality doesn't happen on its own. Someone made it happen and brought others with him or her to ensure that quality would endure. Leadership is action. Leadership moves others.

Leadership begets quality. Leaders are emphasized to take the crucial role in presenting the high quality approach that fosters quantitative methods and the knowledge of people to assess and improve:

   a.   Materials and services supplied to the organization

   b.   Significant processes within the organization

   c.   Meet the needs of the end-user, now and in the future

Leaders are responsible for such things as a sense of quality in the organization, for whether or not the organization is open to influence and open to change.

Leader with sense of quality should address processes central to mission performance, not those that are incidental to it. This emphasis avoids committing scarce organizational resources to less important issues.

Quality leadership is managing themselves and others for maximum effectiveness. The leaders engage the followers in an ongoing honest discussion of the quality of work that is needed for the program to be successful. They do not only listen, but also encourage their members to give them any input that will improve quality. They teach the followers to inspect or to evaluate their own work for quality with the understanding that they know what high quality work is.

The leaders continually teach the followers that the essence of quality is constant improvement. Their duty is as a facilitator – doing everything possible to provide the followers with the best tools and a friendly, non-coercive, non-adversarial atmosphere in which to work.

Organizational processes and attitudes, when managed with the highest levels of dedication to quality, efficiency and conservation will automatically leads to products and services which command superior values and in turn generate superior returns.

Great leaders do not accept such arguments as: "What do you want, production or quality?" Great leaders help the people they lead understand that their jobs have a number of priorities, and all are important. The quality of the people comes down to the quality of its leadership.

Great leaders know it is people not programs that create a quality organization. Leadership qualities and skills can be acquired, and developed through quality information, practice, experience and mentoring from those who have been successful leaders. Leaders in their organizations should ensure quality.

ETHICS

Members can't follow someone who they believe lacks integrity or ethics. If you find yourself questioning when to be honest, you should realize that honesty is always the right course. The secret ingredient of leadership greatness is ethical influence. It is the type of leadership that produces not only great accomplishments but also great people.

Leaders determine to not merely use their people or coddle them, but rather to help them to be better, more ethical people as a result of the leadership endeavor.

A critical ethical dilemma in business today is the rise of individuals demonstrating choice selection in behavior and attitude that reflects minimal effort for maximum pay mentality. This behavior perpetuates an erosion of leadership ethics and becomes toxic to an organization as it permeates throughout all of function-able levels.

Nothing strikes more to the heart of fraudulent leadership than leadership by emergency. Leadership by manufactured emergency; no matter, who commits it, is fraudulent leadership.

Vision without purpose is like a ship without a compass. The focus of ethics of leadership is the ethical challenges that are distinctive to leaders and leadership. Leaders who exert ethical influence relearn and reapply these principles as their experience, knowledge and responsibilities expand. Ethical influence flows from those who align their words and behavior.

Leaders encourage ethical development involves growth, discussion and disagreement. The leaders must affirm ethical behavior in others within the organization. Blatant unethical behavior must be confronted. The leader must never request or manipulate unethical behavior from those that he/she leads. The leader must transparently communicate to those he/she leads an ethical living.

Ethical leaders are self-confident, not self-centered. People will deliver an extraordinary performance for a leader they trust. The leaders must be punctual, forthcoming, honest, and hard-working.

Leaders know their code of ethics and values and take them into account in decision-making. To operate an ethical organization, you have to create an environment for your people that allow them to operate in an ethical manner, by creating the boundaries of acceptable behavior.

Greatness is not manifested by unlimited pragmatism, which places such a high premium on the end justifying any means and any measures. People recognize the need for leadership ethics; ethical behavior as an important characteristic. As a leader, you have to set the standard yourself, constantly keeping your actions above reproach.

Knowing what is right is absolutely critical to personal and business ethics. Yet, ethics only happens when good beliefs lead to good behaviors. Leadership is the process of directing the behavior of others toward the accomplishment of some common objectives. The ethics of leadership rests upon three pillars:

a. The moral character of the leader: To reach excellence you must first be a leader of good character. Your actions should be based on reason and moral principles.

b. The ethical values embedded in the leader's vision, articulation, and program which followers either embrace or reject

c. The morality of the processes of social ethical choice and action that leaders and followers engage in and collectively pursue.

A leader who is credible must be aware of his or her values. These values then serve as a guide or moral compass in decision-making, helping leaders decipher right from wrong and between ethical and unethical conduct and actions. Leadership is a behavior, not a position.

Ethics is about knowing, what one ought to do when no one is watching - it concerns the moral will to do what is right despite the threats to values-based actions. Leadership is an ethic. There are really only two important points when it comes to ethics; a standard to follow; and the will to follow it. Leadership is about relationships, credibility, and what people do.

Unethical behavior, in which people deliberately intend to harm themselves or others, springs from, and is reinforced by, destructive and painful mind states.

Ethical behavior, on the other hand, enhances the well-being of everyone because it comes from, and reinforces, motives and emotions. There are two aspects to ethics, i.e. the ability to discern right from wrong, good from evil, and propriety from impropriety; and the commitment to do what is right, good and proper.

Great ethics is caught from great leaders who inspire appropriate conduct beyond the expectable. Ethical conduct is displayed through one's exemplary behaviors, respect for others, and sense of loyalty and responsibility. It means being honest and accurate in one's dealings with others and not misusing one's position or power against others for selfish gains or personal grudges.

A great leader is one who embodies in attitude, behavior, and action the five core beliefs: respect, trust, optimism, intentionality and service. Leadership in ethics demonstrates:

a. Respect - Treat each member of their departments and organization as important, contributing members who become entrusted with leadership's role that strengthen their leadership skills.

b. Trust and honesty - Set the standard through words and actions that are consistent and hold the same expectation for all members of their team.

c. Optimism - Inspire others by looking for positives in all situations, believing there are more possibilities than obstacles, and embracing change as an opportunity for growth.

d. Intentionality - Exemplify loyalty through reliability, generosity, strength, and keeping commitments.

e. Service - Serve their organizations and not themselves, other-centered versus self-centered. They lead at the request of others. They do not distribute favors to just a few, but provide benefits to many. The leader has a tremendous ability to affect organization and therefore must choose to serve for the common good.

Great leaders surround themselves with greatness in ethics. The great leader will showcase their ethics and values. Followers can't follow someone who they believe lacks integrity or ethics.

Great leaders have great integrity (wholeness, soundness) and assume the role of keeper of ethics. Leaders must articulate the ethical expectations necessary to maintain the wholeness and soundness of the team, as well as the individual members.

MORALITY

Sense of morality is a sense of how we should or should not behave. Morality is behavior that directly affects other individuals. It describes moral behavior;

i.e. be kind to others. Great leader is a man that combines moral foundations with intellectual talents and serves a cause.

Morality is based on reciprocity: the obligation to return a favor done with a similar favor. Morals are not absolute; they are a code of conduct more or less haphazardly developed for group survival, and vary with the nature and circumstances of the group.

Morality is a critical factor in leadership that its absence could turn an otherwise powerful leadership model (i.e. transformational leadership) into a disastrous outcome.

The importance of morality for leaders is self-evident in light of the far-reaching effects of leaders' actions or inaction on other people. Such proposition necessitates the discourse in the objectivity of moral principles as the legitimate basis of a sound understanding of moral leadership.

Morality is a code of conduct that all rational persons would put forward for governing the behavior of all moral agents. Morality is a code of conduct that all persons would put forward for governing the behavior.

Morality as applying to behavior may affect other people. Morality requires doing that act that would result in the best overall consequences. Morality deals with that which is regarded as right or wrong; by which people determine whether given action are right or wrong.

Morality describes the principles that govern our behavior. Without these principles in place, organizations cannot survive for long. Everyone adheres to a moral doctrine of some kind.

When values have been separated from a foundation of morality, they come to mean nothing because they mean everything. Morality as it relates to our behavior, ensure fair play and harmony between individuals; make us good people in order to have a good organizations.

Morality impacts our everyday decisions, and choices. Moral implies conformity to established sanctioned codes or accepted notions of right and wrong

Leaders and followers raise one another to higher levels of morality and motivation. Organizations are in desperate need for persons of high ethical standards to lead the members.

Leadership in an organization, that has separated values from morality, requires clear and reflective thinking. Before a leader puts him/herself forward as an ethical leader, he/she would do well to determine his/her basis of understanding ethics and morality.

A leader inspires others by his or her commitment to not only a sense of purpose but a strong and abiding set of ethical principles. Great leaders use principles as their compass in difficult times. The leader with character is consistently courageous, being imbued with a basic integrity and a firm sense of principle.

Great leaders also obey principles of healthy human relationships. Great leaders lead others with morality, integrity, and service. Honesty and morality are not inconsistent with great leadership. A person who is considered a great leader should stand with a strong sense of morality. Ethicality and morality are common characteristics of great leaders.

DISCIPLINE

Leaders instill a sense of discipline. Sense of discipline is the ability to do what's right even if you don't feel like it. The most successful people demonstrate extremely self-disciplined. They don't need other people cheering them on every step of the way - they perform well because they've trained themselves to do so. A strong sense of discipline is the most important, which evolves:

a. Self-discipline: A certain task or to adopt a particular pattern of behavior. A leader must be extremely self-disciplined. If we fail to practice self-discipline, we will miss the best that opportunity has for us.

A leader is a person who has learned to obey a discipline imposed from without, and has then taken on a more rigorous discipline from within. The leader maintains a climate in which everyone wants to achieve self-discipline. Anyone who scorns self-discipline does not qualify to lead.

Self discipline is when your conscience tells you to do something and you don't talk back. Great leaders always have self-discipline.

b. Encourage discipline for others: Leaders, whose organizations are in order, have a minimum of members' misbehavior. Discipline in organization means teaching the followers to acquire: the great virtues of sound judgment, a sense of responsibility, personal courage, self-control, and magnanimity.

Leaders practice affectionate assertiveness. They assert correct conduct and attitudes by their example, action, and words. The collective performance is more about discipline and individual accountability.

Discipline certainly involves occasional punishment and some control as well as clear guidelines for behavior. The components of discipline are:

a. Commitment: Establish and maintain appropriate behavior.

b. High behavioral expectations: Share and communicate high expectations for appropriate behavior.

c. Clear and broad-based rules: Rules, sanctions, and procedures are developed with input from stakeholders, are clearly specified, and are made known to everyone in the organization. Clearly stated rules and procedures, assures that all members understand what is and is not acceptable.

A leader, one who gives commands, is him/herself under command; is accountable to the organization. Without the essential quality of discipline, all other leadership virtues remain as dwarfs - they cannot grow. Therefore a leader must:

a. Submit to discipline from without: No one achieves and sustains without it. And no matter how gifted a leader is; his/her gifts will never reach their maximum potential without the application of self-discipline. It positions a leader to go to the highest level and is a key to leadership that lasts.

b. Develop discipline from within: Learning about any highly disciplined person should make you realize that to be successful, self-discipline can't be a one-time event. It has to become a lifestyle. One of the best ways to do that is to develop systems and routines.

c. Give discipline to others: Leaders give some examples. Leader who begins to do the hard task himself/herself will see others follow suit.

Discipline is obedience of orders and the timely and accurate execution of assigned tasks. The essence of discipline is doing what we have to, even when it is difficult and painful, and doing it to the best of our abilities.

Discipline means inner strength, self control, mental stamina, physical toughness and perseverance. Discipline creates a sense of ownership and belongingness.

A great leader has both vision and discipline to work towards achieving his/her vision. The leader requires great discipline. Discipline is a serious issue that no great leader will want to take lightly.

VALUE

Values are the qualities and things in your life that you think are important. Leaders know what they value. They also recognize the importance of ethical behavior. The best leaders exhibit both their values and their ethics in their leadership style and actions.

Your leadership ethics and values should be visible. Your value in your organization is tied to what the people around you do, have and give when you're not around.

Leaders assist in the evolution of an organization's values system or culture by calling to and encouraging the elements that are ready to make the leap to the next level.

Leaders are also to an extent a blank canvas onto which their followers project elements of their own values systems. Which values are appealed to and projected; the best or the worst; will depend on what the leader says and does. Leadership was nothing to do with self-aggrandizement, but a necessity for pursuing their cause and acting on their values.

The leadership starts with a thorough understanding of the follower's needs, aspirations and concerns. It starts with a thorough understanding of the value systems of all stakeholders.

Values are the accepted principles or standards of an individual or a group. Values emerge over time, and get consensus over time. The leader's value system must be congruent with that of the followers if the relationship is to prosper.

Values are the principles that enable us to take a moral stand - to do the right thing, regardless of the circumstances. Our core values influence our behavior. They guide how we act on a personal level as well as within our larger organizational framework.

Great leaders know what they stand for and what is important to them. It describes their sense of values, which includes:

a. Personal value: Leaders must first understand and then communicate their own value systems if they are to be trusted and followed.

  Leadership comes from within us, in the sense that deeply held values and principles provide the road map for the way we lead, and the way other people respond. It is always the leader's personal value system that sustains them in their quest, whether they are a person of impeccable moral fiber, or quite disreputable.

b. Organization's value: Values that bind them together within the organization, i.e. Align the organization's value stream with customer needs and desires, prepare the organization for change, focus on breakthrough improvement to beat the competition, be a leaning organization which creates value for its customers and helps them succeed, etc.

Leadership is based on values, vision and vitality. Leaders must have a commitment to personal and organization's core values. They realize how much of the perceived (and real) value of an organization is related to intangibles. These intangibles include: quality of leadership team, ingenuity and ideas of members, unique structural processes, inventions and special procedures, strong relationships with customers and alliance partners, brands, and more.

Leaders should be able to create value. They create value through their ability to bring about change through other people. If leaders fail to engage people in strategic execution, then creating value through leadership will be exceedingly difficult.

Communication is at the cornerstone of creating value through leadership. Communication in leadership entails nurturing and maintaining a workplace environment in which communication flows freely and quickly in all directions with minimal distortion or lag time. Because of their very strong values, leaders will actively seek harmony and commitment and will.

If we use our values to make decisions, our decisions will align with the future we want to experience. Values transcend both contexts and experiences. Therefore, they can be used for making tough decisions in complex situations that we have not experienced before. When we use values in decision-making, we are consciously creating the future we want to experience.

Values are not constrained by the past and are adaptable to new situations. Values are the anchors we use to make decisions so we can weather a storm. They keep us aligned with our authentic self. They keep us true to ourselves and the future we want to experience.

Values are becoming the preferred mode of decision-making in business. It is not surprising therefore to find ample research showing that adaptable and values-driven companies are the most successful organizations on the planet.

When organizations unite around a shared set of values, they become more flexible, less hierarchical, less bureaucratic, and they develop an enhanced capacity for collective action. When followers do not only share the same values, but also share the same vision, the performance of an organization is significantly enhanced.

Shared values build trust, and trust is the glue that enhances performance. A value is a belief, a mission, or a philosophy that is meaningful. Whether we are consciously aware of them or not, every individual has a core set of personal values.

Values can range from the common place, such as the belief in hard work and punctuality, to the more psychological, such as self-reliance, concern for others, and harmony of purpose. Value is a term that expresses the concept of worth in general, and it is thought to be connected to reasons for certain practices, policies or actions.

Value framework focuses on others requirements. It is action oriented that focuses on optimizing organization's value. Value encourages innovative thinking, problem solving and performance improvement.

Whatever one's values; whenever we take them to heart, and implement them in the smallest details of our lives great accomplishment and success shall follow. Individuals subscribe to values; so do organizations and institutions.

Values are the key to our success; commitment to trusting the other; belief in the values of solving problems of society; values of systemization and standardization.

We can energize our lives by making the full effort to implement the values we subscribe to. Once we identify values that are meaningful to us, we can develop strategies to implement them.

Whenever we make the determined effort, to implement those strategies; good fortune is sure to follow; in the form of new opportunities, new sources of revenue and income, and other forms of material and psychological benefit.

We may even notice that as we implement values, we experiences instances of life response; where good fortune suddenly comes to us from seemingly out of nowhere, defying our normal perceptions of what is logical and possible. In order to be the great leader you need to:

a. Follow principles: Leadership that is based on principles is flexible and widely applicable to many situations. Leaders present a framework of principles and tools to help followers navigate the difficult task in the organizations.

b. Develop a character that produce a moral and ethical work force that provides excellent service to the organization's

c. Add value to each process, product and service

Values are what we value and that makes them valuable to us. Higher order values (trust, respect, empathy, etc) are most important in relationships and need to be the ones you strive for. To be distinguished from others, you should

a. Determine your key values - What you stand for and what makes you happy.

b. Determine the values you need to develop to become the person you would like to be and work on developing those values in yourself.

c. Associate with people that display the values that are important to you.

d. Determine what you want in each area of your life and live in congruence with what you want.

The key point to keep in mind about values is that implementing them energizes everything concerned with it. Committing to and applying values releases fresh energies, which always attract success, achievement, and well-being.

By adopting values, individuals become energized, as do its customers, its products and services, and everyone and everything else associated with that organization. If you want the values you identify to have an impact, the following must occur:

a. Demonstrate and model the values in action in your personal work behaviors, decision making, contribution, and interpersonal interaction.

b. Prioritize it in your daily work life - Ensure that you are able to accomplish those things that are of a more urgent nature vs. those that seem to constantly loom over you.

c. Use values to guide every decision – Values display principles and practices which maintains high moral standards of personal conduct

d. Recognize other people who embrace - Values may be different from yours against other's. It's not matter of rejecting other's values or to disregard your own. Values are not bad or wrong. You must also be able to live with other people whose have different values.

e. Enhance personal goals which are grounded in the identified values.

f. Adoption of the values and the behaviors that result performance.

g. Promote others whose outlook and actions are congruent with the values.

Values are attitudes about the worth of people, concepts, or things. Values are important as it influence a person's behavior to weigh the importance of alternatives. Values are activities, those are most important to one's life, others and the organization.

Great leaders recognize when their values are on the line; the thinking about what it means to be a leader who operates based on a clear set of values. Great organizations have great leaders who multiply value.

Great leaders possess the ability to see ability in others. They are willing to invest time and resources to help their followers, opportunities to discover those gifts and talents they might not realize they have.

Great leaders also have the ability to help others develop their ability. The great leaders add value to the lives of their followers and the organization, individually and collectively.

SERVICE

Leaders instill a sense of service in them. Leadership is first of all service. To lead is to serve whom you are leading. It is to be responsible beyond your own existence, and melt your own desires with that off your team (nation, religious congregation, group, or whatever you are leading). A leader is foremost a servant, not in word, but in deed.

Leaders must look not to their own interests but to the interests of others. Great people they all exhibit a consistent trait: their willingness to be of service to a greater good, a higher ideal, a supreme purpose. The first and most important choice a leader makes is to serve.

Leadership is essentially about helping people to achieve a better life. The basis of good leadership is honorable character and selfless service to your organization. In your members' eyes, your leadership is everything you do that effects the organization's objectives and their well being.

Great leaders focus their followers on serving one specific core group. By serving this core group, the organization can better serve other groups as well. Someone we call great rises head and shoulders above the common man - in integrity, maturity, nobility of character, and service to humanity. A great person, though they might end up serving themselves, is not essentially self-serving; his/her intentional actions spring from a desire to help the whole. They may end up serving themselves too, but that's not their primary motivation.

Leadership greatness is about creating new realities in the interest and service of all mankind and to thereby shape our future. If we apply the law of reciprocating to the organization, being of service, cordial, enthusiastic, positive and hard work will generate unexpected good results. In essence, there has to be a strong sense of service.

Leaders know that success depends on high standards of service: a skillful selected variety of goods; highly qualified staff; a pleasant atmosphere in which the customer feels welcome and valued; products which are refreshed, finest quality and innovative.

URGENCY

Crisis comprises a condition that includes urgency and emergency. A crisis becomes a crisis because it becomes an emergent situation. Crisis is a time of great danger or trouble, often one which threatens to result in unpleasant consequences. Leadership requires a sense of urgency to maintain organization. Urgency is needed to avert a crisis.

A leader handles crisis by sense of urgency. Sense of urgency is inner drive and desire to get on with the job quickly and get it done fast. This inner drive is an impatience that motivates you to get going and to keep going. A sense of urgency feels very much like racing against yourself.

One of the biggest mistakes people make when trying to achieve a goal is to plunge ahead without establishing a high enough sense of urgency in themselves and others. Communicating urgency is one of the hallmarks of leadership.

Leaders must continually maintain a sense of urgency in order to compete and win. Sense of urgency wins, as people do it now; have a propensity for action; make decisions quickly.

The quality of your leadership is greatly affected by the level of your reactiveness to events, circumstances and the behavior and opinion of others. The goal is to avoid being blown off course by reactiveness and become aware that you have the ability to appraise people and events in a way that serves your intention.

Successful people are those who have a huge sense of urgency. They always want to get it done sooner and now cultivate the habit of doing it now. Set a pace that you can maintain forever. In the sense of urgency, you need to figure out what gives you strength and energy and focus.

If you believe that business in general is becoming more competitive, then you must also believe that you need more out of yourself. The best way is to create a sense of urgency into all of your goals and plans.

A deadline and strong sense of urgency generates energy toward getting results. They drive people to perform. Sense of urgency causes you to accomplish what today sets before you. Team members need to believe the team has an urgent and worthwhile purpose.

Establishing a sense of urgency and direction will help them know what their expectations are. The more urgent and meaningful the need to reach a goal, the more likely it is that a real team will start to emerge.

The best teams define their performance expectations, but are flexible enough to allow changes to shape their own purpose, goals, and approach. There are seven ways to demonstrate a sense of urgency:

a. Recognize the importance: When people do not understand why the change matters to the organization and how it impacts or benefits them specifically, they do not act in ways that support operational or business objectives.

b. Show the reasons: In a customer-driven marketplace, the need to get things done is critical to winning and keeping business. Leaders constantly communicate urgency to their members. Everyone understands the importance of urgency.

Sense of urgency separates great leaders from just managers, in which the leader could work on this quickly, i.e. Highlight future opportunities, and the current inability of the firm to capitalize on those opportunities; show organization's weaknesses compared to the competition.

Leaders accurately show current and future realities and that positively motivate people to take action. The leader gives guidance in taking steps of action, and brings solutions to the problems of the people and organization.

c. Identify the strategies: Leaders identify the strategies for leading organizations effectively, i.e. recognize individual contributions, define priorities, etc.

d. Discuss with people: Communicate thoughtfully and effectively the urgent need in the organizations.

e. Take action and stay focused: Opportunity is all around you. What you complete by year-end is totally dependent upon the sense of urgency you create beginning right now. Deadlines create a sense of urgency that helps you get things done.

f. Monitor progress: Adjust where and when necessary. An atmosphere of urgency will create an atmosphere of achievement. High achievers

151

work best under a self-determined or externally fixed deadline for achieving objectives.

Those who consciously choose not to 'sleep at the wheel' realize that regardless of the goal being pursued, they must continually maintain a sense of urgency in order to compete and win.

g.   Stick to the deadline: No excuses accepted Things that get accomplished all due to a deadline and corresponding sense of urgency that is either self imposed or other imposed. Everything involves the use of deadlines to create commitment, accountability and most importantly a sense of urgency.

True greatness is only achieved once we develop a sense of urgency and importance of what we are doing. A sense of urgency describes we feel getting results and achieving our goals is a matter of life and death. A deadline and strong sense of urgency generates energy toward getting results. It drives people to perform.

Leaders have to pick and choose when to be urgent. Not everything is an emergency. Just because a client is having an emergency, doesn't mean it has to be an emergency for us. We want to feel a sense of urgency, but we can't do it for every situation.

Great leaders recognize that tough times create a rare opportunity to make dramatic improvements. They see that calamity can crystallize thinking and temporarily paralyze the forces which prevented change in the past. They understand that urgency and stress are limited commodities which need to be channeled into productive action, not squandered on panic and indecision. They know that short term corrections can support long term goals.

Leaders know well the use of deadlines to create commitment, accountability and most importantly a sense of urgency. A sense of urgency is that feeling that lets you know yesterday is gone forever, tomorrow never comes. Today is in your hands. Great leaders are decisive, resourceful, have a deep sense of urgency.

COMMUNICATION

Leader is a master in the art of communication. Communication is the core component and without it one can never be a great leader. Leadership is about being able to organize a group and work to see things through to completion. Essential to being a good leader is having excellent interpersonal skills.

Organizational greatness requires effective communication between people as well as between people and processes, and between processes. Recognizing this concept shifts one's focus from optimizing the parts of the organization to optimizing the relationships between the parts. Communication is the linkage – the web – holding it all together.

Leaders take a simple message and repeat it endlessly. Where it comes to vision and strategy; say it well, often, simply and passionately. They keep communicating the vision to create a strong field which then brings their vision into physical reality.

A leader will embrace effective communication rather than dictate; delegate rather than control; and skillfully guide rather than take charge. One-way communication should be replaced with a two-way interaction of interest, intellect, and understanding.

Great leaders involve their people in the communication process to create the goals to be achieved. If people are involved in the process, they psychologically own it and you create a situation where people are on the same page about what is really important: mission, vision, values, and goals.

Leadership is communicating people's worth and potential so clearly that they are inspired to see it in themselves. They have the interpersonal skills, courage, and determination to do what needs to be done and know how to take the necessary steps when the inevitable mistakes are made. Great leaders keep their teams 'in the know' about information pertaining to their work.

Communication continues to be a significant problem for many leaders and within organizations. If a leader desires to have his or her members make a significant contribution to the success of the organization, then the leader must keep them informed of all necessary information pertaining to their work.

Great leaders do not withhold or assume that they are aware of pertinent information. Great leaders assure through frequent and direct communication with their members that the information members have is current, correct, and complete.

However, simply providing information is not enough. In addition, great leaders engage their members by creating member ownership of the work to be done.

Great leaders communicate in a way that members understand how the information communicated applies to them. Great leaders do more than communicate – they have an ability to connect with members.

You need to articulate your vision clearly and repeatedly. Spell out your plan of action, asking for everyone's support and showing confidence in a positive outcome. Keep those around you in the loop. Arm them with information that helps give them an accurate assessment of where they are, the odds against them, and what they have to do to achieve their goal. Make them feel part of an inner circle. Listen attentively so you are well grounded with your team and the environment that surrounds you. Know who your friends and enemies are and keep malcontents close to you to win their support.

Leader is responsible for effectively communicating their expectations. Members learn they are dependent on one another in the overall success. The leader should provide a trained workforce that follows written guidelines and/or procedures.

Members must be made aware of performance expectations as well as resolutions to poor performance. Both support and communication are key elements to the team's success. Succinct, consistent and optimistic communication to all levels within the organization, regardless of the nature of the messages, is a fundamental attribute of all good leadership. Vital, too, is the encouragement of constructive feedback and disagreement. Active listening (not merely hearing), and being both readily available and accessible is essential if this is to be effective and embraced as a reality.

The great leader is a master in the art of communication. He or she is aware of the strong need for actions to match words. Leaders need to possess a willingness to listen to input with an open mind.

Two-way communication, being approachable and having an open door policy makes for very good team relations. This is crucial in building a trusting and open environment. It must be an established norm that it is okay to ask for help and that players can communicate openly without fear of punishment. The way one communicates with and leads a team may play a big part in their motivation to work hard.

The key to member engagement is for a leader to move members from awareness (through information) to knowledge (really understanding the meaning of the information), and then to action (incorporating this information and knowledge into day-to-day activities). This includes inviting and integrating input into job functions and direction.

It also means that leaders should concentrate on communicating only a small number of key messages to emphasize the critical pieces needed to achieve the goals.

Many leaders are actually quite effective in terms of keeping their members informed. However, it is in terms of engaging people where many leaders fall short from being merely good to great. Great leaders excel in communication and motivation, mutual respect, instilling confidence and enthusiasm, and showing credibility and integrity on a consistent basis.

SPIRITUALITY

Spirituality is multidimensional and is best understood as comprised of multiple dimensions including: behavior and practices; beliefs; motivations and values; and, subjective experience. Spirituality defines belonging, referring or relating to the spirit or soul rather than to the body or to physical things; consisting of, or affecting the spirit, relating to sacred matters.

Spirit itself relates to the deeper sense, meaning, or significance of something. Leadership is based on a spiritual quality - the power to inspire, the power to inspire others to follow. Spirituality in leadership is a holistic approach to leadership in which the leader strives to encourage a sense of significance and interconnectedness among followers.

Spirituality is personal. A leader brings unique and individual spirits to the organization and is highly motivated by the spiritual need to experience a sense of transcendence and sense of community in the organization. The spiritual journey, which leaders must take and inspire others to take, begins with us.

Leadership involves motivating and inspiring members through a transcendent vision and a culture based in altruistic values to produce a more motivated, committed and productive workforce. Members' spiritual needs are met and aligned with organizational objectives.

This higher motivation, commitment and productivity have a direct impact on organizational processes and outcomes which in turn impacts organizational performance. Spirituality and religion are not the same:

a. Spirituality incorporates values that lead to a sense of transcendence and interconnectedness of all life such that workers experience personal fulfillment on the organization's objective.

   The leader who incorporates spirituality into his or her leadership will be one who causes others to seek out and understand their inner selves and who fosters a sense of meaning and significance among his or her followers.

b. Religion is a system of beliefs regarding a greater reality than we can perceive with our five senses, i.e., ultimate reality. Religious beliefs are sets of creeds, rules, dogma, doctrines, principles, teachings and/ or philosophies.

Most religious beliefs involve faith, a trust or confidence that exists in the absence of complete proof, which may include insights derived from direct experience.

Leaders are persons who seek to transform the organizational culture from materialistic to altruistic values that are more idealistic and spiritual must address value congruence across all levels of the organization.

The leaders have the ability to sense the deeper spiritual needs of followers and link their current demands to the deeper, often unspoken, need for purpose and meaning.

Leadership with spirituality involves the application of spiritual values and principles to the workplace. The spiritual leader understands the importance of followers finding meaning in their work and demonstrates a genuine concern for the whole person, not just the follower.

Spirituality in leadership implies that the focus will be less on formal position power and more on people; less on conformity and more on transformation and diversity; and less on controlling and more on partnership, collaboration, and inspiration.

Spirituality in leadership does not require that the leader adhere to a particular religion or that he or she attempt to convince followers to pursue a specific set of religious principles.

Spirituality in leadership is more concerned with the development of employees as whole people - people who exhibit compassion to other employees, superiors, subordinates, and customers.

The leader's spirituality will directly impact his or her ability to define reality for those who follow as well as sustain the process of realizing the vision. Leader's spirituality enhances a leader's ability. Leadership skills alone do not make us great leaders. Individual spiritual development and transformation is the key.

TRANSCENDENCE

A major change is taking place in the personal and professional lives of leaders as many of them aspire to deeply integrate their spirituality with their work; which is leading to very positive changes in their relationships and their effectiveness.

Great leaders make a difference; the minds of their followers can never go back to where they were before the accomplishment. Transcendent leadership changes the world and makes it better. A leader is self-aware enough to be aware of their own personal agenda, to consciously master it and to place it aside in favor of greater principles.

Leadership involves motivating and inspiring followers through a transcendent vision and a culture based in altruistic values to produce a more motivated, committed and productive workforce. In such an organization, where followers' needs are met and aligned with organizational objectives, this higher motivation, commitment and productivity has a direct impact on organizational processes and outcomes which in turn impacts customer satisfaction and ultimately, organizational performance.

Great leadership create the conditions for a vision that might be perceived as impossible and allow it to become a reality. A leader generates a type of commitment among his/her people based on personal trust and transcendent motivation.

People bring unique and individual spirits to the workplace and are highly motivated by the spiritual need to experience a sense of transcendence and community in their work. A leader with transcendence is the leader who really cares for the good of the organization and the people who work in it.

Leaders with transcendence are persons who rise above their ego to build bridges instead of creating polarities. Leadership is about bringing people together in the spirit of some greater outcome, so it's impossible to talk about leadership without talking about how that leader somehow convinced a large number of people to join their cause or mission in order to create something great.

Greatest form of leadership creates the conditions for exponential results. Great leadership is the willingness and ability to transform one's thinking and behavior to serve a higher purpose than just one's own needs.

COMPETENCE

Competence inspires leadership, but a lack of competence destroys it. Low competence leaves the leader unsure where to lead his/her team. Leaders continually demonstrate competence, impressive aptitude, shrewd thinking, resourcefulness and apparently limitless capacity. They delegate with conviction.

Leaders are passionate about teaching and mentoring their followers. And in each successful mentoring relationship there is an expectation for mutual learning - the apprentice from the leader and visa versa. A successful mentoring assists in problem solving, not by becoming the solution provider, but by coaching independence of thought.

A leader finds and places top talent. The leaders seek able men and weigh results over personality. It is leader's responsibility to make sure that exceptionally able men, even though not popular with their contemporaries, should not be prevented from giving their services.

Sometimes the top man or woman for a job is the one who has made the best of a difficult appointment, not someone who has coasted in an easy position.

Leaders may not leave employment and promotion policies to the personnel experts. They promote from within before hiring from outside, and make sure that individuals are promoted irrespective of race and color.

Leaders must be competent and able to do their jobs. They must have both intellect and good judgment. Often this quality is underplayed and the attention goes to vision, but vision and ability go hand in hand.

Ability is not limited to job knowledge, technical expertise, or management skills but must also include the ability to learn, inductive reasoning skills and deductive thinking which lead to better problem solving.

Great results are a by-product of great leadership. Leadership is about stepping up, committing, knowing what really matters, and trusting our ability to find a way. Followers believe in the competence of the leader to get them to the goal.

Great leaders have core competence for which everyone can totally respect. They have the competence and skill to succeed. Each inspires trust and understanding of the perils of reaching their goal.

HUMOR

People need to have fun being around you. Use humor and other diversions to relieve tension. An attribute that is so helpful in any leadership is a sense of humor. Humor is a spontaneous and non-serious perspective of life itself at any given moment. In the past, using a sense of humor in the work place is seen as a sign that people aren't dedicated to their work.

If you had fun, or were found joking, laughing, or showing a playful attitude on the job, it is assumed that you are goofing off, and not taking your work seriously.

The great leaders are the ones who love what they do and have fun with it. Everyone wants to be around a leader who knows how to have fun but still gets the job done.

Humor promotes teamwork and camaraderie and stimulates creativity. Humor is also a powerful form of persuasion. If you can maintain your sense of proportion and humor when the world seems to be falling apart, people who rely on you will show their appreciation in better work and greater loyalty.

Almost nothing is more helpful in dealing with people than a sense of humor. A sense of humor doesn't necessarily mean a knack for telling jokes.

Some problems might be serious - but there's nothing to be gained by exaggerating their importance. Get in the habit of taking yourself and your problems less seriously. Learn to smile at yourself and the world as well. You'll get better results - and actually have more good things to smile about - when you do.

A good sense of humor can enhance your capacity for resilience, adaptation, imagination, and resistance in stress situations.

Humor can also backfire because sometimes people just don't get it and may take it too seriously. There also can be considerable truth in humor which if used skillfully can lead to change.

Great leaders have a charming sense of humor. They laugh at their failures and take their successes in stride. They take the light things seriously and the serious things lightly. They constantly have fun, finding the genuine humor in the tragedy of the situation.

Leadership is always well served by a good sense of humor. Leaders who take themselves too seriously are people who are in danger of losing their perspective. A sense of humor is part of the art of leadership, of getting along with people, of getting things done.

Leadership is being fun to be around. Leaders maintain a sense of humor. A good sense of humor can enhance your capacity for resilience, adaptation, imagination, and resistance in stress situations. Humor can also backfire because sometimes people just don't get it and may take it too seriously. There also can be considerable truth in humor which if used skillfully can lead to change.

Great leaders never take themselves too seriously. Having a sense of humor is not only a great quality for leaders but a sense of humor should not be a quality only for leaders.

CONNECTIVITY

The most extraordinary things about leadership is unites people. Leadership creates a bond in their appreciation of what the organization stands for. Leaders build group synergy and a sense of unity that tie well to the organization. Organization's member lived with a sense of unity.

Connectedness or connectivity is a way to connect us to each other, whether it is through the internet, cell phones, laptops or any other technical device that can connect people to their computers or each other. Connectivity is sense of belonging that comes with the ability to communicate interactively with other.

Connectivity also shapes organization's communication flow and sense of unity. Leadership is a relationship. Leaders are defined by their followers. Leadership is a relationship between those who aspire to lead and those who choose to follow.

Leaders should accept that the value of connecting things with each other is when they are able to connect everything with each other. If they do not accept that everything must be connected with each other, then they are accepting the notion of disconnected information.

The value of connectivity is the amount that the value of information can be increased by connecting it with other uses of that information. Leaders build quality relationships, foster teamwork, collaborate, develop people, and involve people in decision making. Connectivity within the organization includes:

a. Co-dependent: Mutually dependent, dependence on the needs of another. Relationship between leaders and followers is codependent. The followers have effect on a leader; they have control or power in certain situation against the organization and the leadership.

   A leader exists because of followers. Everything they do depends on the successful efforts from one to another. Codependent is an individual who is affected by the actions of others.

   Leadership and organizational effectiveness are codependent. Both leader and followers have a common and shared understanding of how they contribute by what they accomplish to the goals and purpose of the organization.

   On other hand, although codependency usually brings to mind the idea of the relationship issues of a person living with, and putting up with, another person who has a dependency on a particular bad habit or vice, the codependent leader is one who brings to the table the imperfections and limitations that exist as a result of the social system that develops around these types of relationships.

The codependent relationship is based on the codependent following a harsh set of rules in order to conceal the behavior of the dependent. He will take personal responsibility for their substandard performance and make no attempt to correct it for fear of hurting their feelings.

Codependent leadership, as leaders inducing followers to act for certain goals that represent the values and the motivations-the wants and needs, the aspirations and expectations-of both leaders and followers.

b. Interdependent: Leadership is a group activity. There is an implied interdependency – cooperate to achieve something that can be achieved independently.

Leaders recognize the mutual interdependence of all members. There is a profound interconnectedness between the leader and the organization/people, and leaders serve the good of the organization.

Team building creates a sense of connectivity and makes group decisions. The value of a piece of information is proportional to the number of uses that piece information is connected to. This law focuses the value on what connectivity is enabling, an increase in the value of information. Leaders need to find partners, including authority figures, but also members of the factions for who change will be very difficult.

Credibility in leadership comes from competence (what you do), character (who you are), and connection (your relationship with followers). Members who know that you are honest will acquire a sense of connection, and one of the results of this connection is ownership. They will be more creative and take more initiatives.

Honesty enhances ownership. For this to evolve, all of the stakeholders concerned with connectivity need to talk with each other, resolve issues of incompatibilities, understand others needs, appreciate the values that are being brought. It has become 'smaller and faster', when people are working in the sense of connectivity. Sense of connectivity keeps people motivated. It mediates communication among the people.

Connectivity is the ability to make and maintain a positive connection between two entities or more. This is an essential trait for a great leader. Connection inspires the people to believe, that they truly have a leader who cares about them.

Leaders should show connectivity with their people, understand their needs, and create the environment they need to be successful, and with the organization. Being disconnected and non-responsive are hallmarks of poor leaders - They do little to support their people or meet their needs, and the environment they create is far from one where people maximize their potential, it's one where people struggle to perform.

TEAMWORK

To become a great leader, you must develop a great team. A leader who is always looking for credit will soon be a solo performer. No team will follow a truly selfish leader. The team may establish a good work regimen and perform well, but unless the members respect their leader, it will not excel.

Great leaders are not afraid to surround themselves with wise people. The age of the omnipotent, all-knowing leader is over. We need leaders who have the confidence to get the best people around them and have the wisdom to listen to them before making decisions.

Leaders select the people to work for them because they are intelligent, perceptive and empowered. In turn, followers oftentimes follow without having to know the entire story or picture. Their buy-in is for their perceived long-term, not short-term, gains. They tend to inspire others to share their burden (and those of the business that they are supporting) in tough times.

Team work is one of the essence as well as best ingredients in leadership. It marks a big step in your development when you come to realize that other people can help you do a better job than you could do alone.

Leaders are not those who strive to be first but those who are first to strive and who give their all for the success of the team. Virtually all major change involves engaging, persuading, and working with other people.

You have to have the organization's best interests at heart, and really be motivated to make things better for those you seek to lead. With this attitude, and a good practical plan, people will be inclined to follow you.

Team-building describes the ability to develop an atmosphere where different kinds of people with different skills, personalities, interests, and passions can support each other and work together with joy.

Developing a team, means having people work in a joint and cooperative manner. The coordination of that effort toward successful execution solely resides in the leadership of that team.

Leadership must be the catalyst for accomplishment. Although you've just delegated work and truly given your team ownership, you also have to take ownership and responsibility at all times. Your team has to know you'll be there for them through the good and the bad times.

PARTNERSHIP

A sense of partnership in a morally valuable common cause can give organizations a special grace. A great leader sees the value of partnerships and will then seek to team up with others to fulfill the work. The leaders must seek internal and external partnership to add value and drive moments of truth in their businesses.

Visionary leaders promote a partnership approach and create a shared sense of vision and meaning with others. They exhibit a greater respect for others and carefully develop team spirit and team learning.

Partnership is a sound strategic approach, it is not the only one, and is a complement to the others. Because partnership is a relationship between two or more persons who join to carry on shared goals; encourage teamwork; and believe that an active and well-informed team member is necessary to ensure the highest standards.

In a partnership the partners share equal responsibility for the duty, benefits, risks and liabilities. It is a means of better determining and expressing the needs and requests, distributing resources more effectively, obtaining a deeper commitment from those involved, channeling grievances and finding the best solutions.

Partnership tends to be more extensively legitimized and more effective. It is more than dialogue, which does not include joint action, and less than participation, where each has and forms part of something. It differs from co-ordination, where the commitment is weaker and presupposes institutional organization, and co-operation, where there is no mutual involvement.

The great leaders are responsive to the real needs of people and they develop participative strategies to include people in designing their own futures.

Partnership is more often an ongoing process through which the relations of groups organize themselves and join forces, resulting in a formal discussion between the part-taker. Partnerships adopt more structured organizational forms and are set up as an entity, depending on the frameworks.

Partnerships are generally formed and developed to offset disadvantages and to defend the scarce resources of part-taker, turning part of its efforts towards the outside, often adopting more loyalty approaches.

The stronger the feeling of identity will be the less difficulty in lasting partnership formula. Partnership is midway between consensus and conflict. It cannot be set up in those two extremes. It will adopt methods of negotiation, dialogue and decision making.

Partnership should not generate exclusiveness, but involve all the resources, reduce an individual's isolation and the social exclusion of individuals, work in closer co-operation, share other's values, striving to find the general interest, and create synergies.

Collaboration means working with others to complete tasks/goals and make decisions with shared responsibilities, resources and accountability.

COMMUNITY

A sense of community plays an important part in developing one's self-esteem. Members of the organization need to know who they are and how they fit into the organization. They need to become more aware of others and in the community in which they live. A sense of community has five key elements:

a. Meet needs: communities form, grow, and maintain themselves by meeting the needs of their members, i.e. security, common interests, identification, etc. Strategies for building community must make sure that the needs of its members are met on a continuous basis for as long as they are part of the community.

b. Share values: Understand the shared value among community members is one of the important steps. Shared values are things that community members commonly believe are important, such as education or caring for each other.

Values reflect the priorities of community members. Shared values can be changed as the community evolves and members' experiences change.

c. Membership: A sense of community provides a sense of belonging and membership. The stronger the sense of community, the stronger the sense of bonding or belonging individuals experience. A feeling of trust and caring comes from this sense of membership.

d. Influence: Organization's members believe that they can individually and collectively influence their communities as well as be influenced by them. They are responsive to their needs and are influenced by their input.

Organization with a strong sense of community provide opportunities for the members to truly influence and improve their connectivity; and the members adhere more to the norms and commonly held values of the organization.

e. Emotional connection: Positive relations among community members, through positive experiences, strengthen a sense of community.

A community is a group of people who form relationships over time by interacting regularly around shared experiences. Sense of community is able to increase well-being and commitment to the organization. It creates a strong sense of recognition where people want to be and appreciate the contributions of others.

Leaders nurture and promote a sense of community, includes:

a. Community identity: Create a sense of place. Having a clear sense of place, promotes an individual's sense of well-being and level of personal satisfaction.

b. Community interaction: Interaction among members of the organization which allows for sharing ideas, concerns, and information that permits members to know each other.

c. Community involvement: Individual is actively caring about what happens in her/his community. It is a loyalty and concern that comes from having a sense of ownership.

Sense of community is social bonds that increase loyalty to the organization. They must be flexible in their approach and responsive to the needs of others. Leaders have to identify the characteristics of healthy environment at the organization, which may include:

a. Trust: Leaders trust enough to be trusted. They raise difficult issues and solve it with integrity

b. Commitment to each other and to common goals

c. Connections/relationships: Relate with care and compassion Resolve conflicts respectfully

d. Respect: Resolve conflicts respectfully.

e. Collegiality: Create an environment in which the leaders are able to develop a sense of community.

f. Satisfaction: The substance of get satisfaction. It's how you give back to the community.

g. Shared successes and failures People enjoy the strong sense of community, the relationships and the purpose they all share.

Leaders should develop skills of the followers in community building, conflict resolution, mediation, decision making and problem solving. They assist as facilitators for community building within organization. A great leader takes people where they don't necessarily want to go, but ought to be.

FOLLOWERSHIP

Followership is an essential element of leadership. Leaders also function as followers; everyone spends a portion of their day following and another portion leading. A key leadership trait is the ability to inspire followership.

Great leaders create trust. Those who follow them believed in their work and they believe in themselves. These leaders give us the best in ourselves. We risk working with these leaders for we are trusted, and we know that, by virtue of who they are.

Followers, who actively contribute, are aware of their function and take personal pride in the art of followership; therefore the joint purpose of leadership and followership - higher levels of mission accomplishment - is achieved effectively.

Leaders may gain respect, trust and loyalty of his/her followers through his/her well-defined and structured leadership. Great leaders are followers too. If you're a leader without following, you're a dictator. Being a leader-follower means finding value in your team, getting inspired by your team, encouraging your team to communicate, brainstorm and be open.

A great leader is a great follower. Along with the skill of vision and leading comes the skill of ability to follow. It means that you have the ability to identify and follow the patterns of success within your organization-follow the footsteps of others who are great leaders.

Entrepreneurship is vital to any organization. The great leaders are those with a knack for building organizations where both performance and innovation thrive; and see themselves as champions of innovation. They know entrepreneurial people need leaders to share ideas with, to help translate those ideas into action, to acknowledge successes and to put failures into perspective.

Entrepreneurship is the essential counterbalances to efficiency and productivity. Once we do the entrepreneurial spirit starts to bubble up. And that's what makes it all worthwhile. Great leaders are quietly introspective, always asking whether they are a cause of the organization's problems or whether they are doing what needs to be done. Leaders with entrepreneurship make intelligent decisions when business conditions are difficult. W

hen entrepreneurship comes naturally as part of your DNA, you've chosen the right path. Entrepreneurship emphasizes leadership skills that can be used to motivate. They must also be ready for constant change and be adaptable. The field of entrepreneurship is one that relies heavily on the ability to change and exploit new markets and opportunities.

Great organizations require great people. It requires greater systems, processes, culture and organizational structures. Entrepreneurship is usually business-oriented and seeks to develop its own business, rather than entering an existing business.

Entrepreneurs are risk takers who, in an effort to develop new approaches to business, try to stay ahead of the emerging trends by innovating and challenging the products and organizations already in existence. Entrepreneurship relies on creativity, self-initiative and long-term vision. Although all business majors should exhibit these traits, the emphasis in entrepreneurship is related to establishment and management of a small and growing venture.

Entrepreneurship emphasizes leadership skills that can be used to motivate people in a growing business environment, particularly as related to starting and nurturing a new business, and the process of business planning. Entrepreneurial leadership is a boundless font of optimism that never seems to end. When faced with a problem, they view it as a challenge. When faced with a setback, they view it as a new direction.

6TH

SENSE OF AUTHENTICITY

Being authentic is central to trust, and without trust you cannot lead. Authentic in leadership means knowing you were born an original. Leadership won't work when it's artificial, contrived, or insincere. Today's followers might be hypersensitive to inauthentic leadership.

Leadership stems from the heart of the leader. You have to understand who you are and figure out a way to communicate it. No matter how big or small; it's what you stand for, what you believe in, and what reflects who you are.

If you're not fighting to stay true to who you are, people will pigeonhole you in a confining role. It's up to you to consistently position yourself to the areas of your greatest strength and passion.

Authenticity is crucial to gaining the mantle of leadership because it is used to retain talent. Authenticity requires:

a. Consistency between words and deeds: You must be genuine. Don't pretend to be someone you're not. Make sure your actions and words are aligned with your core values.

Guard against doing and saying things that are superficial or intended just to attract attention. Don't make changes just to put your fingerprints on things. The proof is in the follow-through. That's where the level of leadership commitment and influence becomes evident.

b. Communication: Leadership requires authentic and effective interpersonal communication that can realize the full potential of individual and organization.

c. Be comfortable with yourself: Fully accepting and loving yourself and your wholeness allows you to be 100% authentic; and being fully responsible for yourself.

d. Recognize weakness: Leaders recognize their strengths, weaknesses, and limits. Being an authentic leader is about being true to yourself and your values - not presenting a false corporate image or trying to emulate the leadership style or characteristics of others.

The leaders are honest, and able to speak out to right wrongs, admit to personal weaknesses and own up to your mistakes.

The authenticity displays leaders' capability to relate to others in an authentic, courageous, and high integrity manner. It measures the extent to which their leadership is authentic - not masked by organizational politics, looking good, winning approval, etc.

It also measures their ability to take tough stands, bring up the un-discussable (risky issues the group avoids discussing), to openly deal with relationship problems, and share personal feelings/vulnerabilities about a situation. Courage in the workplace involves authentically and directly dealing with risky issues in one-to-one and group situations.

Principled by both high ethics and unwavering integrity, leaders regularly demonstrate a high correlation between their core behaviors, beliefs and principles and those that they expect to be present in their followers.

Consequently, leadership embodies the persona of the leader, and it manifests regularly, consistently and unwaveringly, without hidden agendas or questionable intent.

Leadership is a particular kind of social and ethical practice. It emerges when persons in community, grounded in hope, are grasped by unauthentic situations, and courageously act in concert with followers, to make those situations authentic. Authenticity is a leadership imperative. When individuals stand up for what they believe and deliver on their promises, the payback is loyalty.

Authenticity gives us congruence, a sense of harmony that aligns our thoughts, our words, and our emotions. By giving deeply of ourselves, and remove the filters we keep in place when we withhold, it may require our true selves to come into focus. Most of us think of responsibility as what we should be doing, or living up to someone else's standards.

Responsibility means having the ability to respond, that is, trusting your feelings. Realize that there is nothing to fix. Being authentic is simply being who you are. This authenticity is highly attractive and draws people to you who are "on the same page" so to speak.

Authentic leaders, however, embrace change with a vision of a new day, and such visions are born from both principle and purpose. Authenticity is the willingness to embrace all of ourselves, to hold all of our aspects, even the darkest ones. It demands a high level of courage and commitment to learning.

Great leaders have that special edge of authenticity and consistently demonstrate that they stand for something more important than themselves.

INTEGRITY

Integrity describes steadfast adherence to a strict moral or ethical code; moral soundness; honesty; freedom from corrupting influence or motive - used especially with reference to the fulfillment of contracts, the discharge of agencies, trusts and the like; uprightness, rectitude; the quality or condition of being whole or undivided; completeness.

Leaders must show integrity. This doesn't just mean not breaking the law. That's honesty, which certainly is an important component of integrity. But integrity goes beyond that. It is a matter of being genuine, being motivated by your deeply held values to make your organization and your coworkers better off. This is where the passion, persistence, and teamwork come from.

Without integrity, you're simply promoting yourself, and people will not follow your lead. Leaders have high levels of integrity. The leaders with integrity, respect the rights of other people, and follow their own bliss; and show themselves as they wish to be seen, which includes:

a. Integration of self: Display free of conflict in personality. Act with no inconsistency/ambivalence.

b. Maintenance of identity: Show commitment to trust and expectation.

c. Stand for something: Demonstrate best judgment.

d. Demonstrate moral purpose: Moral obligations, act ethically, and accept responsibility.

e. Show a virtue: Willing to say and act similarly with words.

Integrity is holding true to one's values. It's a quality that characterized by honesty, reliability, and fairness, constructive; self-criticism; self-improvement and personal excellence; proactive; responsibility; developed in a relationship over time.

Integrity comprises the personal inner sense of wholeness deriving from honesty and consistent uprightness of character that can be seen from ethical tradition or in the context of an ethical relationship.

Integrity is knowing what important to you and living your actions accordingly; understand not only as a refusal to engage in behavior that evades responsibility, but as an understanding of different modes or styles in which some discourse takes place, and which aims at the discovery of some truth.

Integrity is used virtually synonymously with 'moral,' we also at times distinguish acting morally from acting with integrity.

Persons of integrity may in fact act immorally - though they would usually not know they are acting immorally. Thus one may acknowledge a person to have integrity even though that person may hold importantly mistaken moral views. Incorruptible explains adherence to a code of moral values.

Completeness means not intruded upon by uncoordinated or unrelated ideas; state of being complete or undivided. Soundness describes unimpaired condition.

Leader has true integrity, which is composed of self-knowledge, candor, and maturity. There are many good and solid reasons why one should live an honest life. When you look for an edge in all of the wrong places; you will sacrifice your integrity in the process.

Integrity emphasizes people to be honest and truthful in what they say or do. You need to put honesty, sense of duty, and sound moral principles above all else. Try to be absolutely honest and truthful at all times; and stand up for what you believe to be right.

Great Leaders are always willing to step aside rather than compromise the team. The leader will never play one member against another as a tactic, realizing that unity of purpose, when grounded in the integrity of the vision, will always lead to increased productivity and progress.

Great leaders are honest, hard-working and conduct all their business dealing with integrity. Integrity appears when something is reliable and can be trusted. It is a measure of the quality of information; that is incorruptibility, soundness, and completeness.

Integrity of a system should refer to the wholeness, intactness or purity of a thing; in which not getting corrupted by development or by the side-effects of development; it remains uncorrupted by error.

Great leaders are persons of integrity. Great leadership is how we cope with people when times are tough. Integrity is what drives us regardless of our situation or position. Too many leaders are ready to assert their rights but not assume their responsibilities. They never come to realize that they lack authority because they lack integrity.

Integrity means that a person's behavior is consistent with espoused values Integrity is also attributed to various parts or aspects of a person's life; i.e. attributes such as professional or intellectual integrity; condition of being free from flaws.

Integrity consists of knowing the difference between what is right and wrong; acting on the knowledge of that difference; and an open and commitment to acting on that difference; acting on what you have discerned, even at personal cost.

Leaders have a guiding vision, a passion that allows them to communicate a sense of hope to followers. The key to this communication is not charisma (as many experts have maintained); what is required is integrity.

Leaders with integrity have a heightened sense of self-awareness and an unshakable understanding of what they believe in and what they stand for. You cannot escape your integrity. It accurately illustrates the depth of your ethics and morality. Integrity can be likened to a shadow on a sunny day, which is clearly visible when exposed to the light of day. It is with you wherever you go for your entire life.

Integrity is more than honesty; it requires actions and a willingness to spurn conformity. Integrity is the virtue that defines good character. It is important that the leader never lies to him/herself, especially about him/herself. It is essential that you truly know yourself - your strengths, weaknesses, know what you want to do and why.

Candor is the key to self-knowledge. Candor is based in the honesty of thought and action, a steadfast devotion to principle, and a fundamental soundness and wholeness.

A leader cannot cut his/her conscience to fit this year's fashion. Maturity is important to a leader, because leading is not simply showing the way or issuing orders. Every leader needs to have experienced and grown through following - learning to be dedicated, observant, be capable of working with and learning from others, never servile and always truthful.

Integrity is the basis of trust, which is not as much an ingredient of leadership as it is a product. The one product that cannot be acquired is trust. It must be earned. Trust is not only getting people on your side, but also having them stay there.

Integrity means aligning our values with principles which do not change greatly simplifies the challenge of walking our talk. Integrity describes how a leader relates his/her values, his/her words and his/her actions. People with integrity are honest, trustworthy and authentic. They are also respectful of others and have a strong sense of personal responsibility.

A vital ingredient in a leader's ability to lead is the confidence, or trust, on the part of those being led, that the result of their efforts is in their best interests. The leader must possess the integrity to be trustworthy and not betray or exploit them. Integrity involves being true to oneself, while honesty means being truthful with others. Each involves being real not fake, genuine not artificial, transparent not deceitful.

You can't spell integrity without the word grit which is defined as a firmness of mind, or unyielding courage. It takes a great deal of courage or grit to be true to self. In the end, though, it's worth the effort because our legacies are going to be impacted greatly by our integrity or lack thereof.

To be a great leader, your integrity will be beyond reproach. Great leaders have character, integrity, and courage. Great Leaders have great integrity (wholeness, soundness) and assume the role of keeper of ethics.

Great leaders walk their talk. They live with integrity and inspire trust. The relationship between the leader and the led is trust, and trust is based on integrity. Leaders must articulate the ethical expectations necessary to maintain the wholeness and soundness of the team, as well as the individual members.

WISDOM

Wisdom describes the ability to discern or judge what is true, right, or lasting. Wisdom and insight are essential to sound leadership. Leadership requires foresight, and it is impossible to imagine foresight without wisdom. Wisdom is more important than power.

While leaders do not have all the answers, they should possess the wisdom and the insight to raise important questions that search for deeper meaning. Such questions are critical because they help leaders and organizations find and determine their direction.

The leaders just profiled asked some powerful questions of themselves and those around them. The virtue of wise person is courage to act on their knowledge, but the humility to doubt what they know.

It can be said that greatness is not a single act, but a way of being that nourishes the self, others, and the organization. It is arising from the unique expression of innate qualities such as love, peace, and wisdom. These qualities are the seeds to greatness, and the true expression of these qualities is greatness itself.

When we awaken and express the simple essence of our being, we are able to create an extraordinary life, a life of greatness that leaves a positive mark on the lives of others, society, and the organization.

Leadership is a quality of those who earn the respect of others through the wisdom of the combination of their words and their actions. True greatness depends on total wisdom. They act as they do because they are what they are - trapped beings, crushed beneath an intolerable burden. A wise person is who learns from everyone.

Wisdom is a kind of meta-knowledge that helps us make better sense of the rest of our knowledge. Here are five marks of wisdom in leadership:

a. Don't care who is getting the credit as long as the job gets done - Great leaders don't draw attention to themselves; they express appreciation for the contributions of others.

b. Willing to put the mission ahead of their personal agenda - Leaders know that what they have done as individuals is far less important than what they can accomplish with and through others.

c. Quick to forgive - Leaders earn respect, but never demand it. They avoid petty squabbles and develop thick skins.

d. Be gratified by the achievements of others - The leaders realize that there's plenty of success to go around, and they help those around them reach for the stars.

e. Give credit where it's due - They know that there are no little people in the organization; every person's contribution is significant. Leaders know how to say: "Well done," and they say it often.

Great leaders in all walks of life comes a wealth of wisdom that provides understanding, guidance, and inspiration for leaders or potential leaders. Kindness, compassion, and wisdom are traits that will make a great leader.

Wisdom is not something a person is born with. It only comes from living, from making mistakes; from listening to others who have made mistakes and learned from them. Wisdom is defined as an ability to make right choices and decisions, which are made without complete information.

We must turn to faculties beyond those of sense and reason in dealing with values; i.e. placement of values within cultures, action towards the achievement, drive towards balance that harmonize in interactions.

Wisdom is a way we take to escape from folly; way of life; way of suffering. Wisdom is our way out; the way we know best, our erroneous pursuit of all that brings us grief and misery, conditions we're inclined to find quite naturally.

Wisdom answers the first question by looking at the situation from a variety of helpful perspectives. Wisdom suggests a sage perspective on life, a sense of balance, a keen understanding of how the various parts and principles apply and relate to each other.

Becoming a wiser person is an exercise in inner development, and there are activities that can help us along the way.

Only by acting transcendentally, we may wing our way to wisdom; in which feeling and intuition are as important as sensation and intellect.

177

Expand your awareness, and attune yourself toward wisdom; calm your mind, and meditate; allow for space within your consciousness, which the wisdom may settle into; use words that energize and motivate; and learn from the experiences of others.

Wisdom doesn't come with position. It arises from one's sense of responsibility.

Leaders will avoid desperation by being excellent judges of the truth. Wise leaders always deal with the truth and will always act on that truth. Their judgment is always consistent and while their choices may not always be the most popular ones, they are always the best choices.

A great leader steps out first and others will follow his/her lead because they have faith in his/her wisdom and his/her judgment. A wise leader will know the mind of his/her followers and act precisely and wisely at the time.

Leaders embody a wisdom that subsumes every leadership. They have the courage to accept the blame and the wisdom to learn from their mistakes.

WIN-WIN

No one has to lose for you to win. Many people go for lose-win rather than win-lose. Sometimes you go for win-win or no deal, which means you agree to disagree agreeably, particularly when there are opposing values.

Sometimes you transcend opposing values by finding a higher, unifying value. Sometimes it's OK to go for win-lose or lose-win if the most important consideration is not the subjects you're discussing but rather the quality of the relationships. This may contribute to a win-win relationship, even though there are some decisions that are win-lose or lose-win.

Conflict can be described as a situation where one person believes that another person's behavior (or anticipated behavior) makes it difficult for them to meet their personal outcomes or needs. The most appropriate model to the solution depends on the situation, therefore leaders may apply differently, i.e.:

    a.   Win/Win - Method of resolving a conflict where all entities feel satisfied that their needs and outcomes were fully met. People can seek mutual benefit in all interactions.

b. Win/Lose - Method of resolving a conflict where at least one of the people feels satisfied and one of the people feels their needs or outcomes were not fully met. It's a competitive paradigm: if I win, you lose. The leadership style is authoritarian. If both people aren't winning, both are losing.

c. Lose/Win - The 'Doormat' paradigm. The individual seeks strength from popularity based on acceptance. The leadership style is permissiveness. Living this paradigm can result pains from repressed resentment.

d. Lose/Lose - Method of resolving a conflict where both people feel that some of their outcomes or needs were met and some were not. When people become obsessed with making the other person lose, even at their own expense. This is the philosophy of adversarial conflict, war, or of highly dependent persons. (If nobody wins, being a loser isn't so bad.)

e. Win - Focusing solely on getting what one wants, regardless of the needs of others.

f. Win/Win or No Deal - If we can't find a mutually beneficial solution, we agree to disagree agreeably - no deal. This approach is most realistic at the beginning of conflict resolution. In a continuing relationship, it's no longer an option.

Win-win nurtures empathy. Thinking win-win is a frame of mind that seeks mutual benefit and is based on mutual respect. It is about bargaining fairly, and being open-minded and reasonable to all parties. It is about compromise and a sincere desire to find agreements that occupy the middle ground.

Win-win is not taking advantage when it is understood that you are being trusted to act with honor. It's about thinking in terms of abundance. Leaders must have the ability to identify and analyze problems, includes:

a. Distinguish between relevant and irrelevant information to make logical decisions.

b. Able to exercise good judgment by making timely and effective, well-informed decisions.

c. Anticipate the impact and implications of their decisions.

    d.   Apply creative solutions based on new insights to make organizational improvements.

    e.   Able to deeply question and investigate the reasoning and logic of ideas and approaches.

The benefits that come from win-win deals, win-win agreements, and win-win decisions often require a long period of patient effort in empathy. In a competitive situation where building a relationship isn't important, win/lose may be appropriate.

If you are to be a great leader in any organization, you must adopt the triumph-lose approach. Some would compare this to what others have called a flawed win-lose technique of compromise. They would be wrong. First, win-lose is not inherently flawed. Being a win-lose leader means using your power of rank and your threat of consequence to get what you want from others.

The win-lose approach is the foundation of triumph-lose. Compromise is the greatest virtue. They emphasize win/win - rather than adversarial win/lose - approaches.

The problem with win-win compromise is identifying the losers. Attempt to reduce the friction, while recognizing that in an effective team, strength lies in diversity. Leaders develop consensus building that create win-win situations that ensure all have been listened to and honored for their expertise and feelings. But to achieve triumph-lose, you must take it further.

To triumph means not just to be victorious, but to be victorious by conquest. Victory is not enough to succeed in today's organization. You must crush and humiliate anyone seeking to sit down and work out a compromise. Treat everyone with a triumph-lose approach, and you will be shocked how quickly you propel to higher-paying positions. Conflict alone does not lead to better decisions.

Leaders also need to build consensus in their organizations. Consensus, as we define it here, does not mean unanimity, widespread agreement on all facets of a decision, or complete approval by a majority of organization members. It does not mean that teams, rather than leaders, make decisions.

Consensus does mean that people have agreed to cooperate in the implementation of a decision. They have accepted the final choice, even though they may not be completely satisfied with it.

Consensus has two critical components: a high level of commitment to the chosen course of action and a strong, shared understanding of the rationale for the decision.

Consensus does not ensure effective implementation, but it enhances the likelihood that managers can work together effectively to overcome obstacles that arise during decision execution.

Great leaders are invariably terrific problem solvers. People bring them concerns and problems knowing that they will come to a viable and win-win solution. They are really good problem solvers, as they will involve you in the solution. All inputs, ideas for possible solutions and opinions are solicited and highly respected.

MATURITY

Mature people may have a lot of ego strength, but they also have high respect for other people. They balance their courage with consideration. Leaders give a degree of maturity to the organization.

Leaders have knowledge of their self-worth, a sense of belonging, a sense of expectancy and a sense of accountability that immature people lack.

Maturity can be seen from one's attitude and appearance. Mature person is one who has grown out of experiences without losing his/her best traits. He/she has retained the basic emotional strengths of infancy; the capacity for affiliation and intellectual curiosity; the capacity for wonder and pleasure; the idealism and passion.

Maturity state is dominated through stability, wisdom, knowledge, sensitivity to other people, responsibility, strength, and purposefulness.

Leaders may grow in self-knowledge and maturity. A mature individual has to be able to love comfortably with his/her own body, whether it is strong or weak, handsome or ugly, healthy or failing. He/she is equipped with the human sensitivities; powerful concern to other feelings.

Maturity is reflection of knowledge which is appealing to culture. Be mature means be prepared for the unexpected situations; never take anything for granted; if he/she does, he/she will be disappointed. Becoming mature means not accept values readymade.

Leaders owe a certain maturity, which is expressed in a sense of self-worth, a sense of belonging, a sense of expectancy, a sense of responsibility, a sense of accountability, and a sense of equality.

a. Personal maturity: The hallmarks of a great leader lie in the ability of the person in charge to bring certain key factors across to the organization. A key component of leadership is emotional maturity or intelligence.

Leaders have good emotional maturity which is an ability to express your feelings and convictions with courage, balanced with consideration for the feelings and convictions of others.

b. Organizational maturity: A central leadership role is increasing the maturity level of the people in the organization.

Leaders understand that setting an untarnished example is not accomplished simply through issuing orders. Their power is derived through past experiences of failure and success and from following examples of great leaders.

Because of the wisdom gained, they allow others to make errors in judgment and grow from them. Their own display of maturity forges the way for others to become confident, observant, dedicated and capable of working with and learning from their own experiences as well as from the input other people provide.

A stable leader is known for his or her maturity. That maturity is seen in the ability to let staff excel, question felt areas of pressure, is open to other's ideas, trusts his/her team, peers and colleagues, and allows others to grow, mature, challenge, take the lead, and learn more and more.

The leader's stability is grounded in a positive sense of his or her own selfhood. The stable leader doesn't carry a chip on his or her shoulders, is not defensive, paranoid, manipulative, angry, passive aggressive or mean spirited. He or she instead is fully confident in his or her strengths.

If you are mature, you won't be concerned with pettiness, trivia, and issues that don't really matter. You will be about being your best, asserting your strengths and growing your team. Leadership is to promote the maturity and responsibility of everyone in the organization. In maturity you are encouraged to:

a. Have capability to listening: Leaders need to sharpen listening skills to become active listening. The leaders must listen - aggressively listen - then synthesize those views into a clear picture. Leaders are able to ask for and welcome input from others, understand what opportunities exist in the future, then shape a direction that will take the group where it needs to go.

b. See your weaknesses: Leaders know their own weaknesses so they can deliberately overcome them.

c. Give yourself appropriate time, and take advantage of discussing ideas with others.

d. Be accountable for yourself. Don't blame the problems on other people. Look inwardly for solutions, judge yourself.

e. Understand what's important to you: Leaders understand of what is important for organization and how to achieve it. They develop their own leadership capacity, i.e. skill development, clarifying priorities, improving decision making, dealing with change, interpersonal effectiveness, following through on commitments, etc.

Leaders must be able to tolerate frustration and stress. They must be well-adjusted and have the maturity to deal with anything they are required to face. Leaders owe maturity. Maturity as expressed in a sense of self-worth, a sense of belonging, a sense of expectancy, a sense of responsibility, a sense of accountability, and a sense of equality. Maturity is not necessarily linked to age.

Maturity implies the ability to control impulse is the base of will and character. The mature individual is to learn when to conform and when not to conform, when to speak out and when to remain silent. His/her values must be so structured and scaled that he can distinguish between what is the priority and inviolable and what is peripheral and expendable.

Leaders demonstrate a sense of maturity that enables them to deal positively and effectively with situations and people. Great leaders can quickly distinguish between right and wrong.

Critical element of maturity is the desire to take personal responsibility. A great leader seeks service to others above self and is willing to be accountable for his or her choices. Making choices for the good of the organization requires the freedom that comes with personal maturity.

Leaders speak up and take personal responsibility for their decisions and refrain from diminishing their own responsibility by blaming others for failures or mistakes.

Leaders need to develop the potential of leading with responsibility among their followers. Followers, who are able and willing to lead upward, enhance their leader's growth to be responsible.

Maturity provides the ability to lead without much noise. Great leadership requires great emotional maturity. Great leader displays a great understanding of emotional intelligence. Completely masters the moment and the emotion of the moment; lives inside the moment easily.

The great leader uses influence not power, seems to follow rather than lead. A great leader uses persuasion not compulsion or confrontation. The great leader knows a crowd and knows the common mood.

A great leader uses collaboration not coercion. He/she invites others to come along with him/her if they so choose, he/she makes coming along voluntary not compulsory.

CONSISTENCY

Consistency is the extent to which a leader treats members consistently and does not play favorites. Consistency critical is to great leadership, simply because it implies an absence of contradictions. People always know what to expect from a leader who is consistent. However, a leader who changes with the weather creates insecurity and uneasiness.

When you eradicate contradictions in your moral standards, actions, and values, you will eliminate inconsistency. When your leadership is consistent and has no contradictions, you have integrity. A high-quality effort starts from intention and commitment, and makes itself evident in skillful and consistent follow-through.

Consistency creates stability. It creates sustainability. What leaders need to do is to be consistent to a higher degree of quality, and we can do this by applying more common sense and practicality to the work.

Leadership is built on authenticity, consistency and a genuine desire to serve stakeholders. Your leadership brand is your identity and reputation as a leader.

A leader has to find consistency in an inconsistent world. Leaders keep things simple and consistent. Great leadership is impossible without consistency.

HUMILITY

Humility is admission of humanity, a sense that leader and follower are in this together. A leader listens to others. He or she values input from members and is ready to hear the truth, even if it is bad news. A humble leader does not promote him/herself to be something that he/she is not. His/her interest is not to serve his/her personal desires or his/her organization. His/her interest is finding and revealing the best in his field of labor.

Followers disdain arrogance and brashness, since they are often associated with self-serving egotism. In contrast, wisdom reveres modesty, humility and reserve.

Great leaders know how to respect the dignity of the least of those who work with them. Nobody should be humiliated. There is a right way and a wrong way to administer discipline. Humility is a core quality found in great leaders. A sense of humility means understanding where we are in relationship to the whole.

Humility makes the leader stronger in his/her convictions. That person can lead others because he/she knows where he/she has been and in what direction he/she is going. He/she is not easily swayed or led by those who do not have his/her sense of direction and would lead him/her astray through flattery, bribery, or those retrogressive qualities related to the personality.

Leaders with humility sun pompous and arrogant behavior. They realize that we are all fallible – a combination of strengths and weaknesses. People who demonstrate humility don't think less of themselves; they just think more of others. A person with the core quality of humility:

a. Listen to others: When leaders truly listen to others they will hear them if they listen non-judgmentally. Ability to listen effectively directly impacts their leadership outcomes.

b. Do not brag or name-drop: leaders with humility don't blame others and are not defensive. They don't brag or name drop. They clearly see and admit their own limitations and failings.

c. Clearly see and admit his or her limitations and failings: Not arrogance and care more about people.

d. Show vulnerability without fear: Leadership is about character - who you are, not what you do. Without integrity, leadership behavior rings hollow. Also notice that the leadership scale is balanced between the qualities of respect and responsibility. Vulnerability in leaders gives them access to the hearts of their people.

Great leaders of the most successful organizations in the world are great stewards. A great steward puts his or her team before self. Great leaders have a profound sense of humility. The great leaders are those who encourage; humble; competent; and kind.

The leaders display that seldom-seen virtue called humility. They discover real worth in terms of their ability to generate team excellence, not personal recognition. Leaders have an acute sense of their own strengths and weakness.

Great leaders set an example in personal humility and possess self-effacing, quiet, reserved, and even shy characters.

EXCELLENCE

Sense of excellence is so important to the fulfillment of one's responsibility, which exhibits excellence in both character and competence. Sense of excellence means always do the best you can. Leaders perform all their normal job duties with excellence, also take initiative and go above and beyond in their contributions to the organization.

As a leader you have the ability to be excellent. In order to develop excellence, a leader must be willing to acknowledge that it is not an accomplishment - it's a never-ending process. Leaders set standards of excellence. Leaders provide motivation and drive towards excellence. Every job is a self-portrait of the person who did it, they must work with excellence.

Leaders are persons who develop their team rise to greatness and take their organization with them. Discover strategies that reap significant results by taking seemingly insignificant small steps that elevate your team to realizable excellence.

Leaders do not command excellence, they build excellence. Excellence is being all you can be within the bounds of doing what is right for your organization. To reach excellence you must first be a leader of good character. You must do everything you are supposed to do.

An organization will not achieve excellence by figuring out where it wants to go; then having leaders do whatever they have to, in order to get the job done; and then hope their leaders acted with good character. This type of thinking is backwards.

Pursuing excellence should not be confused with accomplishing a job or task. When you do planning, you do it by backwards planning. But you do not achieve excellence by backwards planning.

Excellence starts with leaders of good and strong character who engage in the entire process of leadership. And the first process is being a person of honorable character.

The organization should encourage people's inclination to compete against their own sense of excellence. Leaders demand excellence, not perfection. They expect the members to work as hard as they are doing and to be as committed to the goal as they are.

Excellence promotes individual effort and puts a premium on exceptional competence and skill. Excellence is normally gauged by competition and achievement. Leaders should remain engaged and committed to a sense of excellence, and it builds a sense of credibility and trust.

Great leaders demand excellence from themselves, which spurs the people to be like them. The great leaders who surround themselves with excellence display a direct reflection on their own character, abilities, and effectiveness as leaders. Their own success and the success of their organizations depend mostly on hiring and promoting the best qualified, ethical, skilled, responsible, mature, and productive people and giving them the proper resources, authority, and freedom to do what's needed for the long-term benefit of their organizations.

A great leader exhibits excellence in his/her activities and expects only the best of outputs from others. He/she will not tolerate ship-shod work, negligence and oversight. He/she will create the environment where lack of knowledge is bridged through training, mentoring or coaching. Once this is done, he/she will not tolerate incompetence and carelessness.

IDENTITY

Yet a strong sense of self is not about selfishness, or self-absorption. A sense of self is what makes us truly unique. It recognizes both similarities and differences. It allows us to see what we share with others as well as those things that are true only of ourselves or of few others. Sense of self is the foundation for the construction of a life, and for being a stable leader.

A sense of self does not close a person off to the opinions of others. Suggestions and insights, especially from those who know us well and whom we trust, are valuable for our personal growth. A sense of self recognizes not only one's strength, but one's weaknesses. What a sense of self does is steel us against the unnecessary suffering criticism and feedback often cause.

The objective isn't merely to be yourself, but to be your best self. That requires recognizing and eliminating or improving our vices and weaknesses. Being one's self is never a legitimate excuse for being less good to other's than one is capable of being. Organization believes that with a greater sense of self (strengths, weaknesses and desires) come better leader and innovator.

Identity displays the product of many definitions of self that exist. Identity relates to self-image, self-esteem, and individuation. It displays great sense of respect and pride. Identity refers to the capacity for self reflection and the awareness of self. Identity cannot be separated from the culture which builds and structures it.

Identity describes the general aspects of the individual's personality. Identity consists of interpersonal concept (set of roles and relationships); potentiality aspect (concept of who the person might become); values aspect (set of values and priorities).

We form our identity by selecting values, beliefs, and concepts that better define our sense of self. Self encompasses one's feeling thought and sensation.

Sense of self or sense of identity involves having a healthy image of who we are. It's the ability to be comfortable in our own shoes. Leadership experience creates and builds a foundational sense of identity in the organization, i.e.:

a.   Personal identity: Sense of one's role in relation to the organization; which can be influenced by the individual's attitudes, habits, belief and ideas. They internalize its mission, ideology, and values, and they adopt its customary ways of doing things.

b. Organizational identity: A feeling of oneness with the organization; one's outlook and style of interacting with others

Those who rely heavily on a sense of self derived from an unchanging role may fail to accomplish the important relationship building activities with a wide range of stakeholders. Unfortunately, high levels of identification can also produce

a. Lack of organizational flexibility and creativity, over-conformity to organizational dictates, and tyrannical behavior on the part of leaders.

b. Lack of risk taking, loss of an independent self, and burnout.

c. Limit diversity by reducing communication competencies in the area of social perception skills

Sense of identity is also affronted by cultural difference, i.e. working across cultural differences; in which we learn to remain open and inspired, and thus to respond to cultural differences in effective and productive ways.

Diversity makes organizational culture more rich, and insights and innovation more applicable to a wide range of contexts; ability to manage the ambiguity of gaining their sense of identity from shared visions; and creates a safety zone in which people feel free to explore new ideas and new ways of approaching problem solving.

A leader must create a sense of identification with those whom they lead, who in turn must sense this. Leaders realize that their position rests on those below them. They preserve their position and remain connected to those below them by practicing simplicity. They don't aspire to the trappings of honor and prestige.

Leaders achieve sustainable results as they model, teach, and advocate the values of authenticity. To promote collaboration, trust and community building, they embrace diversity.

Leadership is honoring the greatness, and uniqueness, in others. Each organization is unique, as is each individual within that organization.

There is, however, a process that has been used successfully by numerous organizations to improve leadership and with it, performance. Be different. It's your uniqueness that makes you special. If you're not different, you have nothing to offer.

Leaders frequently begin their work by building an inclusive work environment and examining their own personal assumptions. They make everyone in their organizations feel that they are part of the diversity journey.

The leaders' inclusive approach involves creating messages that speak to the entire organization, developing policy for all segments of the organization, and behaving in a way that shows they value individual differences.

Leadership is the act of making a difference. It's the ability to achieve results - through people. Leadership is - who you are when no one else is looking. It's to know what you're best at, what brings a light to your eyes, what you most love to do, and then doing it. Inclusion is a situation that is created to have an understanding and openness to similarities and differences.

Diversity will broaden your cultural and social horizons beyond your usual experiences. Learning to see things from different perspectives will give you greater flexibility in problem solving. In a rapidly changing world, be willing to venture in new directions to seize new opportunities and learn new skills.

Great leaders implement diversity as a business strategy that optimizes the performance of their corporations. They integrate the development of people with innovative products to ensure profitability. Diversity connects all things in a corporation.

Leaders use diversity to build success. They view diversity as a win-win strategy that is good for followers, good for the organization, and good for the community.

ACCEPTANCE

Leaders help others to develop and use their own power for the good of the organization and the achievement of its goals. This begins with a willingness to accept others, which requires a tolerance for imperfection.

Acceptance is the need to accept yourself and be accepted by others. This includes a feeling of belonging. Accept means agree without adverse reaction - take no action against a situation, undertake a responsibility - notions of willingness, or reconcile to situation - experience of a situation without an intention to change that situation.

Acceptance allows change. When acceptance feels so good and is so good for us. It's an agreement with yourself to appreciate, validate, accept and support who you are at this very moment, even those parts you'd like to eventually change. You can accept (be okay with) those parts of yourself you want to change some day.

To set an untarnished example, leaders acknowledge and stress the importance of failure. It is one necessary element in moving forward toward positive achievement. Past experiences of failure and the reasons behind them becoming the cornerstone of success.

Great leaders embrace failure and do not exhibit procrastination or fear because of its consequences. They understand that persisting in the face of failure reinforces their commitments, confidence and self-trust.

To reach base level of acceptance, you need only remove the items that lay on top. To do this, you must first identify all the things you do not accept about yourself. Then, one by one, eliminate them by examining and questioning your beliefs around that issues. Acceptance is the need to accept yourself and be accepted by others, which implies:

a. Self-acceptance: Love of self beyond the evaluation of self-features. Self-acceptance refers to an individual's satisfaction or happiness with himself. Leaders. Leadership begins with self-leadership. Self-acceptance means:

    i. Know your beliefs: Interpret the existence to match the belief.

    ii. Take a good look at yours: Identify any vulnerability and take responsibility. Nobody's perfect and there's a considerable tolerance for errors.

    iii. Know your best: Never let the opinions of others define for you who you are or what you can or cannot do.

    iv. Show value judgment: When we judge something about ourselves as "bad", it becomes impossible for you to accept that part of yourself.

    v. Examine guilt: Examine guilty and resolve it

191

vi. Understand your motivations: Everyone has unique combinations of needs, wants, and values which motivate them to be successful.

vii. Ask what you don't accept: Resolve it, and accept your strength and weakness.

b. Acceptance of others: Expect and give acceptance, get genuine approval and acceptance from others, i.e.:

i. Acceptance of command and control: Acceptance of authority, influence, etc

ii. Acceptance of the concept: Create policies with built-in flexibility, initiative, new paradigm, etc.

iii. Acceptance of full responsibility and personal accountability, risk-taking, etc

iv. Acceptance of differences/diversity: Individual contributions, acceptance of diverse cultural groups, individual identity

v. Acceptance of the purposes and mission of the group: acceptance of the task and objectives, value, norms, etc

Member needs to feel comfortable, not defeated, when he/she makes mistakes or fails. Explain that these hurdles or setbacks are a normal part of living and learning, and that he/she can learn or benefit from them.

Let your supportive, constructive feedback and your recognition of his/her effort overpower any sense of failure, guilt, or shame he/she might be feeling, giving him/her renewed motivation and hope. Accept the present as it is, simply because it is what it is and it doesn't serve you, or anyone else to fight it.

Acceptance sets the stage for forward motion. Once awareness and acceptance are achieved, you can quiet. One of the things, you must accept, are those areas of your life that won't succumb to anything less than hard work.

Great leaders believe that leadership is the most important thing they do. They believe that it's something they'll get better at if they work at it.

For that reason, great leaders are continually doing after-action critiques on their own performance. They pay attention to the items that are under their control and try to do those better and better and better. They monitor the results they get from their actions and then modify their actions to get the result they want. This grows out of the concentration on consequences and behavior. The result is that the great leaders use a wider array of leadership and communication tools and use them more effectively than their less effective peers. These are the behaviors that great leaders do.

If you do them you'll be a great leader to work for. And you'll create a great working environment for the folks who work for you. To achieve greatness, leaders must learn from their mistakes and listen to others.

Great leaders excel by understanding their way may not always be the right way extends to subordinates' acceptance of ideas. They accept that advice is easy to give; it is much harder to take.

CHARACTER

Leadership is the expression of vision, ideas and character and/or position cause others to emulate, work or act in accordance to the leader's direction or philosophy. Character describes the morals, ethics and judgment one shows in making ones decisions and taking actions. Character is your internal makeup, your personal DNA. To develop a stronger sense of character, get to know yourself - assess, evaluate and correct.

Leaders must have character. Without character, all the other keys are for naught. That's because your innate character strengths and limitations play a critical role in your leadership style. To reach excellence you must first be a leader of good character.

Leadership is lifting a person's vision to higher sights, the raising of a person's performance to a higher standard, the building of a personality beyond its normal limitations. Ground yourself in the core values that never change over time: honesty, respect, faith, perseverance, caring, and diligence. Or to put it simply treat others the way you would want to be treated.

Strong moral underpinnings inspire trust and confidence.

Character always matters, especially in the White House. Character counts in decision-making; e.g. in the case of John F. Kennedy with his actions in the Bay of Pigs invasion and his secret war against Fidel Castro. JFK began showing signs of becoming a man who could empathize with others and show a measure of compassion. (Thomas Reeves, Presidency: How do Historians Evaluate the Administration of John Kennedy?, 2001)

Great leaders are reliable persons of character who are committed to compelling principles and purposes, while embodying both empathy and respect for others, as well as inner connectedness and respect for oneself.

Great leaders have that special edge of authenticity and consistently demonstrate that they stand for something more important than themselves. The cornerstone character traits of great leaders are integrity and honesty.

Character is a personality which reflects characteristics such as integrity, trustworthiness, consistency, wisdom, hospitality, patience A leader must possess reliability and strength of character in order to inspire commitment and selflessness within others.

Character is one of the best assets in the leadership. If you want to become a great leader, encourage yourself to nurture your character, for your character will cover and protect your reputation.

Great leaders exhibit behaviors that all of us are capable of but few of us cultivate over the course of a lifetime. These behaviors are manifested by a sense of character that each of us possess.

CONTROL

Control is necessary for a leader to lead in the right direction. The foundation for leadership, then, is the ability to manage effectively. Having control provides us with a sense of achievement, strength and possibility.

When people feel out of control, they experience a powerful and uncomfortable tension between the need for control and the evidence of inadequate control. As a leader, you should demonstrate:

a.   Self-acknowledgment: It brings you to self-love and a willingness to see your own greatness.

b.   Awareness: Know where you are presently. Know there is greatness within you. Gently direct your awareness to this fact and be open to seeing this, for the mind will always attune to whatever you are open and willing to accept

Controlling describes a situation in which leaders establish a sense of personal worth through task accomplishment and personal achievement. It measures the extent to which leaders push themselves and others hard and use overly driven and aggressive tactics to get others to do what they want.

A person, who cannot control him/herself, can never control others. Self-control sets a mighty example for his/her followers. The extreme perception of control is:

a. Too little control - Stop doing things that could improve their situation.

b. Too much control - Control things they can't; responsibility for things outside their control.

By managing their sense of control, leaders can achieve far greater actual control. If they ignore this, they will soon fall into a power battle for control of the conversation and the agenda. Leaders with sense of control demonstrate:

a. Self-control: Lead yourselves first before trying to lead others. Great Leaders know how to gain and maintain control of their own lives. Self-control implies:

i. Self-acknowledgment: It brings you to self-love and a willingness to see your own greatness.

ii. Awareness. Know where you are presently. Know there is greatness within you. Gently direct your awareness to this fact and be open to seeing this, for the mind will always attune to whatever you are open and willing to accept

b. Control others: As a member is striving to achieve and gain more independence, he/she needs and wants to feel that he/she can make it on his/her own. Once a leader give his/her expectations, guidelines, and opportunities in which to test his/herself, he/she can reflect, reason, problem-solve and consider the consequences of the actions he/she may choose. This kind of self-awareness is critical for his/her future growth.

Those who have a high sense of control strongly believe there are things they can do to bring about desired outcomes. Great leadership is the ability to command and control.

AWARENESS

Leaders interact in an environment abounding with needs. They are able to look beyond their own needs to sense and respond to the needs of others. Organizations need great leaders in order to create the performance, future, and fulfillment that everyone desires.

Sense of awareness is the leader's ability to gain respect of those who follow him. If they know the leader is always going to do the right thing, then it's easy to follow him/her to the destination. Awareness consists of:

a. Self-awareness: Leadership's orientation to ongoing professional and personal development, as well as the degree to which inner self-awareness is expressed through high integrity leadership. It is a measure of emotional and interpersonal maturity. Leaders who are more self-aware will experience:

i. Greater self-acceptance: Awareness of their strengths and weaknesses.

ii. Higher autonomy: Have confidence to take responsibility and be more accountable

iii. Positive relationships with others: Leadership is a relationship between those who aspire to lead and those who choose to follow. Leaders are getting along well with other people.

It also measures the extent to which the culture encourages the kind of personal/professional development that results in personal mastery.

Self-awareness is essential for leadership. Self-awareness provides clarification of the personal identity of the leader. Leader is one who possesses a strong sense of self-awareness. It's the ability to lead (as it were) one's own self prior to leading other selves similarly (emotional intelligence competence)

Self-awareness influences leadership behavior. Leaders with self-awareness are neither overly critical nor unrealistically hopeful. Rather, they are honest with themselves and with others.

The leader is comfortable enough with his/her sense of self. A leader who is self-aware may possess a greater than average sense of purpose and meaning.

b. Organizational awareness: Awareness that is focused on whole system improvement and on followers' welfare (the symbiotic relationship between the long-term welfare of the community and the interests of the organization). Leaders should be able to foresee the implications of their courses of action.

c. Situational awareness: Know where you are, what you can do and how to do it. Situational awareness is vital to leadership decision making. A leader must know:

i. Context (what is happening): Knowing the context of your decision will help you make the right choices. Therefore, determining the factors pushing for the decision is vital to making the decision. A leader must know what he or she is up against - that is, what forces are shaping your world and your decisions.

ii. Circumstance (what has happened) and consequence (what could happen): Consider the unfolding situation. Whatever a leader does must be framed within variables.

iii. Consequence: Decisions have outcomes. Those outcomes will dictate what a leader does. Also keep in mind that failure to decide is a consequence. Good leaders who push decision making to the front line are those leaders who want their people to be accountable as well as responsible for outcomes.

Leaders must be having more self-aware and reflective than others; they follow an inner sense of direction, and lead from the inside out.

Leadership is grounded in the extent to which the leader, through a process of self-exploration and understanding, develops a leadership identity. Without self-awareness of one's leadership abilities, self-identity as a leader does not form.

Leadership starts with the individual's discovery of his or her potential. Self-awareness is an important capacity for leaders. It involves a personal understanding of one's strength and weakness, how these strengths and weakness influence others. Leaders must increase their awareness about themselves and organization to maximize their leadership potential.

Great leaders possess the ability to observe their own behavior, are aware of their own actions, and are well-connected to their own thoughts and feelings.

DIRECTION

Directing means telling others what to do; seeking clarification and confirmation about the tack; supervising closely; and follow-up.

Leaders have a broad sense of direction, a vision that others can share to unify their efforts. It represents a clear view of how the organizations for which a leader is responsible can contribute to the strategy of the whole.

Leaders are clearly recognizable as those who affect the direction a person or a group (e.g. parish) will take. Sense of direction is achieved by conveying a strong vision of the future.

Leadership is the capacity to establish direction and to influence and align others toward a common goal, motivating and committing them to action and making them responsible for their performance.

A sense of direction is achieved by conveying a strong vision of the future. You must be trustworthy and you have to be able to communicate a vision of where the organization needs to go. Greatness is not in where we stand, but in what direction we are moving.

Establishing direction requires a clear vision for the future and the development of strategies to achieve it. A sense of direction is important because it serves to define and maintain the focus for follower's efforts.

Furthermore, when times get tough, the direction provided by a leader can lend stability to matters, aiding dispirited followers in regrouping and renewing their efforts. People want to be guided by those they respect and who have a clear sense of direction, which evolves:

    a.   Self-direction: Ability to control personal actions. The leader follows a method of self discipline, goal setting, positive thinking, and intelligently administered self rewards. Self-directed person is a person who can make his/her own decisions and act independently. The principles of self-direction are:

i. Freedom: It is also necessary for a person to continue his/her self-examination, to observe what he/she is, and what he/she is becoming. This is freedom.

When you can be totally objective with yourself, in whatever direction your total experience leads, you are free from the restrictions of a pre-determined truth. To be free, is to be centered, and have the ability to recover your balance, even in the midst of action.

A free person knows where he/she stands, and what he stands for. This is a free person, and a leader. The free persons mind and his/her state of consciousness, create a climate of openness in his/her life, which gives him/her not only stability, but flexibility and endurance.

ii. Authority: The ability to control some objectives.

iii. Responsibility: Leaders set direction in ways that facilitate achievement of organizational goals. Leadership is accountable to others and endeavors to see that individual and organization needs are met.

b. Organizational direction: Leadership gives a sense of direction to the people and organization; and gets people to follow. Leaders who set a clear sense of direction have the greatest impact.

Any effective organization has a sense of direction. It starts with a vision of the future and is embodied in a mission, goals and objectives that drive the organization toward that vision. Organizations require leadership in order to change, to grow in response to problems, challenges, and opportunities.

Leaders give a clear sense of direction, display the ability to make tough decisions, demonstrate the ability to command and control, or, conversely, to inspire loyalty in those led through strong emotional empathy.

Great leaders have a strong sense of direction. They know where they want a group to go and they understand the steps to be taken to get the group there.

Right direction gives followers an unmistakable clear sense of direction. One of the major contributions of leadership is a sense of direction and a focus for action. This sense of direction generally serves the best interests of the leader's organization, their followers and the others.

COMMITMENT

Great leaders surround themselves with great people. Leadership is developed through experience and through a commitment to achieving results. A leader is good with actions as well as words. A leader's ability to generate commitment shapes and is shaped by the broader culture of the organization.

The achievement of high levels of commitment depends both on articulating the values of the organization and on valuing the contributions of others. Making commitment becomes easier when we feel our purpose strongly. The most important factor in organization and individual success is commitment.

Commitment ignites action. To commit is to pledge you to a certain purpose or line of conduct. It also means practicing your beliefs consistently. Leaders foster a sense of commitment to their members.

Honesty develops from commitment that displays a willingness to strive for goals. Nothing erodes confidence faster than a series of broken promises. Since we participate in a show me world, the ability to consistently walk the talk and to deliver upon commitments, are vital in a great leader.

Leaders show commitment to the other person as a beacon for other person vested. Commitment is the act of pledging or engaging; the act of exposing, endangering, or compromising; also, the state of being pledged or engaged.

Commitment is trait of sincere and steadfast fixity of purpose. Before one may lead, he/she must first understand the people who he/she will be leading. He/she must be able to see and understand his/her followers' situation in their point of view. Observe how they act, speak and think. In the long run, the people you are mirroring will feel more comfortable with you as if actually seeing themselves in you.

Leaders show genuine politeness and are friendly. Make your followers feel how willing you are to extend assistance in case they would need it. This builds mutual trust within the group, which will promote a stronger team spirit.

A leader must also provide compelling evidence that he/she can deliver. The leader must be able to concretize ideas and implement them. A good reputation is most important, so build one and maintain it.

If you are unable to reach agreement or get a commitment from another, agree to disagree, summarize your understanding. A leader is nothing without followers. Two fundamental conditions for commitment include:

a. Set of beliefs: A belief and sense of commitment promote the well-being and growth of members as well as that of the organization.

b. Faithful adherence to those beliefs: Commitment is persistence with a purpose

What leaders want and need from others is commitment. This is one's emotional investment to extend great effort toward the implementation of a decision, outcome or goal. Successful leaders need to solicit the commitment and dedication of others to achieve established goals and the group's mission.

A leader makes a commitment to the success of individuals in order to achieve organizational goals, that leader is well on the way to earning trust. Commitment is the engine that generates implementation energy from others. It reflects the leader's ability to get others excited about and dedicated to turning the vision into a reality.

While a leader has or creates vision, commitment is an 'emotional buy-in response' elicited from others. Leaders who are skilled at building and sustaining commitment do so primarily through five types of practices:

a. Communicating with others to share information and elicit their views

b. Involving others in key activities and decisions

c. Supporting others through resource allocation and by managing external factors that threaten to frustrate their efforts

d. Influencing others to integrate their priorities with the broader vision

e. Promoting teamwork to leverage the strengths of the organization in meeting customer needs.

Leadership is a dynamic relationship based on mutual influence and common purpose between leaders and followers in which both are moved to higher levels of motivation and moral development as they affect real, intended change.

Relationship is the connection between people. Mutual means shared in common. A leader builds commitment among followers by doing these actions, i.e.:

a. Gain commitment from others: Build commitment through appreciation and value. The leader values what they do and appreciate their valuable contribution to the organization.

b. Challenge exclusiveness: Demonstrate open and honest communication.

c. Encourage involvement: People feel a greater sense of commitment when they are involved in the decision-making process. A decision will fail without the commitment of others.

d. Ask for the commitment of others: This can be done by vividly articulating a clear vision, and personally requesting their solid commitment.

e. Set example: Demonstrate your own level of commitment. Show others that you are willing to do what you ask of them. The core leadership strategy is simple: be a model. Commit yourself to your own personal mastery.

Talking about personal mastery may open people's minds somewhat, but actions always speak louder than words. There's nothing more powerful you can do to encourage others in their quest for personal mastery, than to be serious in your own quest.

Great leaders are committed. They believe in what they are doing. The word quit simply doesn't exist in their vocabulary. To be a great leader, you need a certain level of intellect, social skills, and a compulsion to be a great doer, and a great reflector. To be a great leader, you need to find what you really like. That's where the passion, commitment, and integrity come from.

The most important underlying factor in leadership is whether a person has searched out and found a great match between what's in his or her heart, which is what he or she really enjoys, and the work situation.

Leadership is a relationship between those who aspire to lead and those who chose to follow. Sometimes the relationship is one-to-many. Sometimes it's one-to-one.

Commitment is founded on trust, respect and a common vision. Vision, along with a plan, continuous action, courage and commitment create some of the "greatest" leaders. Great leaders communicate commitment.

ACTION

Leadership is action, not position. Leaders act. Leaders get it right the first time. Leaders take action the moment it is required and inspire others to do the same.

Take action rather than talking continually about what you are going to do. You focus on specific steps you can take immediately. By employing this technique you concentrate on the things you can do right now to get the results you want and achieve the goals you desire.

Great leader tells the truth with understanding, seeks to learn as much as possible about any issue requiring actions, acts with confidence once a decision is made and then keeps the team motivated and focused toward the desired outcome.

When be successful, a great leader deflects to his/her team. When unsuccessful, a great leader does his/her best to figure out why, takes actions to prevent repeating the failure and, if appropriate, takes personal responsibility.

Great leaders are able to communicate in ways that resonate with others. This doesn't happen by accident. They practice the words that they use to help others see the better future that they imagine.

Great leaders not only see the world differently, they do things differently. They clarify purpose by articulating why goals are established and how individual work contributes to those goals; and defining the job to be done; create a strategic link between the work of the team and the goals of the organization; connecting the work of the team to the organization's model.

Your actions impact upon every aspect and every person in your organization. An action is the output of an organization, in which a leader should:

a. Take action: Get things done, show the ability to act, and continue to act, in focused ways over time, to build and reinforce the productivity of an organization. Practice doing things rather than thinking about them.

A leader displays commitment to his/herself to how he/she acts as a leader. Many leaders have done great things while being unpopular with the people.

b. Encourage others to act: Leaders show their followers the way.

Member should be committed to do as directed and complete the goals or objectives and expect the leaders/managers to support them. To meet these commitments, a sense of action is a priority for all members throughout the organization.

Great leaders take charge and get things done. They take disciplined, organize action. A leader has the courage to act. They learn by taking action. Nothing teaches better than experience. Great leaders act on reality. They act decisively, not recklessly, to maximize lucky breaks.

PRESENCE

Followers are ultimately inspired by a leader's presence and way of being. Leaders with presence assert themselves, offer a hand first, ask questions and appear interested. They are self-confident and gracious and can conduct a conversation with people at a variety of levels. You literally create your future with your present thoughts and actions.

When you are fully in the present, you have 100% of yourself involved, and remain alert to the opportunities which are present. The people you encounter subjectively sense whether or not you are fully with them. This has a great impact on the quality of your personal relationships.

Leaders are awesome - they are dynamic, focused and you feel better when you are around them. Leadership presence is an important factor in your ability to become a great leader. Leaders' presence and comportment affects how others follow them and whether they are open to their ideas. Presence means exhibiting following key factors:

a. Congruity: When our thinking, feeling, verbal messages, and actions all deliver the same message, people are more likely to trust us and work with us in a cooperative manner.

b. Self awareness: Being aware of ourselves lead to greater understanding of what drives our responses and reactions, and greater confidence in both our intellectual and gut decisions.

c. Attuning to others: When we attune to and respect the values, dreams, and desires of others, we vastly multiply what can be accomplished.

d. Courage and commitment: Charting a new course requires that we enter into new and uncharted territories. Heartfelt leaders have the courage and commitment to stay the course.

e. Impactful engagement: Heartfelt leaders need to be able to extend their energy and impact others in a dynamic manner. Great leaders have presence. Every great leader, regardless of his or her personality, has a special, compelling something. They have the sparkle factor in abundance.

What makes people stand out is leaders' presence. Whenever a leader is present, people get motivated. Leadership is manifested each time a person presents a dream of the future in a way that enlists the enthusiasm and commitment of others. Presence is an essential part of leadership.

Leaders with presence would need to be very self-aware, interact effectively with others. They leave their ego at the door, and bring a sincere caring and interest in others to the mix.

The key to satisfaction in any endeavor is progress. It can be accomplished by demonstrating sense of presence. Leaders lead by example, personal presence and involvement.

Followers are overwhelmed by the sense of presence of the great leader. Cutting across all the other competencies is the pure presence that great leaders exude. This is not the same as charisma, but is the ability to be open and authentic enough for people around the leader to personally feel and be impacted by that leader's passion. This is the sense that the leader has a direction, has energy to pursue it, and is genuinely enjoying the pursuit. It is the feeling of confidence in the intention of the leader. It is the recognition that the leader is indeed charting the course and is living towards it. Through this, people around that leader will also be inspired to take creative action towards the goal of the future.

Being authentic doesn't automatically create leadership greatness. Authentic leadership is a calling worthy of continued development. A leader demonstrates authentic care for all stakeholders.

The genuine and authentic leader should be visionary. He/she must be true to themselves and those they serve and to those who serve them.

7TH

SENSE OF TRUST

Trust is the essential ingredient for a healthy organizational relationship between the followers and the leader. Trust is the glue that holds leaders and followers together. Trust is a risk. Trust indicates a depth and a sense of assurance. Trust makes for a sense of being safe or of being free of fear.

Trust breeds confidence and conviction. What followers are looking for is someone in whom they can place their trust. Someone they know is working for the greater good - for them and for the organization. They're looking for someone not only that they can - but that they want to - follow. Because it is only when you have followers - people who have placed their trust in you - that you know you have moved into that leadership role.

Leaders can demonstrate good order, discipline and accomplishment to the extent that their relationships with the followers are based upon mutual trust and respect, i.e.:

a. Be a trusted leader: Leadership should be in the way trusting enough to be trusted. To be a great leader, your followers must have trust in you and they need to be sold on your vision. Leaders are people who were both ethical and who convey a strong vision of the future.

In any organization, a leader's actions set the pace. This behavior wins trust, loyalty, and ensures the organization's continued vitality.

b. Trust other: Your follower needs to feel trust in you. Toward this goal, you should keep promises, be supportive and give your follower opportunities to be trustworthy. This means believing him/her, and treating him/her as an honest person.

206

If people don't trust that you have their best interests at heart, if you don't consistently model stewardship, people will stop following you. A leader must be trustworthy. Trust is the lever of the heart. Persons who are not trustworthy cannot be leaders. The leader must examine his/her motives and intent, and know him/herself to be trustworthy.

We also must not trust someone without cause. A leader must prove his/her trustworthiness. The man who keeps looking over his/her shoulder because he/she doesn't trust those around him/her cannot concentrate on the work h/she is doing or on his/her goal for the future. Trustworthiness is also very important in group work.

Believability is achieved through both honesty and consistency between both the leader's statements and actions. Leaders are straightforward with their subordinates and behave in such a manner that earns the people's respect and trust.

As your members understand that you know them they will feel your trust, then they will come to experience the growth that accompanies that trust and you will find you have developed your most loyal members. It is natural to believe in great men.

You build relationships of trust through both your character and competence and you also extend trust to others. You show others that you believe in their capacity to live up to certain expectations, to deliver on promises, and to achieve clarity on key goals. You don't inspire trust by micromanaging and second guessing every step people make.

You must have honest understanding of who you are, what you know, and what you can do. Also, note that it is the followers, not the leader who determines if a leader is successful. If they do not trust or lack confidence in their leader, then they will be uninspired.

To be successful you have to convince your followers, not yourself, that you are worthy of being followed. When leaders extend them a fair recognition, communicate openly with them, and express gratitude for their efforts, they're likely to earn our trust along with their peak performance.

Trust begets trust. When we extend it, we'll reap the benefits in abundance. If you don't have high trust, none of those things will happen. You can't fake high trust by willing to risk in your relationships by reaching out with trust. In response, you'll earn respect and devotion. Leaders must instill mutual trust and confidence, which includes:

a. Create a culture that fosters high standards of ethics.

b. Be accountable and reliable to ensure that duties within areas of responsibility are completed in a timely manner.

c. Be open to feedback from others and use this feedback to make corrective changes as appropriate.

d. Must be flexible and open to change: Have the ability to adapt behaviors and work methods in response to new information, changing conditions or unexpected obstacles.

Great leaders create personal credibility and earn the legitimate trust of others. If people anywhere are to willingly follow someone – whether it be into the battle or into the boardroom, the front office or the front lines – they first want to assure themselves that the person is worthy of their trust.

Great leaders know that if they are perceived by followers as both highly competent at their job and genuinely caring about people – and they are able to demonstrate these two qualities again and again over time (i.e., they are perceived as dependable), then these leaders are well on their way to building high trust relationships with their followers.

For a great leader, high trust relationships are the foundation to fostering high performance work relationships. Trust is composed of three dimensions: credibility, respect, and fairness. Sense of trust implies two conditions include:

a. Get to trusting others first. One of the most valuable things you can do to create higher levels of trust is to trust others more. Don't wait for them to prove themselves to you. Trust them and become more trusting and you will begin to build your trustworthiness immediately.

b. Leadership that is based on earned trust. Trust is earned up close and personal and excepting extraordinary circumstances, requires an extensive investment of time: years, decades, and a lifetime. Trust is never permanently earned. It must be continuously re-earned.

Trust is earned by placing the welfare of your followers before your own welfare. Trust is earned by actions that demonstrate, unequivocally, your reliability. Trust is earned by taking personal risks to benefit your followers. Trust is earned by making personal sacrifices to benefit your followers. Trust is earned by demonstrating competence.

Trust is earned by accepting responsibility and accountability for your actions. Trust is earned by demonstrating integrity, sincere, and displaying courage – bravery and moral courage. Moral courage is an indispensable aspect of leadership.

Leaders use the positive aspect of trust, communication, and respect. They give people 100% of their trust, communication, and respect. They also act respectfully towards people, never limiting them, giving them the full opportunity to be who they are.

Leaders grasp at simple patterns where none exist, and plan a development program to those assumed to be responsible for failure, where the true causes lie in the organization itself.

Leaders, in words and in actions, must be consistent. One of the reasons people trust others is because they know what to expect – they know that people are consistent. As a leader this is definitely true. One of the best ways to be consistent is to operate from your values and principles.

When we do this we are more consistent – they anchor our words and deeds. When we share these values and principles with others, we help them see that consistent anchor.

Real leadership requires a belief in the people on the team. That belief can be demonstrated through the offering of awards for outstanding achievement. Sense of trust is enriched or diminished throughout our lives by experience. Trust makes people vulnerable to being hurt and to looking foolish; therefore they might be unable to trust anything or anyone.

Leaders must learn to trust themselves. If leaders do not believe in themselves and in their own abilities, trust in others is distorted into a relationship of dependency or subjugation, or worse. The more trusting leaders are; the more likable and the more trustworthy they are. Trust is a better option than mistrust.

HONESTY

When ones have a sense of pride in their honesty; so, honesty pays. Having a sense of honesty implies having a reference point of truth. Honesty inclines people towards integrity; which include:

a. Preference of trueness: Trueness means do not say what you believe to be false, and do not say what you can not prove. Honesty and sincerity avoid any bias or prejudice. Foundation of leadership consists of honesty, truthfulness and straight dealing.

b. Choose valid reasons: Leadership makes what they feel are the right decisions for the right reasons; shows trust with valid views; and do the right things for the right reasons, and long-term results will tend to be achieved.

c. Crave fair play: Practice leadership that is guided by justice, fair play, honesty and what is best for all.

A leader who is considered honest is one who displays integrity, is genuine and not deceptive or fraudulent. Honesty is characterized by truth and sincerity. Honesty denotes the quality of being upright in principle and action.

Honesty implies truthfulness, fairness in dealing with others, and refusal to engage in fraud, deceit, or dissembling. It is the responsibility of leader and every person in the organization to ensure that dishonesty is not tolerated. Exude an unwavering sense of honesty and integrity in your leadership.

Two of the most admired leaders are Abraham Lincoln and Martin Luther King Jr., people who contained a set of values and were honest. (Eric Papp, The Making of a Leader, USA, 2007)

Honesty means display sincerity, integrity, and candor in all your actions. Honesty should also show fair treatment to all people. It elicits a sense of respect. Being honest to your followers also generates within them a feeling of being respected. In return, they will give you their enhanced respect as well.

Leader commitment to honesty cannot be measured by bragging but, rather, by doing. Honesty and trust are crucial in organizational relationships. It enhances trust. If followers know that you tell the truth, they will trust your words and actions more. Sense of honesty includes:

a. Personal honesty: Becoming a leader requires a healthy dose of courageous, self-honesty, i.e. telling the whole truth, including those elements that are perhaps less flattering to the person or supporting arguments they may be making. Be sincere so others can trust you. Carry out your responsibilities carefully and with integrity, never claims credit for someone else's work and willing to acknowledge mistakes. Share ideas openly in a climate of trust. Be honest in all things in your words and in your work.

b. Organizational honesty: Organizational sense of honesty of being factually accurate as far as the statement goes, with the possibility, if not the probability, that elements less flattering to the organization or not supporting the organization's cause, are being suppressed or even distorted.

Organizational honesty requires that a person be as accurate at least as far one goes. Where the testimony is not even accurate as far as it goes, and turns out to be inconsistent with facts that the person giving the testimony must have known, then it risks crossing over the line from merely organizational honesty into explicit dishonesty.

Great leader will be generous and merciful to his/her opponents, as well as to those who are weaker than him/herself. Sometimes people don't say what they mean in order to hide something, protect themselves or someone else, or simply because they are trying to deceive in order to gain from circumstance.

Great leaders are honest, the need to establish a strong reputation. Great leaders have found it profitable to be honest. Honest means honorable in principles, intentions, and actions; treat other truthfully; adhere to ethics; be transparent and maintain a high degree of disclosure levels. Personal truth-telling is your time to get honest with yourself, and to consider others' best intentions.

We must be willing to be honest with ourselves, explore alternatives, and act with courage and leadership. Seek feedback from neutral people to help you gain a new perspective, or they're so vested in the outcome of your decisions that they can't be objective.

Honesty is the only way that people will ever come to understand each other. Commitment to honesty with ourselves and with other people encourages us to take another risk. Without honesty, your best efforts to resolve conflicts will be wasted because you will not understand each other well enough to find mutually acceptable solutions.

We need to practice honesty; learn how to talk to each other about our thoughts and our feelings and our needs; to talk about our struggles and failures, about our dreams and our successes.

The first step toward honesty is to pay attention. It brings forth shared responsibility. This is another outcome of the connection that honesty draws out. Co-workers will sense the manager's openness, obtain a greater sense of meaning, and dare to step up and claim more responsibility. The cornerstone character traits of great leaders are integrity and honesty.

CREDIBILITY

Credibility is the foundation of leadership. Leadership itself consists of management skills, personal credibility, and the ability to motivate. For an organization to be truly successful, it has to have credibility. Building up the credibility of the organization takes time and effort, i.e. create a strong reputation through a superior quality product or service; or develop a keen sense of the credibility of information.

If you can't deliver what you promise, then people won't trust you. Be honest in your capacity to fulfill others' expectation; and respond quickly and positively to any problems or issues against organization reputation. Believability is achieved through both honesty and consistency between both the leader's statements and actions.

Credibility in leadership comes from competence (what you do), character (who you are), and connection (your relationship with followers). Credible leaders are straightforward with their subordinates and behave in such a manner that earns the subordinates' respect and trust. Leadership credibility includes:

a. Personal credibility: It is necessary, since leadership is personal. People follow because they believe. They believe that the person has a positive vision and direction. They believe that their leader is going to be successful, and they want to be a part of that success. And finally, they believe that their leader cares about them, collectively as a group, and individually. Individual credibility is crucial to organizational credibility.

b. Organizational credibility: It is important towards successful cultures and climates. Trust is a key dimension to organizational credibility. Credibility has a significant positive outcome organizational performance.

Definition of leadership that makes sense is the successful combination of effective management practice, coupled with the personal credibility and the ability to motivate others.

A leader who is seen as honest, committed and caring has credibility and integrity and can be trusted. It is likely that people will follow this leader. Leaders aspire to create the same sense of credibility for the organization and followers.

Leaders create credibility that results from trust and knowledge. If you have created trust, then you need only demonstrate your knowledge. It is not enough merely to show others how smart you are, but that you can use that knowledge to educate and help individuals grow.

Leaders with credibility are those who by their actions and behaviors demonstrate that they have the best interests of the organization. When a leader makes a commitment to the success of individuals in order to achieve organizational goals, that leader is well on the way to earning trust.

Great character results in credibility and moral authority. The great leaders also obey principles of healthy relationships. They are very ethical, extremely credible and competent, excellent skills, visionary and charismatic.

COMPETENCE

Trust is about competence and accountability. Trust implies to leaders show egos don't get in the way. They have the competence and skill to succeed. They inspire trust and understanding of the perils of reaching their goal. Leadership is about your ability to inspire trust, loyalty, commitment, and collegiality among team members.

Leaders focus on increasing the speed and magnitude of their individual and organizational results by improving trust and increasing influence with their key stakeholders.

Poor leadership at the top of the organization can translate into millions in lost profits and missed opportunities. A leader creates an opportunity for individuals to prepare themselves to fill this leadership shortage and provides a proven process for organizations to increase the bench strength of their organization by developing critical leadership skills in their key people. The leader must earn the trust and respect of his/her followers.

Greatness involves both character and competence. Trust is a unique which occurs when a person perceives sincerity, commitment and competence on the part of the other. Leaders inspire trust that builds credibility as a leader, so that people will trust him/her with their highest efforts.

Leaders have the personal characteristics that engender trust and commitment. The leaders not only have to respect others, but must have a high level of competence in working with and supporting people, especially when things are difficult, conflicted or uncertain.

Followers typically trust leadership that inspires a compelling vision (competence), offers meaning, purpose and excitement (commitment) and is sensitive to individual awareness, expression and interaction (sincerity).

Trust is the core imperative of great leaders, since it affects their ability to do everything else. Trust is a function of personal credibility and behaviors that build trust.

INTELLECT

Intellect describes ability to view an issue from many different perspectives. Aspect of greatness is greatness of mind. One study of great leaders found traits such as intellect, determination, and courage to be most important.

Great leaders are often scholars in their field and are intelligent. Like all great scholars, they aren't know-it-alls, they feel there is always more to learn and have a willingness to admit mistakes.

Great leaders apply scientific and rational approaches towards presenting new innovative ideas and healing scars of internal divisions. The key of great leadership is having the capacity to generate intellectual capital--and great leadership is the key to realizing intellectual.

KNOWLEDGE

Leaders demonstrate sound knowledge as well as abilities such as being able to communicate with their followers. Learning is process of acquiring modifications in existing knowledge, skills, habits, or tendencies through experience, practice, or exercise. It demonstrates continuous personal improvement; apply knowledge to provide the best services; individual performance and development; and passion.

Knowledge must be acquired, digested, integrated and applied. This knowledge must range from the hard technical skills of leadership, to the much more elusive goals of self-knowledge and self-awareness. Knowledge is a key element of leadership. Sense of knowledge is about acquiring:

a. Self-knowledge: Understanding one's self is a difficult task to achieve. Leaders never lie to themselves because it destroys their chances and opportunities to lead others successfully.

   Setting a good example takes courage and confidence. It requires individuals to admit to specific flaws in their personalities, skills and characters.

   Self-knowledge assists in understanding personal strengths as well as shortcomings. Leaders need to be able to draw upon their personal strengths and skills to the fullest while continually working to minimize weaknesses. They need to have the wisdom to draw competent, trustworthy individuals into their world to fill the gaps and voids their own personal weaknesses tend to create.

   Without self-knowledge this becomes an impossible task. The more leaders gain knowledge, the better they are able to find the truth. One way that we enhance our being is to practice self knowledge. Before we can influence others, we must understand what motivates them. But first we must understand ourselves.

b. Organizational knowledge: Acquiring the knowledge of others - through reading, attending workshops or presentations, and questioning experts; and putting the learning into action through practice on organizational issues/case studies.

The increase in leadership skills will result in the development of exceptional leaders, which in turn will have a significant impact on individual and organizational performance.

A leader has true integrity, which is composed of self-knowledge, candor, and maturity. Self-knowledge provides the personal integrity to engage in powerful action. Learning and growth constitute the essential foundation for success; which can be distinguished from behavioral changes.

The purpose of learning is growth, and our minds, unlike our bodies, can continue growing as we continue to live. The more educated, you would become more independent-minded and rational. One certainly must possess knowledge in order to grow wisdom.

The gift of knowledge perfects a person's practical reason on matters of judgment about truth. As a leadership philosophy, one uses practical reasoning to decide how to act, i.e. how you will undertake a task. From a cognitive position, strong leaders ignore the unproductive possibilities in favor of productive ones.

The more leaders gain knowledge, the better they are able to find the truth and make decisions consistent with that truth. The goal of leadership development is to produce confident, knowledgeable and courageous leaders, which implies:

a. Skill development and knowledge acquisition: This facilitates the doing of leadership - knowing what to do as a leader.

b. Personal insights: This self awareness facilitates the being of leadership - being comfortable enough with your sense of self so you can truly be an effective leader

Great leadership demonstrates knowledge, skills, and talents combined with the inner qualities of a leader that drive noble actions. All great leaders, in any field, maximize their strengths to achieve their potential. Leaders have a thirst for knowledge. They must have the knowledge and expertise to help others accomplish results.

THOUGHT

Success comes to those who habitually do things that unsuccessful people don't do. Achievement comes from the habit of good thinking. Great leaders come to the party with a sense of wonder and awe. They restlessly and repeatedly ask questions. People admire and respect leaders who are dynamic, uplifting, enthusiastic, positive, and optimistic. People expect them to be inspiring.

Yet it is not enough for leaders to have dreams of the future. They must be able to communicate those dreams in ways that encourage us to sign on for the duration and to work hard for the goal.

A leader whit sense of thinking, one who is in organization that thinks, in which others will look to for leadership, requires:

a. Demonstrate learning and focused thinking into their daily routine: Leadership requires one to always be a step ahead in their thought processes.

b. Practice of realistic thinking: Actions always have consequences; realistic thinking helps you to determine what those consequences could be. The thinker always does what is best for the organization by seeking to understand the consequences of his actions.

Therefore the leader should listen to different voices in an organization. It leads to true insight into the organization. They nurture creative and critical thinking skills necessary to effect personal and organizational change.

c. Look for opportunities to be a coach: Coaching must become a key component of the leader's repertoire. It emphasizes people and an investment in others for the betterment of the organization.

The leader wonders about everything, wants to learn as much as he or she can, is willing to take risks, experiments, and tries new things. Leadership requires thought and planning. Great leaders plan time to think and to process information before making major decisions.

Leaders create and inspire new leaders by instilling faith in their leadership ability and helping them develop and hone leadership skills they don't know they possess. The leader becomes the chief thinker in the organization and the teacher of those he/she leads.

The leader becomes the sage of the organization, delegating the implementation of the vision while coaching others up to become great leaders. Integrity is based upon honestly examining and evaluating one's thoughts and actions.

Leaders continually display a steadfast devotion to principles and values. They never attempt to trim these in order to please others. Leaders believe that the way to become self-defeating is to compromise their conscience to fit another's expectations and desires. They chose to maintain proper and appropriate actions, thoughts and responses even if it means relinquishing personal gain, praise and acceptance.

A leader never arrives at a destination; he/she is always looking for new paths to explore and new territory to conquer. As a thinker, the leader will always remain fresh and will be willing to try new and innovative ideas.

Great leaders have an extraordinary sense of perspective. The great leaders adopt a different way of thinking. The spend time thinking strategically with your management team. They think big and small.

The leaders must possess key critical thinking skills that steer organizational strategy and decision making. Critical thinking is a differentiator, and as such, it should play a prominent role in both the selection and the development of the people. Critical thinking is a necessary skill for great leaders.

LEARNING

Without learning, organizations, teams, and leaders are stuck in yesterday's world. Leaders are responsible for building organizations where people are continually expanding their capabilities to shape their future --that is, leaders are responsible for learning.

There are built-in tensions between learning and performance, which organizations must learn to recognize and deal with. Leadership entails learning. Leaders are more powerful role models when they learn than when they teach.

Leaders take time to learn from the greatest examples of historic leadership. As we, the leaders, deal with tomorrow, our task is not to try to make perfect plans. Our task is to create organizations that are sufficiently flexible and versatile that they can take our imperfect plans and make them work in execution. That is the essential character of the learning organization.

Leadership is to develop a field that encourages learning. There is a natural relationship between learning and performance in a changing world. That is, performance cannot be sustained over time without learning, because yesterday's performance is inadequate in today's world. So, to maintain or improve performance, learning is required.

Learning organizations must be willing to learn from the past and the present in order to create an exciting, and worthwhile future - a place to be great. A great leader is someone who is interested in constant learning and growth.

Learning leaders can become absolutely indispensable to the success of their organizations by thinking, speaking, and acting strategically. People can become not only great leaders, but great coaches.

Leaders must strive to continually learn, and learn to be more effective. They must step outside the box and look beyond the horizon of the current situation.

Great leaders learn from other great leaders. They are constantly reading books by other great leaders, as well as listening to them and reading about them. They know who the great leaders in their profession are and they stay current with what they are doing and with the knowledge that they are creating.

Self-coaching will help you acquire useful leadership skills, clarify your values and guiding principles and actively build your reputation.

Self-knowledge will provide you with the personal integrity to engage in powerful action-oriented relationships. Anyone who stops learning is old, whether at twenty or eighty. Anyone who keeps learning stays young.

The greatest thing in life is to keep your mind updated. By applying what we learn, we can become better leaders. Self-directed learning creates a great leader

Great leaders of learning create leaders of learners. Great leaders develop the same way that great performers in other fields develop which needs aptitude or talent and a combination of training and developmental experience to improve your ability to perform.

FAIRNESS

People want to be treated as unique individuals and to know that their leader cares for each of them in a personal way. Fairness is marked by impartiality and honesty; it is free from self-interest, prejudice or favoritism; it conforms to the established rules.

A sense of fairness should make us cautious. We feel we have acted justly when we treat someone as we feel they ought to be treated. Justice is defined as state of being just; the practice of being fair and consistent.

A just person gives consideration to each side of a situation and bases rewards or punishments on merit. Be honest with yourself about why you make a particular decision. Avoid favoritism. Treat other adequately, fairly, or with full appreciation. Try to be fair at all times and treat all things and people in an equal manner.

Justice should not only aim at controlling the negative traits in human nature, it should work to promote a sense of fairness, compassion and universal brotherhood. Justice can be achieved from following states, i.e.

    a.   Just and fair - In the way people are treated or decisions are made

    b.   Moral rightness in action or attitude - Do yourself justice to display your own abilities fully or perform to your full potential often used in the negative

    c.   Reward in accordance with honor - True qualities, especially the merits, of somebody or something

    d.   Conformity to truth - Speak of the good

The cumulative effect of poor judgment can erode an organization's intangible assets and undermine its potential. Justice is virtue in having to do with our treatment of others. No one can be discriminated on the grounds of religion, sect, belief, gender, color, caste, wealth and social status. It also reflects rule of law for all without considering their position in the organization. Leaders use justice for enhancing people and develop excellence.

Everyone has a basic sense of fairness, since everyone can distinguish between equal or unequal returns, or at least thinks he/she can, and therefore is capable of distinguishing between fair or unfair actions. Treat everyone in a just and honest way. Needs should be treated without favoritism or prejudice. Opportunities will be open to all and be appropriately distributed.

True fairness is not based on equality but on meeting individual needs. Fair equal to just, equitable, impartial, unbiased, dispassionate, or objective, that means free from favor toward either or any side.

Fairness implies an elimination of one's own feelings, prejudices, and desires so as to achieve a proper balance of conflicting interests; and treat equally and without prejudice or bias and in a timely manner.

Fairness defines the cultural rules in which you treat other the way you want to be treated; take turns; tell the truth; play by the rule; think about how your actions will affect others; listen to people with an open mind; don't blame others for your mistakes; don't take advantage of other people; don't play favorites.

Fairness involves a comparison between what a member is experiencing to what is happening to others in the organization. Organizations need leaders whose character profiles comprise an element of courage and passion, as well as integrity and a sense of fairness.

Leaders with a strong sense of fairness like to give everyone a chance. Everyone must be treated fairly and injustice frustrates and horrifies. Such people set aside their personal prejudices and will see the good in others. Leaders develop a personal sense of fairness and helped others do the same.

Sense of fairness is related to trust, which is a key to relations, high morale and productivity. Without a sense of fairness and justice, no leader can command and retain the respect of his/her followers.

OPENNESS

Leaders provide a forum for candid and honest discussion of important issues; for hearing different perspectives and opinions; and for learning from each other. Openness enables the creation of new ideas and initiatives to address organization's major challenges.

A leader creates a sense of openness that encourages people's ideas; atmosphere of openness in weaknesses and challenges faced

Great leaders display characteristics such as self-awareness, valuing others' opinions, willing to learn and change, sharing power, having the ability to hear the truth and admit mistakes, and working to create a culture of openness where dissent is encouraged in an environment of mutual trust and respect.

JUSTICE

Justice is an important principle and virtue. Justice is the principle which should guide how laws are applied. Justice maintains fair and harmonious relations and should be treated so. Justice makes sure that no one is above or below the law that applies equally to all.

Justice is what is right for everyone, and it is best applied by someone who is neutral, objective, unbiased, and detached from irrelevant considerations while being devoted to treating all equally and according to the facts.

Justice resolves conflicts in ways that are fair for all, which concerns for equality and non-discrimination of people. Individuals should be treated with equal rights and entitlements; and discrimination signs should be avoided, i.e. identity as a source of discrimination in organization; discrimination that occurs on account of one's religion, race and gender, and multiculturalism points to discrimination of minority cultures. It needs encouragement in which equality for diverse cultures requires a system of special, group-differentiated rights.

To preserve justice, organizations must have great leaders. If you wish to be a great leader, then practice justice for all. Justice is truth in action. A leader must excel in justice and display high degree of justice. Race, creed, belief, sex, nationality, tribal affiliation and other considerations should be set aside when the leader is administering justice.

Great leaders can quickly distinguish between right and wrong. If they don't know, they find out. Only then do they dispense justice. And their sense of justice is unwavering. They set the same standards for themselves as they set for others. Not doing it amounts to hypocrisy. Great leader must be in the pursuit of equal justice under the rule.

SINCERITY

Leadership is the ability to lead without managing, motivate without manipulating, doing what you say you will do and generating results without fear and intimidation.

Sincerity is the virtue of speaking truly about one's feelings, thoughts, and desires. Without this sincerity, without trust, no one can achieve anything worthy of note. It is only sincerity that can inspire men to greatness.

Your greatness is measured by your kindness. Those who lead in the business organization must also possess a sense of sincerity. Great leaders come in many forms.

Leaders are not only highly driven and intrinsically motivated but also foster that same enthusiasm in their associates. Leaders display sincerity, integrity, and candor in all your actions.

A leader sincerely wants what is best and that sincerity arouses enthusiasm so people are inspired to do better than they thought was possible and that discovery of their own greater selves gives them a deep sense of satisfaction.

A great leader has the ability to see where the organization needs to go. A leader must possess reliability and strength of character in order to inspire commitment and selflessness within others.

Great leaders are reliable persons of character who are committed to compelling principles and purposes, while embodying both empathy and respect for others, as well as inner connectedness and respect for oneself. Respect for others is clearly demonstrated by sincerely caring for others, paying attention to who they are.

Leaders have a deep concern for people. A leader's words and deeds always convey sincerity. Sincerity is an important part of the positive treatment. Weak people cannot be sincere. Sincerity gives wings to power.

Great leaders genuinely care about and show a sincere interest in what their followers have to say and take the time to listen to them. They are active listeners who pay attention to what is being said, concentrate on the ideas and issues their followers raise, and take appropriate actions that demonstrate their understanding and concern. Great leaders spend time among their employees and empathize with their followers.

RECOGNITION

Leaders recognize and appreciate the efforts of their followers. Recognition is important; it builds positive self-esteem. Benefits are achieved when the member feels the job could not have been done without them. This means they were faced with a challenge, which means, they had the responsibility and authority to take action.

Giving people recognition generates energy within them. They will then direct that energy toward increased productivity. The flip side of accepting responsibility when things don't work out as planned is to give the credit to others when things go right. Nothing will stifle their future contributions more quickly.

Leaders give thanks. For they appreciate the efforts of their team. They are generous in praise, not criticism. They respect team members and let them know. They are also quick to support and defend their team. When leaders give awards and praise in front of others, they send important signals to the organization.

Praising is a form of leadership, but it needs to be used carefully. When they praise and select individuals that will be viewed as heroes by others, great leaders explain why these individuals are selected - who they serve, how they score and what actions they take. In doing so, they embed these behaviors in the organization.

Rewards are more than financial. Recognition fosters a real sense of personal achievement, self-reliance and respect as an entrepreneur. These are things that money cannot buy.

An important part of interpersonal success is the creation of positive relationships with others. When you recall that an important communication norm in the organization is reciprocity. It's easy to understand that good relationships are built on recognition of each others' positive efforts.

Recognition is a process of acknowledging one's adversary with his or her own legitimate situation and concerns. It is something one gives, not something one gets. Recognition feeds upon each other, creating a constructive, connecting, and humanizing interaction.

People who display greatness rely upon others who are able to see as they do, to listen, encourage, and support. Without those people who recognize greatness and move in to support it, even the greatest ideas, works of art; and political movements would remain unborn.

Probably the single most important step in encouraging members' involvement is recognizing those who contribute. Having pride of belonging to a good organization is recognition. Leadership values even the smallest moments of inspiration. Recognition motivates higher levels of commitment and in taking on the additional challenges. Leaders give genuine recognition and praise. Pay attention to what people are doing and catch them doing the right things. When you give praise, spend a little effort to make your genuine words memorable.

Recognition may change behavior, increase people's motivation, redirect attention, or build social cohesion and allegiance. In other instances the organization may want to foster a sense of engagement and commitment or influence members' attitudes and feelings.

Appreciation and celebration enriches your everyday relationships. Recognition of this is a call to action that, if heeded, will inspire others to see in you the greatness they also possess. This creates a chain reaction of greatness unfolding itself endlessly into the future.

A carefully defined task, suited to the particular person involved, with finite scope, milestones, resources (if any) and limitations, is best. The clearer the understanding of what is to be done and the clearer the measurement of success is the better.

Success is the continued expansion of happiness and the progressive realization of worthy goals by honoring others. It is a life filled with appreciation and gratitude. Living on purpose creates success. Leadership is about the success of your people, not about you.

Good communication creates a powerful sense of recognition. The more one is recognized and praised, the more he or she is likely to contribute. Certainly you need to thank a person for doing a good job. Few people will continue giving of themselves unless their efforts are recognized and appreciated.

Recognition must be consistent so that people do not suspect favoritism. Team accomplishments can also be celebrated, giving equal credit to all team members.

People with a sense of connectedness have a sense of 'we' as well as a sense of 'I'. The more special the we, is the more special the individual feels as part of the group, and the greater the self-esteem that is generated. This is why it is important to have high standards for becoming a group member.

Throughout our lives many events shape who we are. The events that touch us the most are the ones that give us a sense of pride and earned recognition for our efforts.

Recognition promotes loyalty, member satisfaction and retention. Recognition is not simply motivation or persuasion. On other hand, people will do things because they are forced to do so, but without any choice in the matter or any sense that their actions are helping others, the threats will not create a positive relationship with the leader.

Recognition is a message that builds a sense of teamwork with the leader. The key to keeping good members is recognizing their efforts. Good organization, management and performance breed success and good communication allows and encourages it to happen.

A leader makes other people feel important and appreciated. The leader excels at creating opportunities to provide rewards, recognition and thanks to his or her followers. A leader creates a work environment in which people feel important and appreciated.

Great leaders also realize that they cannot make change happen alone. The great leader for the future will be his or her ability to get along with people, to show compassion, and to make others feel good about them. People love to be recognized for their accomplishments, and this will instill a sense of pride in your people.

Great leaders understand recognition. They will seek to create environments where their followers are rewarded for their hard work and success. Average performers tend to believe money and material possessions are their. However, investing money in the productivity of your followers is useless if the leaders do not understand how to recognize and reward those who are under them.

HARD WORK

Leaders aren't born they are made. And they are made just like anything else, through hard work. Becoming a great leader isn't an overnight process. You can definitely learn how to improve your leadership qualities over time. Great leaders don't sit around telling others what to do. Great leaders are created through hard work, dedication and experience. People do their best work when they're motivated by a sense of purpose.

Hard work creates opportunity. People want to know they're working for an organization that is challenging, innovative and important to organization.

Leaders should be able to take things one day at a time, and can work towards goals. They should be able to 'hang in there' and appreciate that things often do take a while to change; also be able to try different approaches when things don't always work the first time around.

Great leaders come in many forms. In one sense, leadership is a subjective thing, in another there are certain characteristics that are, typical of quality leadership.

Leadership is the process of influencing members to work hard towards, and be committed to, organization's goals. Leaders are usually seen as active, expressive, and energetic. They are often very optimistic and open to change. Overall, they are generally quick and alert and tend to be uninhibited.

Work is used as the primary means to achieve an identity, a sense of self-worth, etc. Leadership is hard work; therefore leaders should:

a. Never fear failure: The fear of failure defeats many who would otherwise be successful leaders. Most successful people will never feared failure.

b. Never quit: Give the objective to the bitter end. Your determination in failure may be the inspiration for another to succeed.

c. Desire to achieve: Achievement is the driving force behind the budding entrepreneur. It is not money. Success of the endeavor was the object of the labor, not money.

Committed and dedicated hard working leaders will eventually develop dedicated and hard working organizations regardless of who they start with or the experience they bring to the job.

Great leaders often inspire their followers to high levels of achievement by showing them how their work contributes to worthwhile ends. Being a great leader is hard work, and this insight is what makes it possible for you to work hard and work long - the other insights are what help you work well.

LOYALTY

Loyalty means that you are devoted to your country, the organization, and to your seniors, peers, and subordinates. You should show your loyalty by never discussing the problems of the corps or your organization with outsiders. Never talk about seniors unfavorably in front of your subordinates.

Once a decision is made and the order is given to execute it, carry out that order willingly as if it were your own. It expresses itself in both thought and action and strives for the identification of the interests of the loyal person with those of the object.

Leaders wisely take care of their organizations and their people first. Since humans are social beings, one of our strongest emotions involves attachment to a group, and there are several different ways to appeal to that emotion.

One is the general appeal to loyalty, which operates on the notion that one should act in concert with (what is claimed to be) the group's best interests, regardless of the merits of the particular case being argued. No man can serve two masters; loyalty is devotion to a person. In loyalty one shows:

a. Dependability - Bring meaning, direction, and purpose into his/her life and unifies his/her activities

b. Allegiance - Willingness, in which ones cooperate with others; invest his intellectual and moral resources

c. Bind oneself to their course of action - Attachment to a particular object

d. Faithfulness - Hope to fulfill his/her destiny

e. Duty and obligation - Tasks to be performed and   with commitments

Sense of loyalty should not reduce to blind obedience. Great leaders build his/her organization's capability to consistently achieve its goals, attract and retain talent, improve work processes, and develop intense customer loyalty. Great leaders develop loyalty by:

a. Clarify values: It is important for leaders to be concerned about strengthening the value systems and how this can be done, that help guide a leader's decisions and actions toward the ethical high ground.

b. Trust people: Leadership cannot take place in a culture where people distrust each other, doubt other's motives, and pursue independent action agendas.

Trust is central to leadership in organizations because followers are people who choose to follow leaders. The trust of followers allows leaders to lead. Leaders build trust or tear it down by the cumulative actions they take and the words they speak.

c. Care: Leaders must take care of their followers. Care about the employee first as an individual, than as a follower.

True loyalty from a follower comes when the leader is able to build a relationship with the follower based upon deep trust. This means that a leader may perceive that he or she has loyalty, but without the follower feeling a bond of trust, the two of them will never have true loyalty.

Loyalty and responsibility may give you fulfillment and peace. Loyalty evolves also to social function. Leaders must first display an unquestionable sense of loyalty before they can expect members of their unit to be loyal.

DUTY

Leaders have high sense of duty, honor, loyalty and courage. Leaders give commitment to the organization. They have a sense of obligation to the organization - a sense of duty to give their best.

Leaders are often dominated by a sense of duty and tend to be very exacting in character. They usually have a very high standard of excellence and an inward desire to do one's best. They also have a need for order and tend to be very self-disciplined.

Leaders give commitment to the organization. They have a sense of obligation to the organization - a sense of duty to give their best. Leaders don't inflict pain; they bear pain.

DEVOTION

Great leaders are willing to sacrifice for the team - They will never let on, that they had to sacrifice for the team. They consistently display a strong sense of devotion to duty. They must symbolize (display the courage of his or her convictions, can move the followers towards its common goals) and show commitment to core values of honor, respect, and devotion to duty (display the courage and supreme devotion to duty - to complete the mission and achieve the goal).

Leaders inspire a deep devotion in their followers. The effect they have on their followers seems to be their greatest achievement. High-commitment organizations begin with a strong sense of devotion, which expresses itself in a life of discipline. Group organized around devotion and discipline tends producing abundance.

Great leaders consistently display a strong sense of devotion to duty. Success can only come to you by courageous devotion to the task. Leaders with outstanding personalities serve the organization in their respective spheres with a sense of devotion, dedication and selflessness.

SERIOUSNESS

Seriousness is marked by dignity; sincerity; deeply interested; concerned with important matters; not trifling; appealing to the mind; and requiring effort. When life becomes serious, a man becomes less cause and greater effect. There is a direct connection between insanity and seriousness.

Getting too serious may create problems: stress, worry, anxiety, emotional pain, drudgery and failure. And being in a continuous serious mood does not help us to deal with them most efficiently. We can easily become over-burdened, stressed out and even unpleasant to be around.

If you feel you are too serious, it helps to find a good role model. We are most effective when we are well balanced with seriousness and joy. Seriousness will help self-growth, i.e.

    a.   Get stronger - Make great gains and get into the good habit. It can happen when your life is well-organized and disciplined.

    b.   Get running - Focus must be in tip-top shape.

c. Get competitive - Strive to play with better players, and serious players; take advantage of the opportunity.

d. Carry a good attitude - Be respectful and responsive to your goal.

When problems are easier to solve, people are more cooperative and you feel more relaxed; work is a lot more fun and a lot less stressful if you have a positive attitude.

Negative attitudes are usually reflected in the quality of a person's outcome. People who have a good attitude are more relaxed, are able to concentrate, and are better able to recognize opportunities to do the real work. Their awareness is higher.

People who are stressed have difficulty controlling their attention. Usually their attention is fixed on something. And it's the something that draws their attention out rather than their deliberately placing their attention on something.

CARE

No one cares how much you know until they know how much you care. Leaders genuinely care about people. They make time for them and they are passionate about helping others develop their true potential. Members also need opportunities to develop a sense of care for each other. When leaders take great care of their followers, they display:

a. Empathy: People need to be accepted and recognized for their special and unique spirit.

b. Constructive feedback: If you really care about someone, you give them constructive feedback - both positive and negative comments. Providing feedback actively states that you really do care.

c. Support their growth and development: Grow the people; deeply committed to the growth of each and every individual within the organization. If you really do care about someone, you want the very best for that person. This means providing him or her with an opportunity to grow.

d. Stewardship: Play significance roles in organization. Leaders feel a sense of responsibility and strive to promote organization's greater good. They value service to others, as well as to self. They take ownership for the outcomes of their acts, including successes and setbacks.

e. Listening: Listening and understanding your members' concerns, you indirectly tell them that you really care about them and value their opinions. Instead of telling them anything, take time to hear their message and fully understand what they are trying to convey.

Great leaders would rather be respected than liked. They have the resolve and character to make the tough decisions even when polls do not support them.

Leaders care enough to make those tough call brings respect. No person can be a true leader unless he/she takes genuine joy in the successes of those under him/her. Without such caring, those who work with a leader lose interest, enthusiasm ebbs out.

Caring is the basis of leadership, the work upon which a good organization is built. Caring requires not only compassion and concern; it demands self-sacrifice and tough-mindedness and discipline.

The leader fosters a sense of care for one another. Sometimes it requires a gentle touch, bringing hope and renewed commitment to discouraged followers. Some times it involves demanding that others be accountable for their actions so that they are stretched and pushed to be their best.

A great leader emphasizes the importance of caring deeply about what people are doing, about the welfare of them, and about doing things with a strong moral fiber. Great leaders have a deeply rooted concern for those whom they lead. The leaders care about the success of others. They care about the well being of those in their charge. They do not use people as simply as a means to an end. They genuinely want others to develop to their full potential.

EMPATHY

Empathy means cultivate a sense of compassion and responsibility for others. You have a bigger impact on the lives of those under you than you can imagine. Always nurture and protect those around you. Empathy implies that the leader would share in the anxiety of the follower.

Empathy is the ultimate corporate secret. It is the most powerful resource and a skill that is critical for leadership. The ability to sense and respond to the feelings of others sets leaders apart from their people. Empathy can be used to form strong relationships, pick up early warning signs, and recognize opportunities to influence.

Leaders take care of their people. He/she knows everyone who worked for him/her as an individual. He/she knows their strengths and weaknesses, their aspirations, their fears. He/she always takes the criticism from outside the group, but let each of them take the praise for what they contribute.

One of the attributes of a truly great leader is empathy - the ability to walk in other persons shoes, to understand their needs and dreams and so on. Respect for others is clearly demonstrated by sincerely caring for others, paying attention to who they are and what they say and respecting them for their own guiding principles and purpose.

Leaders that have empathy are kind, loving, and understanding. Leaders take a personal interest in people. Show people that you care, and genuine curiosity about their lives. Ask them question about their hobbies, their challenges, their families, their aspirations.

Great leaders will be able to help followers identify the situation and then develop a plan to improve it. Leaders empathize passionately - and realistically - with people, and they care intensely about the work followers do. Being a great leader means listening and understanding, and helping them to understand.

Leaders are reliable persons of character who are committed to compelling principles and purposes, while embodying both empathy and respect for others, as well as inner connectedness and respect for oneself. A person who cannot genuinely empathize with others can never excel as a leader.

To be a great leader, you must have a believer's heart. Great leaders show great empathy towards others, always seeking to understand diverse points of view, and encouraging collaborative problem solving. The caring aspect of empathy is what inspires people to stay with a leader, even when times are challenging. Empathy breeds loyalty.

Great leaders are able to see and feel what their people are experiencing. Great leaders possess a passion that touches that noble impulse in each of follower, and they have empathy and love for people.

EXAMPLE

Role modeling is critical. Leadership is an active ability to inspire by example – to ardently motivate others to achieve with integrity and accountability their greatest potential.

Leaders may adopt a persona that encapsulates their mission and lead by example (it should always be – do as I do, not only do as I say). He/she pushes his/her people hard. He/she demands a lot of them. But no one ever works harder than he/she does. He/she is the first one in and the last one to leave. And he/she works hard the whole time he/she is there.

Lead by example means you don't ever ask anyone to do anything that you wouldn't or couldn't or haven't done yourself. From the lowliest of assignments, pitch in and do the work. That will help provide an understanding of what you need others to do, plus it will underscore the can-do spirit focused on getting things done and inspiring your team.

Leaders are those whose good habits serve as an example to others. The greatness of leadership does not depend on position, and a great position does not guarantee a great leader. Leadership is grounded in others, not self. It gives to get the best from others. It inspires by commitment and example, not by exhortation. It inspires and aspires for the greater good.

A great leader is one who sets an outstanding example by the way he or she consistently behaves. This individual does not necessarily have to be a high-level executive or have a powerful title, but this leader must demonstrate by example what it means to lead. You must never expect others to do what you would not do. You must be fair, firm, friendly and dependable.

If you have to correct someone, do it in private. You have succeeded as a leader when your team works just as well in your absence. Be constantly on the lookout for heroes in your own life to admire and emulate. Adopt their styles. Then, lead by example.

Be a good role model for your followers. They must not only hear what they are expected to do, but also see. We must become the change we want to see.

Great leaders lead by example. When leading towards a great vision, you must do so in the reality. The best motivation is always example. The example of a great leader is always a greater motivation than any other single thing.

Great leaders can see the potential in others and encourage them. Leaders create standards of excellence and then set an example for others. The great leaders set great example. Example is the foundation of everything else that makes a truly great leader.

LISTENING

One of the most important skills you need as a leader is the ability to listen. Being a good listener is quite crucial. Active listening focuses entirely on what the other person is saying and confirms understanding of both the content of the message and the emotions and feelings underlying the message.

A leader listens emphatically. He/she welcomes ideas and inputs from his/her members. This promotes consensus building within the team. He/she creates enough opportunities for open communication then he/she capitalizes on the ideas shared within the group but making sure that he provides recognition for these ideas. Though he/she places a high value on dialogue and feedback, he/she knows when to take action.

Listeners have a big leadership advantage over those who do all the talking, because they may:

a. Highly respected because they've shown they care about others.

b. Tend to be better informed because active listening results in greater learning.

c. Likely to be listened to because they'd made others feel important.

Great leaders make an emotional connection with the people they lead. Leadership is about understanding people, and about getting people pointing and acting in the same direction. The unique role of a leader is then to provide the energy and commitment to see this job through, and ensuring execution is perfect.

Leadership is about listening, and making a real connect with others. By leading into a culture of deep inquiry and skillful listening, leaders can strengthen the foundation from which all else stems.

Leaders develop the vital skill of active listening. This is part of an overall need for effective oral communication. Active listening is the ability to listen intently to what others are saying, understand what they are communicating and show a response of positive affirmation that we are hearing and comprehending their remarks.

Listening connects us with others. It is through listening that we learn the needs and motivations of others. This knowledge provides us with the reasons people will follow. As leaders we discover how we may move and serve our followers. Real leadership - leadership that endures - requires the skill of listening includes:

a. Listen to self: Listen to voices of head and heart of him/herself. Listening also connects us with ourselves. By listening inwardly we discover our mission and passion, the forces that compel us to lead. Great leaders are great leaders because they have the ability to listen to themselves.

   The ability to listen to him/herself - to make the connection between head and heart - is certainly the most valuable resource of leadership. It also is a kind of a barometer for the degree of self-respect that a leader has for him or herself.

b. Listen to others: Great leaders put both the attributes of empathy and respect on display when they truly listen to others. The Leadership job starts with a thorough understanding of the follower's needs, aspirations and concerns, which needs excellent listening and facilitation skills.

Leaders strive to be an effective listener by listening attentively to what other is saying. They show open attitude to other through body language and attentiveness.

To be an effective listener, you must be composed when relating with the speaker. In this way, they feel more accepted when they are with you. Don't fidget or frown when looking at the speaker because he/she is trying to get a response from you, so giving a negative attitude makes him/her feel defensive, insecure and not confident.

Leaders who have the knowledge before hand usually will make a person complacent about note taking and listening. If we see it, hear it, and write it down, we have a much greater chance of remembering it.

As a leader you both get and give information. You must be able to do both of these well. Learn to take notes when there is a lot of detail. Recognize their concerns: Use of rational persuasion should not be seen as a form of one-way communication from the leader to members.

Great leaders listen carefully to the concerns and uncertainties of their team members, and make sure that they address these in making a persuasive appeal.

Listen – truly listen to people. Listen with your ears, eyes and heart. Pay attention to others' body language, to their tone of voice, to the hidden emotions behind what they are saying to you, and to the context. Practice naive listening. Don't talk, just let people explain why they are doing the types of things that they are doing. You will learn many things. If you would like to become a listener, you need to:

a. Commit yourself to understanding what others say and mean - We often in engage in conversations in which our listening is inhibited because we are looking for a chance to express ourselves and our own viewpoints, rather than using all our senses to understand clearly what the other person is saying. Quieting our own urge to speak is often the most difficult skills to practice and achieve.

Hearing only becomes listening when you pay close attention to what is said and how it is said, and when you check whether your interpretation of what was said is correct.

b. Practice - Practicality is acquired through practice or action, rather than theory, speculation, or ideals. To be practical, the thing should be practiced, implemented into work; and ease of use.

Through listening we discover our call to lead; through courage we nurture our will to lead. Listening gives us a reason to lead; courage provides us with the strength to lead. Listening is the most important component of communication for leaders.

The leader listens so as to fully understand the perceptions of followers, their needs and concerns. This requires asking probing questions and feedback, as well as reflective thinking to enhance understanding.

Leaders display a willingness to be influenced and to use their understanding to further shape the vision, ever increasing the shared nature and support for the vision.

Whenever we listen deeply to what others need we learn more about ourselves and the environment around us. Listen fully to what other say before interrupting; that gives you an opportunity to obtain all the information you need to give a meaningful response. Your active listening also encourages others to do the same. To truly listen is to open ourselves to being changed.

Listening requires loosening our focus on self. It is allowing ourselves to be influenced by what we hear. Listening requires silence. We must stop talking to hear. Listening to others also builds understanding and trust.

When followers feel listened to, they are more apt to support the leader's decision. Followers feel their input has been considered an`d perhaps even incorporated into the final decision. Followers will trust, though, only if they experience the leader as having genuinely listened.

Sincere listening means the leader is willing to be influenced by what is heard. This does not mean that the leader will necessarily change. The leader may decide to continue on the original course of action.

Leaders take self and followers to the edge of the known and move into the unknown. Leaders may lead by listening. It means they learn, grow, experiment; and always with an ear to the messages experience sends to them.

A leader who listens is one who knows that is going on around him/her. Listening enables followers to communicate more directly. Leaders who listen expect their people to tell them the facts, especially when things are not going well. Leaders who listen expect their people to share ideas, even when those ideas may conflict with the leader's stated point of view.

The habit of listening, as a pillar of leadership, finds its ethical foundations in empathy and respect for others. To empathize with another person is to feel with another person, to come alongside them, to enter briefly into that person's world and to see things from his or her perspective.

Great leaders put both the attributes of empathy and respect on display when they truly listen to others. Great leaders listen. The great leaders understand and accommodate the needs of their people.

COUNSEL

Counsel means providing encouragement and guidance, assisting with problem-solving, developing a personal quit strategy, and offering support. We might also call this being able to provide the right judgment. Those we lead look to us for guidance on how things should be done. And, they expect decisions to be properly weighed before made and then made in the best interest of all people affected by the decision. The reason for counseling is to help members develop in order to achieve organizational goals.

At times, the counseling is directed by policy, and at other times, leaders should choose to counsel to develop members. Regardless of the nature of the counseling, leaders should demonstrate the qualities of a counselor (respect, self-awareness, credibility, and empathy), which includes:

a. Understand that the behavior might be undesirable, not the person. Counseling sessions should be conducted in private immediately after the undesirable behavior. Do not humiliate a person in front of others

b. Understand you care about him or her as a person.

c. Do not punish members who are unable to perform a task. Punish those who are able to perform the task but are unwilling or unmotivated to succeed. Ensure that the member understands exactly what behavior led to the counseling or punishment.

Leaders should be able to put themselves in 'someone else's shoes' and appreciate how a member is feeling or better understand the reasons for his/ her behavior. They should be able to listen and talk to the member. Leaders mentor others and have a mentor or two. The leaders are valuing both giving and receiving feedback.

A leader with followers who always agree with him/her reaps the counsel of mediocrity. Behind every great leader you'll probably find at least one great advisor. The need to take counsel is not the same as government by majority vote.

The great leader likes to hear alternative solutions, discover the desires of all concerned, and then seeks a solution which will satisfy as many as possible.

As far as possible the great leader has already achieved agreement about a new direction before the decision is published.

PROTECTING

Protecting is a quality in which leaders act to protect themselves and organization and establish a sense of worth/security. If dangers within or from outside the organization begin to threaten their well-being, leaders should act to protect.

People sometimes even need to be protected from the damage they may do to themselves. Leaders are protecting their flock from harsh surroundings, which evolves:

a. Self-protection: Leader may protect himself/herself and establish a sense of worth through withdrawal, remaining distant, hidden, aloof, cynical, superior, and/or rational. It is composed of:

i. Arrogance - Project a large ego - behavior that is experienced as superior, egotistical, and self-centered.

ii. Critical - Take a harshly critical, questioning, and cynical attitude.

iii. Distance - Establish a sense of personal worth and security through withdrawal, being superior and remaining aloof, emotionally distant and above it all.

Character is one of the best assets in the leadership. If you want to become a great leader, encourage yourself to nurture your character, for your character will cover and protect your reputation.

b. Organizational protection - Leadership responsibility includes protecting the organization from danger, guarding and protecting others, i.e. Protect emerging leaders to assure continuing leadership in your group against criticism, fear of failure, or being overwhelmed, protect organization's assets, reputation; protect human rights, etc.

Leadership requires foresight; that is contingent on leader's ability to evaluate the current state, assess, and predict trends and act to prevent those actions that will lead to crisis. The leader should help members to develop the sense of protecting the organization.

Great leaders have the mind-set, skill-set, and tool-set necessary to enable members engage in to protect their interests.

SIMPLICITY

Complexity is bad, simplicity is good. Simple indicates a condition which is not complicated; ordinary or common; humble in condition; composed of only one thing; easy of use; not guileful or deceitful; sincere to the user; free from vanity; not sophisticated.

It may also imply a degree of intelligence inadequate to cope with anything complex or involving mental effort. In this time of great complexity and hurry, there is no more important personal value than simplicity.

The essence of profound insight is simplicity. Simplifying a work not only streamlines it, but makes it more effective and productive, leading to greater results when compared to its former complex arrangement. Simple things are usually easier to explain and understand than complicated ones. Simplicity can mean freedom from hardship, effort or confusion.

Leader seeks to realize simplicity by design. In character, in manners, in style, in all things, the supreme excellence is simplicity. The greatest lesson in life is to know that even fools are right sometimes.

Practicality is acquired through practice or action, rather than theory, speculation, or ideals. To be practical, the thing should be practiced, implemented into work; and ease of use.

Practical things offer useful result to the people. Otherwise it is idealistic when no regard to practicality. It should be able to solve problems in the natural state, and emphasize the practical aspects of thinking.

Leaders have a unique ability to make things simple. Often people with great talent, artistic temperament, or other qualities fail to achieve because they are not practical in their thoughts and deeds.

When important opportunities come their way, they shun them; or they have a prejudiced view about the value of money, i.e. they shun it. Any attempt on one's part to be more practical will rapidly catapult one from one's current status towards the pinnacle of success.

List two to four ways you have been or are impractical in life. Now make an effort to your ways. Keep reaffirming your new approach till it becomes part of your being. If you are not sure if and how you are impractical, why not be brave and ask those who are looking out for your best interests.

Leaders need a talent for simplicity. Everything should be made as simple as possible, but not only simpler. Leaders make decisions based on facts, and apply common sense and simplicity to complex tasks. Great leaders are almost always great simplifiers.

GIVING

Leaders transmit energy to people, giving them a new sense of hope and confidence in achieving the vision. Leading is giving. Leadership is an ethic, a gift of oneself.

Your quest as a leader is a journey to find the treasure of your true self, and then to return home to give your gift. The quest itself offers great rewards: the capacity to be successful in the world, knowledge of the mysteries of the human soul, the opportunity to find your unique gifts in the world and to live in loving community with other people. The greatness of a leader is measured by the sacrifices he/she is willing to make for the good of the group.

FORGIVENESS

Forgiveness, however, is about recognizing conditions as they are, complete with all the hurt, disgust, anger or other emotions, moving beyond current circumstances and not carrying the past into the future. A sense of forgiveness leads to feeling calm and at peace with his/herself. Sense of forgiveness demonstrates:

    a.   Forgive yourself: You will grow into your own greatness when you forgive yourself for being human. Anyone who has never made a mistake has never tried anything new. Humans will make mistakes.

    b.   Forgive others: Organizations must create a context of forgiveness if they expect to have quality leadership. And leaders must embrace their own vulnerability and offer forgiveness to followers if they want to contribute to that context of forgiveness and nurture the leadership abilities of their people.

Forgiveness may be the most important gift an organization can give to its leaders, and the most important gift a leader can give to the people for whom he or she is responsible. Forgiveness offers people the chance to take risks, to learn and to grow in their own leadership within the organization. Leaders need forgiveness given their own vulnerability and it is something they must offer others, even though others' failures increase the leaders' vulnerability.

Leaders must be able to forgive themselves. This may be the hardest of all. All of us are haunted by the foolish things we have done, the mistakes we have made, the failures of yesterday.

Our ability to lead is directly proportional to our ability to forgive ourselves and risk failure again. If our actions are circumscribed by fear of failure, we cannot lead. Failure must be forgiven and learned from.

Without forgiveness, we would never commit ourselves to the interdependent relationships of our communities. But forgiveness comes with the gift of leadership. It is the empowering side of accountability.

Leaders don't wear the golden crown of a ruler, but a wreath of thorns known as responsibility. They are responsible for their team's success. And whenever it is achieved, they make sure the team receives the credit. Yet, when problems appear, they have the courage to accept the blame and the wisdom to learn from their mistakes.

Great leaders learn to love others. They sense the need to build others up, many times even at their own expense. They can fire you and make you feel good about the process. The reason is they always deal with the performance and never the performer. Love the person, regardless of the person's behavior. If their behavior is unsuitable, then speak to that, never be the performer.

If a leader is not able to forgive mistakes from followers, there is no room for acting freely within a group. Opportunity should always be connected to accountability, as when there is lack of accountability, there are no true opportunities and risks. Therefore, in order to make subordinates take responsibility, they need to face opportunities.

Leaders learn to forgive. Forgiveness requires true faith in oneself and others. Punishing another person because you are in power requires no great effort.

Forgiveness touches people's hearts, while punishment merely brushes people's memories.

Since true change comes from the heart, forgiveness offers greater chances of transformation. Forgiveness and letting go can lead you down the path of healing and peace.

ENCOURAGEMENT

Encouragement is a word, statement, or gesture that conveys an attitude of approval of, appreciation for, and a desire to see another person continue with what he/she is doing, seeking to do, expressing, or feeling.

Encouragement grows confidence and plants the seeds of self-esteem in the people. For followers to successfully execute organization's goals (including enhancing patient safety and satisfaction), they must feel as though they are capable of performing the work required of them.

Great leaders encourage their people by making them feel that they can successfully accomplish their job tasks. Everyone, even the best people, needs encouragement. Encouragement is the fuel that brings out everyone's best effort. In addition, great leaders acknowledge their people (both individually and as a team) when they have successfully completed specific tasks.

Praise is an essential, but often overlooked strategy that great leaders know has significant impact on people performance. The effective use of praise is a great way to also get great performance in the future.

People will be able to do real work when they are under the stimulus of encouragement and enthusiasm and the approval of the people for whom they are working. Encouragement is characterized by:

a. Encourage others: Giving encouragement to others will lift spirits, increase self-worth, and a hopeful future. Tell a sincere message of approval and appreciation and continued best wishes for what they are doing.

Encouragement helps people feel a sense of belonging. Not only does followers need to achieve, but they also need positive feedback and recognition - a real message that they are doing well, pleasing others and making it. Encourage and praise them, not only for achieving a set goal but also for their efforts, and for even small increments of change and improvement.

b. Not to exercise power excessively: Punishment may work if all you are interested in is stopping misbehavior for the moment. But in the long-range results are negative.

Commitment offers a sense of encouragement and well being. Encouragement lets people know what they've done well and recognizes or rewards them for it. People feel good when they receive words of encouragement from their leaders.

Encouragement helps them to develop self-confidence, self-respect and, a sense of accomplishment. Leaders must instill a sense of pride and confidence through encouragement.

Great leadership results from both individual efforts and the collective support. Great leadership inspires and enables others to do their absolute best, together to realize a meaningful and rewarding shared purpose. Leaders encourage people; align the people with them; solve a problem for them; and ending something that's distracting them.

HARMONY

Harmony is a condition that comes about when all the parts of one's life are balanced with each other and the world around him/her.

Harmony is an alignment or congruence among four elements: what we say, what we think, what we feel and what we do. When there is harmony, alignment, and congruence between our thoughts, feelings, actions and words we experience an inner and outer sense of peace, called harmony.

When we're in harmony, the pieces fit. You get a sense of harmony by working in a positive manner with others, by working on teams and helping build a better organization. Harmony is built on collaboration and trust.

Harmony supports one to act from a place of authenticity and integrity; there is no fakeness or phoniness, no self-deception. Sense of harmony evolves:

a. Personal harmony: Keep yourself in harmony with your deepest self, discover and develop your strengths, define and promote your vision, and create a life in harmony with both achievement and satisfaction.

b. Organizational harmony: Ensure all parts of your organization work in harmony, act to restore harmony to the leader and follower, in the pursuit of peace. Harmony believes in the importance of personal relationships.

Since leaders lead people, the style with which you do is important. It must truly represent you and must fit with the situation, the results you wish to achieve and the people you hope will follow your lead.

Leaders create a sense of harmony within the organization. Harmony is the metaphor of an orchestral conductor to describe the quality of the leadership process. A leader resembles an orchestra conductor in some ways. Organizational structure should not be duplicative in nature and confusing in responsibility and accountability. It may create disharmony.

Harmony can reduce stress. Harmonizing means negotiating or reliving tension when appropriate; suggesting ways of accommodating differing views; helping others explore their disagreements; seeking appropriate compromise solutions that split the difference or make some type of trade-off.

The ease with which the organization is able to accomplish its goals is dependent upon the ability of the leader to evoke a sense of harmony within the organization. Leaders have to be committed to create harmony between organization's demands and high performance with the individual's needs for wellbeing, freedom and fulfillment at work.

Great leaders are committed to harmony. They foster behaviors that allow follower to live in peace and harmony.

BALANCE

Balance is defined as equanimity, satisfactory distribution of elements, comfort, stability, a calm emotional state. Balance exists if sentiment, beliefs about events or people, is equally positive or negative.

The two main factors affecting balance are the sentiment (e.g. liking, approving, admiring) and unity (e.g. similarity, proximity, membership) qualities of beliefs.

Leadership is based on a balanced expression of the spiritual, mental, emotional and physical dimensions. It requires core values, clear vision, empowering relationships, and innovative action. We need a sense of balance to deal with multiple interest groups, whilst also achieving our goals.

We must first understand and communicate our own value systems, and must focus on balancing the interests and concerns of others, helped by understanding their value systems.

Balance between vision, commitment, execution and personal/professional qualities is critical to effective organizational leadership. This balance ensures the vision remains grounded in reality, that key players are on board and that results achieved in a focused and disciplined manner. If the behaviors of people are not in balance, the leadership team must provide it.

Success comes to organizations by balancing managing and leading. Too much managing brings about stagnation. An excess of leading creates chaos. By understanding how leading and managing differ, we can better ensure that both functions are fulfilled. Great leaders have to be ambidextrous.

On the one hand, they have to be able to execute capably within the current business paradigm, the way we do business. On the other hand, they must be able to reflect on the current paradigm, find ways to fundamentally improve it, and manage the large-scale change to a successful conclusion. Sense of balance implies:

a. Personal balance: Leaders have a balanced life. Your mind, body and soul can feed upon and grow from each other.

   Balance your body, mind, and spirit; and be equally physical, mental, and spiritual fulfilled. Have other interests besides your routine job. Take time to be with your family and friends. Be true to yourself and to others. Plan your own future, and don't try to be like someone else, who is not you, just to getting ahead.

   Leaders make people feel that they're at the very heart of things, not at the periphery. Everyone feels that he or she makes a difference to the success of the organization. When that happens, people feel centered and that gives their work meaning.

b. Organizational balance: Perform and maintain stability through dynamic balance within the organization Explore the steps needed to contribute to organizational balance from the individual in the basic work unit to the macro organization and all its stakeholder environments. Maintain balance is both an obligation of a leader to those they serve and themselves. The leader should know when that balance is out-of-balance.

Leader must first understand and communicate organization value systems, and must focus on balancing the interests and concerns of others. He/she needs a sense of balance to deal with multiple constituency interest groups, whilst also achieving organization goals.

Balance is multifaceted. Balance applies to many elements of life, work and leadership, includes the balance of work and personal life, the balance between individual needs and organizational needs, the balance of opinions that needs to occur within teams, the balance required to moderate disagreement.

Leaders need great balance - The ability to balance the in and outflow of communication with the ability to create thinking time to allow the creativity of growth. Balance is not the same as equilibrium; that is a condition in which all acting influences are canceled by each other, resulting in a stationary system.

Leadership has to do with sense of balance, i.e. balance between inner and outer leadership, between personal growth and organization development, between holding the vision and enabling others to achieve it, between serving and leading, between the head and the heart, between economy and ecology. The leader becomes the bridge between old traditions and new ways.

Organization needs leaders with vision and integrity, who are balanced in their judgment and actions as well as balanced within themselves.

Leadership is based on a balanced expression of the spiritual, mental, emotional and physical dimensions. It requires core values, clear vision, empowering relationships, and innovative action. Leadership fosters awakening to the importance of heart, soul, and spirit to being a real leader.

Great leaders have a clear picture for what they want to achieve and/or what they want to create; and having vision for the future which can be attributed to understanding and organizing the present.

Great leaders balance between understanding what happened in the past and why, and based on what's happening now, they think what could the future look like. By knowing these situations, therefore the great leader has focus and self-discipline that allows him/her to carry out the action steps.

OWNERSHIP

A sense of belonging (sense of ownership) generates its own sense of motivation. Ownership motivates members through the chance to build assets, to make their organizations more fulfilling places to work, and for all of us to have greater control over their own destinies.

Ownership develops when members play a key role in formulating and implementing tasks and understand the benefits of participation. The recognition comes when a leader is able to achieve his/her own goals by collaborating and helping his/her members reach their respective goals is the best way to ensure partners are committed for the long haul. Conditions that foster a strong sense of ownership, i.e.:

a. Participatory process: A sense of ownership stimulates commitment and participation. Leaders create an open organization where people believe in collaboration and feel free to say what they think, and encourage a sense of partnership and ownership from everyone.

b. Know each other: Know your people. The more you know your people the more common ground you're likely to find, the more you'll be able to connect.

c. Share: You need to share information. If you think it's appropriate, social activities can be planned. Hold meetings to know one another.

d. Goals discussion: Open people up to each other and make people realize they have common interests in working together.

e. Access: Give access to information. Display open information flows and an environment that encourages teamwork, conversation, and constructive differing.

f. Empowerment: Encourage education about ownership which increases the sense both of reward and of risk.

You can't do everything. A great leader needs to be able to delegate effectively. The key to delegating successfully is giving members ownership of the work you assign them. They can't just feel like they own the work, they really have to.

People need a sense of ownership in order to take care of things. Sense of ownership means people are completely engaged. Leaders build a partnership culture that motivates each employee to treat the business as if it were his or her own.

A great leader is able to rally their people and give them hope and a sense of ownership.

RESPECT

Leadership qualities is exhibited by people who are willing to tell other people what to do but have the respect of other people as well, or gain that respect. Respect is not merely a distasteful marker of submission to authority, but others see respect as more egalitarian, recognition of shared values and an acknowledgement of the essential dignity of all.

Leaders are not necessarily liked. They are respected. If you are a person who has a strong need to be liked, it will be difficult for you to make the tough decisions leaders make. Do not strive to be liked. Take those actions that earn respect.

Leaders are respected. Leaders treat people with respect, give support and challenge as appropriate. Respect is developed by the component qualities of empathy, emotional mastery, lack of blame and humility.

A leader must create an environment of trust and mutual respect for what each person contributes to the organization. This includes the belief that individuals are responsible for their own actions and ideas. It includes an awareness of a person's individuality by recognizing their unique values, attributes, and skills. As you attempt to develop people with counseling, you must refrain from projecting your own values onto them.

Leaders naturally garnish respect primarily for who they are, rather than for what they know. They are evenhanded in their dealings with others and relate to and validate them regardless of domain, tenure, seniority or context.

When it comes to defining executive leadership, the wicked leader is he/she who the people despise; the good leader is he/she who the people revere; the great leader is he/she who the people say: "We did it ourselves." Sense of respect is a responsive relation, which includes:

a. Self-respect: Pride and dignity toward yourself; liking yourself the way you are; able to take responsibility for one's own actions, accepting the consequences without worrying about the opinions of others.

    Self-respect is a product of your esteem for yourself and your respect for others. It is an amalgamation of self-love, confidence, independence, courage, and responsibility. Respect yourself, if you would have others respect you.

b. Respect others: Respecting those around us is the key to gain their support and cooperation. Great leaders who have left their mark on human history and remembered even today are true fans of other people.

    Giving undivided attention, listening, taking effort to understand others and giving importance are some of the signs of respect. Treat others the way you would want to be treated.

It is part of everyday wisdom that respect and self-respect are deeply connected, that it is difficult if not impossible both to respect others if we don't respect ourselves and to respect ourselves if others don't respect us.

Respect is the moral conscience of the great. Respect and recognition incline one's self-esteem which describes the way in which he/she perceives him/herself, in other words, his/her own thoughts and feelings about his/herself, and his/her ability to achieve in ways that are important to him/her. It is impossible to be a great leader without a respect for diversity and an ability to work with people from different walks of life.

EQUALITY

A sense of equality is, paradoxically, one's true greatness. Hierarchy and equality are not necessarily incompatible, as hierarchy provides connections while equality makes hierarchy responsive and responsible. Leaders display equality in the relationship, a desire to give of what you know so others can move forward.

Leadership is a product of a culture of equality and mutual accountability Leaders foster a sense of equality among the members. Leaders utilize their ability to lead and inspire others in a shared vision of equality, which includes:

   a. Equality of opportunity for welfare or advantage: Leaders promote equality of opportunity for all members and provide them welfare services with adequate numbers.

   b. No special privileges accorded to any member: No special treatment for nobody. And there is nobody with special privileges in the organization.

   c. Display resources devoted to each person should be equal: Organizations provide leadership and guidance in acquiring and maintaining resources that equal for each person.

Leaders demonstrate a commitment and leadership on equality and diversity. The leader who commits to a 'strong' sense of equality must challenge discrimination among the followers within the organization. Leaders unleash capability by empowerment through equality in responsibility and authority.

COURAGE

At the heart of extraordinary organizations are leaders who inspire Greatness. Leaders make courageous decisions in what they perceive is the best interest of their people. Neither won the popularity contest, yet both, given the opportunity to decide again, would probably make the same decision today. Leaders don't make decisions based on what's going to make them popular. They analyze the situation and decide what's in the best interest of the majority concerned. Many times, that decision is very lonely.

Leaders have a clear sense of purpose, exhibit discipline and determination, elicit trust, display courage and through their example inspire those around them to overcome obstacles and achieve greatness.

CHANGE

A leader inspires others by his or her commitment to not only a sense of purpose but a strong and abiding set of ethical principles. Leaders never outgrow the need to change.

The ability to respond to change with a clear vision is founded by a set of principles and purpose. They embody innovation and progress. Adaptive challenges require leadership. Solutions to adaptive problems come through experiments, discoveries, and adjustments from many persons or organizations.

Innovation without differentiation seldom produces optimal appeal to optimal results. When these innovative differentials are significant, whole new categories of business opportunities can be created.

Leaders produce change by establishing a vision and a direction, and then by aligning, motivating, inspiring, and empowering people to collectively desire, seek, and attain the shared vision. Along the journey of leadership, you'll meet all sorts of people, and bump into a few critics.

Most people are settled into a comfortable status quo and resent being challenged to break out. But if you aim to lead people to get great results, they not only have to be pushed but more importantly, they must be challenged to push themselves. Trying to appease everybody invites trouble. They're afraid to make waves, and therefore, they avoid changes.

Leadership begins to take flight when the leaders press people to change - whether they thanked or cursed them.

When you become a leader, you take on a great responsibility; you promise to change the world for the better. Leaders cause change to happen, through people. The organization needs great leaders. A photograph never grows old. But as people live on, they change completely.

Leaders challenge comfort zone. You can't move forward if you don't grow and you can't grow if you never leave your comfort zone. When possible, give your members challenging assignments. Help them prepare by providing them a safe environment to learn from the mistakes that they are bound to make.

Adaptive challenges require leadership. Solutions to adaptive problems come through experiments, discoveries, and adjustments from many persons or organizations within the organization. Avoid becoming closed to new ideas. It needs to pursue innovation and refinement in yourself and the organization.

Great leaders step outside of their comfort zone on a regular basis. They know that only by stretching themselves will they become even greater leaders. Minor leaders or non-leaders stay inside their comfort zone and are too scared to try new things. They rationalize and make excuses as to why they cannot achieve their goals.

Leadership through change must provide meaning, encourage practical wisdom about how to do things differently in particular circumstances and build in review so that learning becomes the norm. Hand in hand with being a risk-taker is being innovative.

Great leaders know that the old ways of doing things aren't always the best ways. It's critical that you stay open to new ideas. Think of managing change as an adventure. It tests your skills and abilities. It brings forth talent that may have been dormant. Change is also a training ground for leadership. When we think of leaders, we remember times of change, innovation and conflict. Leadership is often about shaping a new way of life. To do that, you must advance change, take risks and accept responsibility for making changes happen. Unfortunately, the ability to embrace change is not enough to make a great leader.

Leaders help others to understand the necessity of change; in order for them to be willing to change. Great leaders are in a constant state of innovation that forces them to look at old problems with new solutions.

CREATIVITY

Becoming creative is not necessarily about become very intelligent. Creativity is a mental process involving the generation of new ideas, concepts or associations between existing ones. Being creative represents both the greatest opportunity and hardest challenge.

Creativity considers having both originality and appropriateness. To simplify, it is an act of something new. People long to escape from boredom and routine. When people work with a sense of creativity and help of knowledge;

then that means that they are at their peak performance. All people work with a help of creativity, but only minority with a sense of creativity.

Creativity depends on a number of things: experience, including knowledge and technical skills; talent; an ability to think in new ways; and the capacity to push through uncreative dry spells. Creativity is the ability to invent, imagine and predict.

Creativity (being innovative) may arise when leaders question traditional assumptions and continually experiment with how things are done, courageously embracing and initiating change. They need to re-think the means by which work gets done in ways that force a results-driven focus and provide flexibility with choice in how, when, and where work gets done.

They must experiment with new work methods and communications tools to better meet performance expectations. They must reduce reliance on traditional work methods, such as face time and co-location of resources, while using them more wisely to build trust when needed and, at the same time, taking advantage of the flexibility and control afforded by virtual media.

They appreciate leaders who are open to unexpected insights, new ways of doing things. Like artists and musicians, great leaders are not afraid of change, variety, playfulness. They can be quirky without losing their dignity.

Great leaders embrace imagination. They foster innovation. If they themselves don't possess those attributes, they surround themselves with people who do. They exude impatient with the status quo. The leader inspires others to have confidence in him or her; but a great leader inspires them to have confidence in themselves.

Leaders are positive. They are positively enthusiastic. They give hope and inspire others to make things happen. Leader's performance first off all depends on beliefs. They should come with new ways of thinking and willingness to innovate.

A sense of creativity will make the organization great. Creativity is more than a soft leadership skill, and then you may have wondered how one can foster a leader's ability to turn organizations around by shedding new light on old problems, generating good ideas from staff, and successfully implementing new programs.

As an aspect of leadership, creativity is often expressed in problem solving. Fundamental to leadership is your ability to stimulate someone else's creativity.

Leadership encourages a great deal of creativity and independence in others. An organization that relies on innovations would value the leadership competency of creating a climate of creativity. Great leaders give the world ideas that change the existing order. They exude creativity and imagination. They embrace an uncertain future.

FLEXIBILITY

Flexibility is important in leadership; it should not be interpreted as weakness. It's critical element of a high performance team and its members.

The first leadership characteristic needed in organization is flexibility. Even when you plan constantly and meticulously, things often can and do go wrong. Evaluate why something isn't working, replace it with a better plan and move on. Don't stay stuck on the same plan if it's not working.

The role of leader is ridden with contradictions. Paradox and uncertainty are increasingly at the heart of leading organizations. A lot of leaders don't like ambiguity so they try to shape the environment to resolve the ambiguity.

Leaders are flexible, responsive to new situations. They surround themselves with people who are proficient and strike a balance. Successful organizations are willing to challenge themselves, and their members, and react appropriately. Flexibility is a key to organization evolving within its business.

Leaders let their followers' voices be heard; listen to suggestions; be open to new ideas and not be afraid of change. The Leaders value flexibility, innovation, and adaptation. They create a much higher degree of flexibility, adaptability, and creativity by focusing on the maturity, character, and capability of each team member.

Great leaders are amazingly flexible. They possess flexibility and resiliency. They bend but never break. The leaders maintain flexibility by engaging in lengthy inquiry into alternative actions. They understand that no single method can fit all situations. They are flexible, and have the ability to decide which method is best and to act upon it, or are able to modify a particular method to suit the situation.

ADAPTABILITY

Adaptability means reacting in an effective manner to shifting circumstances in your business environment. Given the current complexities of work, the sheer volume of information flowing in, and the rapid changes taking place, it makes sense for leaders - and the people they lead - to be adaptable.

A leader, who is flexible and adaptable, should be able to learn new things, experience new situations and be prepared to have days that don't always turned out as you had planned. If adaptability is not your strongest asset, then hone your skills by:

a. Learn to accept difference as just that – Difference, not a problem.

b. Develop ways to anticipate problems and prepare backup plans to effectively cope with those problems.

c. Keep an open mind and committing yourself to learning constantly, learning quickly and reacting accordingly.

d. Adopt an approach of flexibility when faced with any situations that require adaptability.

Flexibility and swift reactions are essential to cope with rapidly changing situations. Don't fence your strategy in with too detailed instructions. Leave a loose rein for those charged with producing results. Only then can they exercise their initiative and react to the changing circumstances without needing further guidance.

Granting people leeway in achieving objectives demonstrates your confidence in them. Brief instructions encourage success and succinct reports, and only deal in detail when you thing necessary.

Many times leaders will have to alter what they originally planned due to changing circumstances, so flexibility and having an open mind are crucial to leadership. Even when you plan constantly and meticulously, things often can and do go wrong. Evaluate why something isn't working, replace it with a better plan and move on. Don't stay stuck on the same plan if it's not working.

In today's business world the complexity and pace of change can be daunting. In this environment of rapid change, leaders are coming to recognize that they need to develop adaptability. The process of developing adaptability begins with learning and practicing three types of flexibility, i.e.:

a. Cognitive flexibility: Use a variety of thinking strategies and mental frameworks

b. Emotional flexibility: Vary one's approach to dealing with one's own emotions and those of others

c. Dispositional flexibility (or personality - based flexibility): Remain optimistic and at the same time realistic.

Leaders create organizational alignment around organization objectives, while encouraging adaptability in the face of discontinuous threats or opportunities. Alignment and adaptability create the environmental conditions for followers to do the right thing. It may encourage the behaviors that drive superior organization performance. On other hand, adaptability without sufficient alignment and control of risks leads to chaos. Adaptability is a core competency for leadership.

Leaders build adaptability and agility into the organization to sense and respond to change. In the highly dynamic environment, leadership innovation and adaptability are critical, especially the leader's capacity to channel the right knowledge to the right people at the right time in the right organization.

Great leaders are adaptable. When a coaching method does not provide fruit, they change the approach. When they are not connecting with the team members, they examine and modify their leadership style. Great leaders are situational adapters based on the needs of team members and the need of the organization.

A leader inspires people to have confidence in the leader. A great leader inspires people to have confidence in themselves. Greatness needs setting up the conditions and then letting the form emerge. It can be seen as superior in one or more things.

Great organizations are created by great leaders - leaders who can unleash the highest and best contributions of their team toward their organization's most critical strategic priorities. Every organization - and every leader - aspires to greatness. At the heart of every successful organization there are great people who do great things.

Leaders spend their energy on finding solutions to the problems of change. Their passion and energy grow in a culture that fosters great things. Great leaders can be developed. We can predict how our best leaders will behave in a variety of situations. Great leaders take charge and get things done. They take disciplined, organized action. They use their power and authority objectively, and they influence others using optimism and self-confidence.

We are all moved by greatness when we see it, and although the experience is to some degree subjective, we know the feeling of it. When we encounter it, it is as if something in us stirs, awakens, and comes forth to meet what was inside us all along.

When we respond to someone else's greatness, we feed our own. We may feel called to dedicate ourselves to their vision, or we may be inspired to follow a path we forge ourselves.

Either way, we cannot lose when we recognize that the greatness we see in others belongs also to us. Our recognition of this is a call to action that, if heeded, will inspire others to see in us the greatness they also possess. This creates a chain reaction of greatness unfolding itself endlessly into the future.

Greatness is not a single act, but a way of being that nourishes the self, others, and the community. It is intrinsic to every human being, arising from the unique expression of innate qualities such as love, peace, and wisdom. These qualities are the seeds to human greatness, and the true expression of these qualities is human greatness itself.

When we awaken and express the simple essence of our being, we are able to create an extraordinary life, a life of greatness that leaves a positive mark on the lives of others, and organization.

Leaders don't have to be perfect, but to be great. Leaders may take time to learn from the greatest examples of historic leadership. If we can develop leaders who can withstand and embrace the changing times by deeply rooting themselves in sense of greatness, then we can develop great people, great teams and great results.

Greatness comes from living each moment as if it was the only moment that exists; and in actuality – it is.

We should commit to encouraging great leadership. Some great managers struggle with change and fail to be great leaders, while a great leader might fail to create a sense of stability in an organization and not measure up as a manager.

Great leaders are reliable persons of character who are committed to compelling principles and purposes, while embodying both empathy and respect for others, as well as inner connectedness and respect for oneself. Great leaders have that special edge of authenticity and consistently demonstrate that they stand for something more important than themselves.

None of us are so perfect to be able to do all elements of leadership, all the time in all situations. You can do all of the above some of the time and some of all the time, but you can't do all of the time. Sometimes the situation is the wrong battle at the wrong time.

It is important though for you to know when you are modifying or deviating from leadership and why you do so. Be honest with yourself.

Organizations need great leaders in order to create the performance, future, and fulfillment that everyone desires. Management skills alone do not suffice. Leadership is crucial. Leadership skills alone do not make us great leaders.

Great leader can recognize a weakness, and still trust us to develop into excellence. Trust is indeed, we believe, the foundation of all great leadership. Great leaders see greatness in others.

Those who want to be a leader can develop leadership ability. Leadership itself can be performed with different styles. Different leaders have different ideas about leadership.

Some leaders have one style, which is right for certain situation, and wrong for others. Some leaders can adapt and use different leadership styles for given situations.

REFERENCE

1. Bernard L. Erven, Becoming an Effective Leader Through Situational Leadership, The Ohio State University, Ohio – USA, July 2001

2. Donald Clark, Leadership Styles, infinity internet inc., Vancouver, WA – Canada, 1997

3. Sooraj Mittal & Associates, Creative Leadership, Summitforthefuture, Amsterdam - Netherland, 2006

4. Tom Bartridge, GASCO, Competence-Based Training & Development, AME Info FZ LLC / Emap Limited, Dubai Media City - United Arab Emirates, 2004

5. Leadership Theories, North Georgia College & State University, GA – USA, 2004

6. Richard Barrett, Values-Based Leadership, Cultural Transformation Tools®, North Carolina – USA, 2008

7. Lars G. Harrison, What leadership type should I choose!, ALTIKA Corporation, GA - USA, 1997

8. Sankar, Y., Character not charisma is the critical measure of leadership excellence, Journal of Leadership & Organizational Studies, San Francisco, CA – USA, 2003

9. Ron Jasniowski, Character-Based Leadership, Integrity Training Institute, 2004-2005

10. Joseph Krivickas, Character-based Leadership: 3 Steps to Win the Battle for the Soul of Your Organization, LeaderValues Ltd, UK, 2006

11. Cheryl Alexander Stearns & Associates, Why Character?, The Center for Character-based Leadership, Minnesota – USA, 2008

12. Murray Johannsen, Different Types of Leadership Styles, Legacee Management Systems Inc., USA, 1996-2008

13. Roy E. Barnes and associates, Preparing And Supporting Diverse, Culturally Competent Leaders: Practice and Policy Considerations, Institute for Educational Leadership, Washington, DC – USA, 2005

14. Sterling Speim and Associates, Leadership Development, W.K. Kellogg Foundation, Michigan – USA, 2002

15. Ben Timberlake, Leadership Styles, Emporia State University, Kansas – USA, 2000

16. Vadim Kotelnikov, Principle-Centered Leadership: Building Natural Principles Into the Centre of Your Life and Work, GIVIS C/O NCR, USA, 2008

17. Stephen R. Covey, Principle-Centered Leadership, Covey Leadership Center, Inc., USA, 1994

18. Tri Junarso, Comprehensive Approach to Corporate Governance, iUniverse, USA, 2006

19. Tri Junarso, 7th Principle of Success, Trafford Publishing, Canada, 2007

20. Holly Culhane, SPHR and Associates, Ignite!, The Ken Blanchard Companies, Bakersfield, CA – USA, 2005

21. Carmine Coyote, The Narcissistic Organization, Pusch Ridge Publishing, Australia, 2007

22. Katherine Lockett, Authenticity: Feeling the Fear, but Going It Alone Anyway, Pusch Ridge Publishing, Australia, 2008

23. Sam Vaknin, Narcissistic Leaders, Global Politician, New York, N.Y – USA, 2004-2008

24. Dr. Sam Vaknin, Narcissists in Positions of Authority, Narcissus Publications, USA, 1998

25. Surinder Kapur, What Makes a Visionary Leader?, Rediff.com India Limited, India, 2007

26. Corinne McLaughlin , Visionary Leadership, The Center For Visionary Leadership, CA – USA, 2001

27. Captain Bob, Elements of Visionary Leadership, Robert L. Webb, South Carolina - USA, 2003

28. Frank Martinelli , Encouraging Visionary Board Leadership, Creative Information Systems, USA, 2008

29. Gordon Davidson and Corinne McGlaughlin , Visionary Leadership for a Sustainable Age, State of California, USA, 1999

30. Vadim Kotelnikov, Strategic Leadership: Providing the Vision, Direction, the Purpose for Growth, and Context for the Corporate Success, GIVIS - C/O NCR, USA, 2008

31. Michael Cieslak, An Overview of Leadership, Rockford Diocese, Rockford, IL - USA, March 2003

32. Pete Reilly, Leadership: A Personal Journey, Lower Hudson Regional Information Center (LHRIC), Elmsford, NY - USA, August 2004

33. Susan M. Heathfield, Leadership Greatness Summit Take-aways, About.com, USA, April 2008

34. James M. Kouzes and Barry Z. Posner , Christian Reflections on The Leadership Challenge, LeadershipNow / M2 Communications, LLC, USA, 1996-2008

35. Michael B. Colegrove, Ph.D, Leadership Essentials, Hutton Center for Leadership Studies, Williamsburg, KY – USA, 2004

36. Michelle Neujahr , Developing Excellent Leadership, Developing Excellence, United States , 2 0 0 6

37. Rabbi Stephen Baars, Where Did All the Greatness Go?, Aish HaTorah, Jerusalem – ISRAEL, 1995 – 2008

38. Robert Knowles , What's Below Your Water Line?, Association of College Honor Societies , USA, 2003-2005

39. Roger E. Herman , Lessons in Leadership, The Herman Group, Greensboro, NC – USA, 2001

40. Gene Saalwaechter, Today's Challenge Is "True" Leadership, California Park & Recreation Society, CA – USA, 2008

41. Ezra Billinkoff , What It Takes to Be a Leader, Scholastic Inc., USA, 2008-1996

42. Maura Wolf & Rebert Lewis, Jr., Cultivating Greatness, CYD Journal , Boston, MA – USA, 2001

43. L. Ron Hubbard, What Is Greatness?, Church of Scientology International, LA – USA, 2003-2008

44. Gail Gunderson, Encouraging Leadership from the Inside Out, the Ohio State University Extension Leadership Center, USA , 2000

45. Jonathan Farrington, Some Thoughts About Greatness And Leadership, b5media Inc., Canada, 2007

46. Neil Curry, The quest for greatness, Cable News Network LP, LLLP, USA, 2007

47. LT Steve Kee, What's Your Definition of Leadership?, US Department of Homeland Security, Washington, DC – USA, 2008

48. J. Donald Walters, The Art of Supportive Leadership, Ananda Portland, Beaverton Oregon – USA, 2006

49. Colin Hutchinson, Effective Leadership, Edwin Datschefski, 1999

50. Lisa Dewey, Five Qualities Good Leaders Express, Girl Scouts of the United States of America, USA – 2004

51. Paul McGillicuddy and Associates, Leadership Traits: Small Business Administration, AL – USA, 2007

52. Jim Martin & John C. Kunich, Surviving at the Top of the Heap, Unisys, USA, 2008

53. Karlene Sugarman, M.A, Leadership Characteristics, Psych Web, USA, 2007

54. Chuck Gallozzi, Great Leaders, Personal-Development.Com, CA – USA, 2008

55. John Baldoni, Recognition: A Leader's Responsibility, Self Improvement Inc., Marlboro, NJ – USA, 1996 – 2007

56. Dr. John C. Maxwell, The Challenge of Change, Mi & Giant Impact, Duluth, GA – USA, 2008

57. Pat Townsend and Joan Gebhardt, Leadership and Quality, QCI International, USA, 1997

58. Donald Clark (2004), Concepts of Leadership, USA, May 21, 2008

59. Ralph Shrader, Risk Taking in a Tentative World, Booz Allen Hamilton Inc., Virginia – USA, 2008

60. Kevin Grauma, Leadership - Top 10 attributes for greatness, American City Business Journals Inc., USA, May 2005

61. Jack Stevenson, Leadership, iscribe.org, USA, 2002

62. Michael A. Aun, CSP, CPAE, 15 Characteristics of Great Leadership, NSA Central Florida, USA, 2002-2007

63. Ronald A. Heifetz and Marty Linsky, Leadership on the Line: Staying Alive through the dangerous of Leading, ShearonForSchools, USA, June 2003

64. Gerald L. Atkinson, Leadership and Ethics Training, .S. Naval Academy©, USA, June 1999

65. Michael Olivares, Wisdom, Vision, Leadership - Mapping our Youth's Future, Los Angeles Police Federal Credit Union, USA, 2008

66. Dr. Thomas Mc Weeney and Associates, CSM Accountability, Center for Strategic Management, MD – USA, 2008

67. Robert L. Turknett and Associates, The Leadership Character Model, Turknett Leadership Group, USA, 2007

68. Gina Hernez-Broome & Richard L. Hughes, Leadership Development: Past, Present, and Future, Center for Creative Leadership, NC - USA, 2008

69. Susan Church, The Principle Difference: Key Issues in School Leadership and How to Deal with Them, Stenhouse Publishers, ME – USA, 2005

70. Wally Bock, What Do Great Leaders Do Differently?, Port City Publishing, USA, 2003

71. Tom Nies, Entrepreneurial Leadership, CINCOM, System Inc., OH – USA, January 24, 2007

72. Murray Johannsen, Nine Characteristics and Qualities of Successful Entrepreneurs and Business Leaders, Legacee Management System Inc., USA, 1996 – 2008

73. Jonathan Farrington, Final Thoughts About Greatness, Theb5media Blog Network , Toronto, Ontario – Canada, April 24th, 2007

74. Jagdish Parikh, The Zen of Management Maintenance: Leadership Starts with Self-Discovery, President and Fellows of Harvard College, USA, 2005

75. Jamie S. Walters, The Elements Of Courageous Leadership, Ivy Sea Inc., CA – USA, 1997 – 2006

76. Martha Lashley, Courage is the Foundation of Leadership, Leadership that Works, PA – USA, 1999

77. Jamie Walters, Courage: Tap Greater Potential and Thrive Through Challenges, Ivy Sea Inc., USA, 1997-2002

78. Oren Harari, The 6 C's of Leadership, Oren Harari, USA, April 27, 2006

79. Michael McKinney, The Courage to Initiate, LeadershipNow / M2 Communications, USA, April, 13, 2007

80. Robert K. Cooper, PhD, Uncommon Reminders for Bringing Out the Best in Others and Ourselves, Society Scope, Vol. 5 No. 1, USA – 2002

81. David M. Boje, Douglas MacArthur, New mexico State University, USA, January 16, 2001

82. Robin Chew, Mahatma Gandhi, Lucidcafé, USA, 2008

83. Sedivy, The Life of Napoleon Bonaparte, Highlands Ranch High School, Colorado – USA, 2002

84. David Leigh and Rob Evans, Shah of Iran, Guardian.co.uk, England, June 08, 2007

85. CHRISTOPHER MATTHEWS, Churchill's Greatness: The Very Model of a Democratic Statesman, The Churchill Center, Illinois – USA, 2008

86. John C. Maxwell, Look Out Below, PDI, USA, 20 June 2005

87. E.S. Reddy, Olof Palme: Introduction, African National Congress, South Africa, June 1989

88. Stellan Andersson, Olof Palme's Archives, Labour Movement Archives and Library, Stockholm, Sweden, 2007

89. B.V. Krishnamurthy, Bill Gates: Entrepreneur, Manager, and Leader, Harvard Business School Publishing Corporation , USA, June 27

90. Vontz, Thomas S. - Nixon, William A., Teaching about George Washington, ERIC Digests, USA, 1998

91. Thomas Reeves, Presidency: How do Historians Evaluate the Administration of John Kennedy?, History News network, USA, 2001

92. Eric Papp, The Making of a Leader, Voice Of Generation Y, USA, 2007

93. Leading Teams From Above: Leadership of Autonomous Work Teams, Wharton Leadership Digest, Volume 7, Number 12, Wharton Center for Leadership and Change Management University of Pennsylvania, USA, September, 2003

94. Rolf W. Habbel, The Human(e) Factor: Nurturing a Leadership Culture, Booz Allen Hamilton Inc., New York, NY – USA, 2008

95. Albert A. Vicere, On Leadership: Great leaders inspire troops, Pittsburgh post-gazette, USA, February 24, 2004

96. James T. Berger, How I Became an Entrepreneur, The Wiglaf Journal, USA, 11 May 2005

97. Bill Breen, The Three Ways of Great Leaders, December 19, 2007

98. Dale M. Turner, CHA, On the Matter of Leadership, Hospitality Internet Media, L.L.C, GA – USA, April 2002

99. Pat Townsend and Joan Gebhardt, Leadership and Quality, Quality Digest Magazine, USA, October 1997

100. Pat Townsend, Qualityworld, The Chartered Quality Institute, London – UK, 2007 – 2008

101. Archester Houston, Ph.D. & Steven L. Dockstader, Ph.D., Total Quality Leadership:A Primer, TQLO Publication Number 97-02, Arlington, Virginia – USA, 2002

102. Partha S. Ghosh, Beliefs on Leadership, Partha S. Ghosh and parthaghosh.com, USA, 2003 – 2005

103. Bud Bilanich, Great Leaders Know "The Genius of the And", bbilanich.typepad.com, USA, December 19, 2006

104. Geoffrey Brewer, The 7 Traits of Great Leaders: An Exclusive Study Reveals What Separates Motivational Leaders From Mere Managers, Caliper Insights Newsletter, Princeton, NJ – USA

105. Jeff Magee, Ph.D., PDM, CSP, CMC, Leadership Ethics: Modeling It Daily!, Performance Magazine Live, Linked Assets, LLC, USA, 2007

106. Robert K. Cooper, PhD, leadership, Society Scope, USA, 2002

107. Kevin Grauman, Leadership - Top 10 attributes for greatness, East Bay Business Times, American City Business Journals Inc., USA, May 6, 2005

108. John M. Gerber, Leadership, University of Massachusetts Amherst, MA – USA, 1993

109. Allan L. Schoenberg, What it Means to Lead During a Crisis: An Exploratory Examination of Crisis Leadership, Syracuse University, USA, 2004

110. John Felitto, The Top Ten Spiritual Principles for Evoking

111. Ed Ruggero, What Makes A Great Leader – Character and Ethics, Academy Leadership LLC, 2008

112. Margaret Thorsborne, The Seven Heavenly Virtues of Leadership, Australia Institute of Management, Australia, 1998 – 2008

113. Jonathan Byrnes, The Essence of Leadership, September 6th, Jonathan L. S. Byrnes & Co, USA, 2005

114. Trevor Gay, Leadership and Management – Chalk and Cheese, Rattle-The-Cage.com, USA, 2004

115. Damian Cox, Marquerite La Caze & Michael Levine, Standford Encyclopedia of Philosophy: Integrity, Metaphysics Research Lab, CSLI, Stanford University, USA, 2001

116. Karin Syren, 10 Leadership Qualities + 1, Karin S. Syren & Solu'shunz Management Services, IL – USA, 2006

117. Linda Hatcher & Associates, The Virtues of Great Leaders, Leadership Development, USA, June 2005

118. Kenneth Rice, Four Dimensions of Leadership, RightToLead.com, USA, 2006

119. Bruce A. Pasternack, Dreamers with Deadlines, Booz Allen Hamilton Inc., USA, 2008

120. Bill Gaw, Traits of strong leadership, Milo Media, WI – USA, 2008

121. Dr. John C. Maxwell, Leaving a Legitimate Leadership Legacy, Injoy Inc., GA – USA, 2006

122. Rodger Dean Duncan and Ed J. Pinegar, What Great Leaders Are, Meredian Magazine, Washington DC – USA, 2002

123. Chris Banescu, Key Characteristics of Great Leaders - Part II, ChrisBanescu.com, USA, June 21, 2008

124. Naseem Mariam, Top 10 Qualities Of Great Team Leaders, iEntry, Inc., KY – USA, 2003

125. Kenneth W. Phifer, TRUST, First UU Ann Arbor , USA, May 1, 2005

126. Robert Longman Jr., Faith, trust, faith experiences, belief, confidence, conviction, credence, credibility, credit, dependence, reliance: Word Definitions and Meaning, Spirithome.com, USA, 21 February 2008

127. Leslie L. Kossoff, From Manager to Leader, About.com, USA, 2008

128. Hal Halladay, Leaders Empower, Know More Media, USA, October 06

129. Marjorie Garber, Symptoms Of Culture, Apple Inc., New York – USA, 2000

130. Richard C. Huseman, Ph.D and Associates, Coaching for Great Leadership in Health Care, The Baptist Health Care Leadership Institute, Florida – USA, 2008

131. Jonas Clark, Encouragement: The Christian Leadership Connection, JonasClark.com, Fla – USA, 2004 – 2008

132. Ron Kurtus, Honesty Pays, The School for Champions, USA, 14 February 2006

133. Marques, Joan, Top 10 Reasons Why Honesty Pays Off in Management, CNET Networks, Inc., USA, 2007

134. Mary FitzPatrick, Carolyn Costley, Lorraine Friend, On honesty and trust, gods and mortals: Gendered experiences of honesty and trust in patient-practitioner relationships, the Journal of Research for Consumers, Perth – Australia, 2001

135. Dr. Condoleezza Rice, Organizational and Business Storytelling In The News: Story #114, Stephen Denning, USA, April 9, 2004

136. Vince Lewis, 4 Key Leadership Characteristics!, Rough Air Associates, OH – USA, November 20, 2007

137. Dale and Juanita Ryan, Honesty, Christian Recovery International, CA – USA, 1991